THE ULTIMATE GUIDE TO
PUPPY CARE
and TRAINING

Tracy Libby

i-5 PRESS

The Ultimate Guide to Puppy Care and Training

Project Team
Editor: Andrew DePrisco
Copy Editor: Amy Deputato
Designer: Mary Ann Kahn
Index:er Elizabeth Walker

i-5 PUBLISHING, LLC™
Chief Executive Officer: Mark Harris
Chief Financial Officer: Nicole Fabian
Vice President, Chief Content Officer: June Kikuchi
General Manager, i-5 Press: Christopher Reggio
Editorial Director, i-5 Press: Andrew DePrisco
Art Director, i-5 Press: Mary Ann Kahn
Vice President, General Manager Digital: Jennifer Black
Production Director: Laurie Panaggio
Production Manager: Jessica Jaensch
Marketing Director: Lisa MacDonald

Library of Congress Cataloging-in-Publication Data
Libby, Tracy, 1958-
  The ultimate guide to puppy care and training : house-training, life skills, and basic care from puppyhood to adolescence / by Tracy Libby.
    pages cm
  Includes index.
  ISBN 978-1-62187-089-0 (alk. paper)
1. Puppies. 2. Puppies--Training. I. Title.
SF427.L6664 2014
636.7'0835--dc23
                    2014015366

This book has been published with the intent to provide accurate and authoritative information in regard to the subject matter within. While every precaution has been taken in the preparation of this book, the author and publisher expressly disclaim any responsibility for any errors, omissions, or adverse effects arising from the use or application of the information contained herein. The techniques and suggestions are used at the reader's discretion and are not to be considered a substitute for veterinary care or professional behavioral consultation. If you suspect a medical problem, consult your veterinarian.

i-5 Publishing, LLC™
3 Burroughs, Irvine, CA 92618
www.facebook.com/i5press
www.i5publishing.com

Printed and bound in China
14 15 16 17   1 3 5 7 9 8 6 4 2

PART I

PUPPY
BASICS

CHAPTER 1

SELECTING A PUPPY

So you are thinking about getting a puppy. Or maybe you have recently acquired one. Either way, the rewards of dog ownership are immense. After all, they say that a dog is man's best friend, and a lot of studies indicate that owning a dog (or two!) can be good for your health. Lower blood pressure and increased exercise are noted benefits, as are unconditional love and companionship. Many owners refer to their dogs as "family members," and many times, a dog is a person's only family. Hopefully you are, or soon will be, part of the 72 percent of US pet owners who consider their pets as part of the family. However, before you rush off to acquire a new puppy, you need to keep in mind that puppies—despite their cuddly good looks and charming antics—are a lot of work.

A puppy is an enormous responsibility that goes well beyond simply feeding your four-legged companion. Your precious bundle of fur will quickly grow into an adult dog that will live with you for ten to fifteen years or longer, which is longer than some jobs, mortgages, and marriages last. Your puppy will depend on you for his food, water, shelter, exercise, grooming, training, and regular veterinary care. He will look to you to provide companionship and affection and to never put him in a position where he can get himself into danger. In return, he will track mud through the house, refuse to come when called, commit unspeakable acts against your personal property, and provide plenty of opportunities for public humiliation. The good news is, if you open your heart, your puppy will change your life. He will touch your soul, provide you with years of unconditional love, fill your heart with joy and devotion, and make you laugh harder than you ever thought possible.

The Right Dog for You

Acquiring a puppy on a whim is never a good idea. You must consider this decision carefully because you will be making a commitment to provide for all of his needs and to love him for his entire lifetime.

Responsible ownership starts with finding the right puppy to suit your personality, temperament, and living conditions. Think about all of the pros and cons of each breed—big or small, shorthaired or longhaired, energetic or low-key. You may be attracted to a particular breed, such as the turbo-charged Border Collie or one of the tenacious terriers. Maybe you have fallen in love with the shaggy coat of an Old English Sheepdog, the unique spots of the Dalmatian, or the petite size of the Chihuahua. It's important to note that size is not always an indication of energy level. Parson Russell Terriers, for instance, are small, but they are dynamite in a small package! On the other hand, Saint Bernards are large but not high-energy dogs.

While considering all of these unique breed characteristics, keep in mind that the puppy you choose could be around for ten to twelve years or even longer—so you want a dog that is compatible with your family and suits your lifestyle, and vice versa. Small dogs do not always make great lap dogs. Some breeds, such as the Chihuahua, are too delicate for rambunctious toddlers. Many herding breeds—especially Border Collies and Australian Shepherds—have become popular pets because they are fast, energetic, and enthusiastic with type-A personalities. These dogs like to go, go, go, and that's terrific if you are equally energetic. However, all of this activity can be daunting, and your dream of dog ownership can quickly turn into a nightmare if your personality is bent more toward being a couch potato. If you prefer calm and quiet to boisterous and excitable, perhaps a slower paced dog, say, a Bulldog, is better suited to you.

Do You Have the Time and Patience?

Be realistic about your circumstances and your expectations before you acquire a puppy. This point can't be stressed enough. How much time do you have? Are you already struggling to juggle work and family? If so, consider an aquarium rather than a puppy because puppies are hugely time-consuming. They require enormous amounts of attention—at all hours of the day and sometimes in the middle of the night. They can be inconvenient. They want to eat and potty even when you are, well, dog tired. They want to play when you want to nap.

Puppies need plenty of physical and mental stimulation. If left to their own devices, they will get into all kinds of mischief—barking, chewing, digging, and peeing from one end of the house to the other. Dogs are social animals and often become stressed when left alone for extended periods of time. You will need to spend a lot of time playing with, training, and socializing your puppy by going places, meeting people, and exposing him to all sorts of different situations. Puppies can be expensive, too, because they need food, toys, bedding, training classes, leashes, collars, flea and tick control, and regular trips to the veterinarian—the list goes on and on!

A puppy's early days—the first sixteen weeks—are critical for instilling all of the desired behaviors and discouraging unwanted ones. Bringing a puppy into your home if you do not have the time, energy, or patience is unfair and will result in a puppy that is at a higher risk of developing behavioral problems, as well as being denied the best start in life.

For most people, the benefits of owning a dog outweigh the cost and responsibility.

Breed-Specific Legislation (BSL)

Some breeds, despite their intelligence and trainability, have been labeled as "aggressive" or" dangerous." The image of certain breeds, perpetuated in popular culture, has created a negative and stereotypical bad-dog reputation for many breeds. When negative stereotypes run amok, breed-specific legislation and dangerous-dog laws appear. From small towns such as Manly, Iowa, to large cities including San Francisco, Denver, and London, politicians are mandating how dogs must be walked in public or contained on their property—just because of their breed. Worse yet, many cities have banned pit bull ownership—making it illegal to own a pit bull, a pit bull mix, or any dog that resembles a pit bull. Be sure to do your due diligence before you choose a specific breed. You may find yourself facing an eviction or, worse yet, a confiscation notice for your four-legged friend.

Where Do You Live?

Dogs need space to run, play, and explore their environment—to be dogs. Where you live and how much space you have will help you decide what type of puppy best suits your lifestyle. Or maybe help you rethink dog ownership.

Do you live in the city or country? Do you have a large yard or a small patio? Do you own your home or rent? Plenty of landlords, as well as some housing communities such as condominiums, co-ops, and active-adult communities, do not permit dogs or limit dogs to a certain size. Some even go as far as to ban specific breeds, such as pit bulls, Rottweilers, and Doberman Pinschers.

Will your puppy have access to a fenced yard? Do you need to install a new fence or reinforce the one that you have? Maybe you need to add a dog run to keep him safe?

Also consider the size as well as the breed of your prospective puppy. Will the size of your new dog suit your children, as well as your home, furniture, and car? For example, a Great Dane is a big, but not super-active, dog that may do well in a large apartment or smaller house but might not fare so well in a studio apartment.

What Is Your Lifestyle?

The dynamics of your household will have a huge impact on the type of puppy you choose. Do you live alone? Are you quiet or reserved? Do you have a boisterous family of toddlers or teenagers? Is your household nonstop with friends, kids, and video games? If you have an active and noisy household, you will want to search for a puppy with a solid temperament and personality that can adjust to the domestic hustle and bustle of your home.

Are you looking for an energetic jogging or hiking companion that can keep up with you on extended outings? Do you prefer a field dog for hunting and retrieving? What about a calm companion for leisurely strolls around the neighborhood?

Do you have other pets? Have you considered how they will get along? A docile toy dog is not likely to wreak havoc on livestock, but larger dogs, be they purebred or mixed breed, have been known to chase and sometimes kill cats, chickens, and sheep. Many counties have provisions allowing farmers and ranchers to kill any dog chasing their livestock. Can you keep your dog safe?

You must also consider who will be in charge of feeding and cleaning up after the puppy. (Hint: Thinking that your children will scoop poop on a daily basis is a lofty goal but not likely to happen.) How long will the dog be left alone each day? Who will play with and train him? Take him to obedience class? Walk him? How much are you willing to budget for dog food, vet bills, toys, and other canine necessities?

Time to Groom?

Many of today's breeds retain the coat for which they were bred. Are you a neat freak? If so, you might prefer the wash-and-wear coat of a Boxer, Boston Terrier, or Doberman Pinscher rather than a four-legged shedding machine such as the Shetland Sheepdog, Golden Retriever, or Chow Chow. Seriously consider the amount of time and energy you want to spend on grooming. All dogs require regular grooming, regardless of their coat type, but some coats require more maintenance than others, including clipping, trimming, or stripping (think Poodle, Cocker Spaniel, and Miniature Schnauzer). Are you willing to learn to do it yourself? Do you have the funds to pay a groomer on a regular basis to do it for you?

Do you have allergies? Does dog hair floating around your house make you panic? Are you willing to abandon the notion of ever owning dark-colored clothing or furniture, which is a magnet for dog hair? These are important points to consider when choosing a breed.

Male Versus Female

When it comes to the "battle of the sexes," personal preference is usually the driving force when choosing between a male and a female dog. Some people simply prefer males to females, and vice versa. Some people are attracted to the larger size and ruggedness of the males. Others love a smaller, more feminine companion. Some owners swear that males are easier to train and that females are more protective.

Both sexes have their pros and cons. It is true that females tend to mature faster than males, with many males remaining goofballs for what seems like an eternity. Both sexes can and do make wonderful, loving companions. Behavioral

A true ball of fur, the tiny Pomeranian will fill your life with endless billows of doggy coat.

differences depend on the individual breed and temperament of the puppy's sire and dam. Some dogs are naturally more affectionate or aggressive because of their environment and upbringing.

Intact females come into season very four to six months if not spayed. Intact males can be more dominant, may challenge their owners, and may roam and fight...and they can smell a female in season a mile away.

If you already own a dog—regardless of the breed—consider getting one of the opposite sex that is (or will be) spayed or neutered. Dogs of the opposite sex are less likely to create chaos and turmoil in terms of fighting and squabbling. Some dogs, despite your best intentions, simply will not live together happily. Much will depend on how well you implement and reinforce canine rules and boundaries. A dog's individual breed, temperament, and personality will also influence how well he gets along with canine siblings.

We Just Want a Great Pet

A dog is a dog, right? Not quite. Dogs, like people, have different personalities, temperaments, quirks, and idiosyncrasies—even within the same breed. Golden Retriever puppies, for example, look strikingly similar in appearance, yet each puppy will develop into a unique individual with his own spirit, personality, and genetic makeup. The genes that a puppy inherits and where he comes from will have a huge impact on his future health and well-being, too.

Generations of selective breeding have produced over three hundred breeds of dog with a wide range of appearances, temperaments, and personalities. Many of today's pampered pets were once hard-working dogs with full-time jobs. Early breeders—primarily farmers, ranchers, and hunters—selectively bred dogs based on working ability and mental soundness. A dog used for hunting fast rabbits and gazelles required a certain body type, including long legs and a deep chest for speed. Good scenting ability was a prerequisite for tracking dogs that hunted in heavily forested regions. Guard dogs needed to be strong, brave, and aggressive, with imposing body structures and powerful jaws to intimidate intruders. Retrievers needed soft mouths to fetch downed birds without damaging them. Herding dogs had to be powerful enough to move a stubborn bull or cantankerous ewe across a creek bed and fast enough to chase down a 1,000-pound running bull—and they had to be physically and mentally capable of doing it all day long.

Generations of selective breeding have yielded littermates that appear practically identical.

By selectively breeding dogs based on their most favorable or desirable traits, such as instinct, agility, stamina, trainability, size, strength, temperament, and so forth, the genetic factors responsible for desired traits tended to become *fixed*, or concentrated, in succeeding generations—meaning that certain traits could be reproduced with uniformity. The process is slightly more complicated, but it is why a German Shepherd Dog looks like a German Shepherd Dog, why terriers are crazy about "going to ground" (digging for vermin), and why retrievers are manic about water and love to pick up and carry stuff, be it a downed bird, slipper, or favorite toy.

What does all of this have to do with you? Many purebred dogs retain the traits necessary to perform the jobs for which they were originally bred. These jobs required enormous amounts of energy, drive, stamina, courage, tenacity, and intelligence. The qualities that make them superior working dogs are the very qualities that can make them unsuitable as pets for certain owners.

Too often potential owners make the mistake of thinking that they can change a dog's inherited traits. Taking the sheepdog off the farm or the terrier out of a vermin-hunting environment does not squelch the dog's drive, energy, or desire to work. If you want calm and quiet, do not get a Siberian Husky. A Siberian Husky will never be a Basset Hound. If you want a dog that behaves like a Basset, get a Basset. In the absence of physical and mental stimulation, dogs quickly become bored, which leads to unwanted behaviors such as shredding furniture, digging, excessive barking, ransacking trash cans, and so forth—a very frustrating situation for human and canine.

Consider what a dog was originally bred to do and whether you are prepared to make a commitment to deal with the associated behaviors. Border Collies, for instance, which are popular everywhere, have been bred for hundreds of years with one primary goal in mind: improved herding ability. They are the working stiffs of the herding world, and they live to herd morning 'til night. Physically and mentally capable of doing his job and doing it all day long, a Border Collie is never going to be satisfied with a ten-minute walk around the block. Researching a dog's history and origin will give you some insight into his behavior and why he does what he does, be it barking, digging, jumping, running, and so forth. The advantage of choosing a purebred puppy is that selective breeding gives you a pretty good idea of how he will act—temperament, personality, activity level—and what he will look like—size, coat color, and coat type—when he is fully grown.

Mixed Breeds

In your search for the perfect puppy, don't discount a mixed breed. Often referred to as mutts, crossbreeds, curs, mongrels, Heinz 57s, or, the more modern term,

The most popular "designer dog," the Labradoodle boasts the best qualities of its two parent breeds, the Poodle and the Labrador Retriever.

DNA Testing for Mutts

If curiosity gets the best of you, DNA testing is readily available and may provide some interesting insight into your mixed-breed dog's ancestral background. Canine DNA testing has expanded considerably since the first tests became available in 2007. However, before throwing open your wallet, be sure you understand what you are getting.

Two types of tests are available: A *swab test* is simple enough to be done at home and involves collecting a sample of cells from the dog's inner cheek with a swab brush. A *blood test* involves your vet's drawing a small sample of your dog's blood. With both types of tests, the samples are sent to a lab for analysis, and then owners receive reports of the results. Some companies have a DNA database of more than 130 AKC-recognized breeds, while others have between 50 and 100 breeds. Accuracy of the tests varies, so first decide what and why you want to learn about your dog's ancestry.

All-American, mixed-breed puppies grow into adult dogs that can do pretty much anything that their blue-blooded cousins do, with the exception of participating in conformation dog shows. As ancient as any dog, mutts make wonderful pets and have gone on to excel in performance sports such as agility, flyball, and obedience. What separates the purebred dog from the mixed breed is the inheritance of genes. Purebred dogs inherit fixed genes that reproduce true to type. Mixed-breed dogs inherit random, unfixed genes from their parents, which is why they have a potpourri of physical traits. Sometimes, but not always, the breed of the dam (mother) will be known, while the sire (father) remains a mystery. Because fixed genes produce a certain type, you can sometimes visually identify a mixed breed as having specific characteristics, such as the coat of a West Highland White Terrier, the body length of a Dachshund, or the head shape of a Doberman Pinscher.

Identifying specific characteristics of purebred dogs, such as size, coat type, tail set, or behavioral traits, can shed some light on what breeds might be milling about in your mixed breed's DNA makeup. More often than not, these are educated guesses because while your dog may look like a Saint Bernard, he might behave like a Border Collie, or vice versa.

Bottom Line: Purchasing the wrong type of dog can make life miserable for you and your dog. Plenty of resources are available, and the more informed you are, the better your chances of choosing the perfect dog, thereby helping you avoid personality clashes and future disappointment down the road.

Where to Find Your Puppy

Once you have decided on the right type of puppy for you and your family, the next step is finding a healthy puppy with a good temperament. Finding the perfect puppy may seem daunting. However, doing your homework and understanding your options will make the journey much easier and increase the odds of a better outcome and a fulfilling long-term relationship.

Breeders

Breeders often get a bad rap—especially in the press and from animal-rights activists—for perpetuating genetic problems and, of course, pet overpopulation. Granted, unethical and irresponsible breeders do exist, and you should avoid them at all costs. However, many excellent, responsible breeders have spent a lifetime—not to mention astronomical amounts of money—breeding and improving the quality of their chosen breed. These are the people you want to talk to.

Sorting the good breeders from the questionable ones involves research and footwork, but the payoff is well worth the time invested. Reputable, responsible breeders are the future of purebred dogs. Conscientious, dog-smart, and passionate, they care about the welfare of their dogs and their chosen breed. They are trying to improve all the time by doing their homework, studying pedigrees, planning litters, and breeding only to improve the quality of their dogs and the breed as a whole. They understand anatomy and genetics, and their breeding stock is tested for genetic problems, including hip and elbow dysplasia, cataracts, heart issues, and so forth. Puppies are exposed to environmental enrichment and are regularly and affectionately socialized to everything they are likely to encounter as adult dogs. Many of these breeders are top-notch when it comes to evaluating temperaments.

While a good breeder can help you pick the best puppy for you and your family, he or she will sell only to clients who meet their criteria. You will need to answer some questions regarding your dog-rearing know-how, including why you're interested in a specific breed, whether you've ever owned or currently own a dog, whether you have ever surrendered a dog to a shelter, whether you have kids, a fenced yard, other dogs, and so forth. Some breeders require references, too. While this may seem a bit intrusive, good breeders feel personally responsible for every dog they produce. They want assurances that their puppies are going to the best homes for their entire lives.

In return, you will want to know a lot about the breeder. Don't feel shy asking questions, including:

- How long has the breeder been breeding dogs? Many years in a breed alone does not guarantee quality, but look for a breeder with longevity in the breed.
- How long does the breeder keep the puppies? Most breeders do not let puppies go to new homes until they are at least eight weeks old (or longer for some breeds).
- What clubs or national organizations does the breeder belong to?
- Does the breeder compete in canine sports,

Purchasing a puppy from a reputable breeder offers the most advantages to a puppy buyer.

If you have purchased your puppy from a reputable breeder, you should receive, at the very least, the following documents:

- sales contract that includes your puppy's name, sex, color, birth date; your name, address, and telephone number; and the breeder's information, purchase price, and date; and possibly breeding rights or restrictions, spay/neuter requirements, description of ownership basis, refund and/or return policy
- registration certificate, enabling you to register your puppy in your name with the national kennel club
- inoculation records for canine parvovirus, distemper, hepatitis, and leptospirosis
- three- or five-generation pedigree that details the puppy's ancestry
- health certifications/clearances, depending on your breed, for eyes, hips, or elbows and/or heart

such as conformation, agility, herding, tracking, or obedience?

- How many litters does the breeder breed yearly? (More than three or four litters per year may indicate a problem.)
- Can you contact the breeder if problems arise?
- Does the breeder have references?
- Is the breeder willing to take back the dog if it doesn't work out?
- What is the breeder's policy regarding inherited health issues (hip or elbow dysplasia, eye problems, or other genetic problems) that might arise?
- Does the breeder have a refund policy?

Equally important, you will want to know specifics about the puppies. A good, knowledgeable breeder is happy to answer questions. At the very least, you will want to know:

- Are the dogs—sire, dam, puppies—registered with the American Kennel Club or United Kennel Club in the United States or the Canadian Kennel Club in Canada?
- Have the eyes of the sire, dam, and puppies been examined by a canine ophthalmologist?
- Have the sire and dam been tested for inherited genetic problems, such as hip and elbow dysplasia and heart problems?
- Have the puppies been wormed and vaccinated?
- Have the puppies been checked by a veterinarian?
- Will the breeder provide you with copies of the medical records and genetic testing results of the parents as well as your puppy?
- Will the breeder supply a pedigree (three generations minimum)?

Good breeders welcome questions and willingly answer them. If they don't, scratch him or her off your list and continue searching.

Where to Find a Breeder

A dog show is an excellent starting point. Dog shows provide the perfect forum for talking to breeders, learning more about the breed, and finding out who's planning a breeding. You may even be able to find out whether anyone may have suitable puppies available in the coming weeks or months. Veterinarians are often familiar with local breeders and the health of their dogs. They can usually provide you with the names of several people who are involved in different breeds.

National clubs and registries, such as the American Kennel Club (AKC), the United Kennel Club (UKC), the Canadian Kennel Club (CKC), and The Kennel Club (England), can provide you with information on a specific breed as well as their parent or affiliate clubs. These clubs usually have breeders listed on their websites. Membership in a parent club is not a guarantee that the breeders are responsible or ethical, but it is a good place to start. Be sure to talk to many breeders and ask a lot of questions, and always, *always* visit the breeder's facilities.

But what if the breeder is several hours or several states away, you ask? It's completely possible that you may not find the puppy you're looking for close to home. You can purchase a puppy and have him shipped to you by the breeder, be it across the state or across the country. However, unless you personally know the breeder, or the kennel has outstanding references from people you trust, it is always prudent to meet the puppy in person.

As puppy mills have come under increased scrutiny, many disreputable puppy brokers (who misleadingly call themselves "breeders") have moved their operations online. Sadly, not all people who breed dogs are trustworthy, and the puppy you choose from an online source may be a far cry from what arrives at your doorstep. The best way to be certain you are acquiring a puppy from a responsible breeder is to visit the kennel personally. If a breeder tells you that you can't visit his or her house or facility or see the mother and the littermates—or if the breeder makes excuses—do not buy a puppy from this breeder.

In your search, you're likely to come across breeders who are not interested in the well-being of their dogs or the betterment of the breed. "Backyard breeders," as they are called, are easy to spot once you know what to look for and understand the characteristics of a responsible breeder. The bottom line for these sellers is almost always money, and they usually sell their dogs on a first-come, first-served basis with little regard for the future welfare of the dogs. Purchasing your puppy from a backyard breeder is no bargain, because it's highly likely that you will pay a good deal more in vet bills down the road.

Be smart. Purchase a puppy from a responsible, knowledgeable breeder who understands and cares about the breed—someone who will be

If you're interested in rescuing a dog, visit your local animal shelter or humane society. Many wonderful homeless dogs are just waiting to meet their "forever" owners.

Signs of a Healthy Puppy

When you know how to recognize the signs of a healthy puppy, it won't be too difficult to spot red flags. At first glance, a puppy may appear healthy, but always look for the following:

- clear, bright eyes with no discharge or swelling of the eyelids
- pink, odor-free ears free of discharge (healthy ears have a slight doggy smell—a bit like the smell of beeswax)
- a clean, healthy coat, shiny and bright with no signs of excess scratching, inflamed skin, rashes, hot spots, or bald spots, which could indicate fleas, mites, ringworm, other parasites
- sweet-smelling "puppy breath"
- healthy, pink gums (pale gums usually indicate anemia or possibly parasites)
- cool, moist, and clean nose, free of nasal discharge, and no frequent sneezing or wheezing
- free movement when walking or playing; no limping

there to help you through the transition periods, offer training advice, and help you make serious decisions regarding the care and well-being of your new puppy.

Rescue Organizations

Rescue organizations are a viable option, although they tend to have more adult dogs than puppies. That's not to say you won't find the puppy of your dreams via rescue. Sometimes pregnant mama dogs or young puppies find their way into rescue.

Dogs end up in rescue through no fault of their own. Too many of these dogs are surrendered because their owners made an impulse purchase, did not give sufficient thought to taking on a dog, or did not understand the time and effort required in owning, training, and caring for a dog. Some owners failed to research their chosen breed thoroughly and got a super-active Irish Setter when what they really needed was a low-key Pekingese. Some dogs in rescue have been abused or mishandled. Others are given up or abandoned after they outgrow the cute puppy stage. Many of these dogs are strays or have been voluntarily surrendered to animal shelters because of their owners' personal or family illness, divorce, death, or other changes.

Numerous rescue organizations exist—large and small, independent and breed-club supported. Most national breed clubs sponsor their own rescue groups. If you are looking for a particular breed, consider contacting the breed's national parent club, which can put you in touch with a rescue coordinator.

Rescue organizations carefully evaluate each dog for health and temperament issues. Some dogs are placed in experienced foster homes, where they receive veterinary attention, training, grooming, and lots of love until they can be placed in permanent homes.

Plenty of wonderful, loving companions have come out of rescue. Many go on to excel in canine sports, including obedience, agility, herding, flyball and more—proving that dogs can flourish in the hands of responsible people who are willing to love, train, and provide for their dogs' physical and mental needs.

If you go this route, be sure to go in with eyes wide open. Understand that many of these dogs were not trained properly in their prior homes and may have behavioral issues. Are you prepared to commit to a rescue dog? If so, find out as much as you can about the dog—his history, training, behavior, and so forth. If no history is known, and oftentimes it is not, be sure to consult an experienced trainer or behaviorist for advice.

Pet Shops

Best advice: steer clear of pet stores that sell puppies. Your heart instinctively will go for the adorable but shy, skittish puppy. It is human nature to feel sorry for sad pups in a store window, but these puppies are risky business. Responsible breeders—who usually belong to a parent club and abide by a code of ethics—would never sell their puppies to pet stores or any other third-party dealer. Therefore, the majority of pet-shop puppies come from puppy mills. These dogs are unhealthy and receive little or no veterinary care, and the puppies are taken at very young ages and sent to dealers or directly to pet stores. Because the puppies are taken from their mothers too soon, they receive no socialization and are often timid, fearful, and downright spooky.

Don't be fooled by the kennel-club registration papers. Many a pedigree has been faked, and none of the documents accompanying a pet-store puppy is an indication or guarantee of quality. Purchasing a puppy from a pet store only encourages irresponsible breeders to produce more litters—purely for financial gain.

Humane Societies and Shelters

Puppies often find their way into humane societies and animal shelters for the same reasons that they end up in rescue organizations. Oftentimes, puppies are whelped and reared in shelter or foster-home environments. Not surprisingly, a particular behavioral problem is the primary reason that most dogs are surrendered to shelters.

Shelter employees and volunteers do their best to work with these dogs to prepare them for adoption. Some shelters work with local rescues, placing some puppies and adult dogs in foster homes for future adoption. Shelter dogs can and do make excellent companions, but they sometimes have behavioral issues and require special care and training.

Pet-Supply-Store Adoptions

A relatively new trend is for large pet-supply stores to work in conjunction with local animal shelters by offering in-store adoptions. These pet superstores open their doors to local animal shelters that bring adoptable dogs to the store for "meet-and-greet" events where the public can interact with all types of dogs in need of homes. Unlike pet-shop dogs, these adoptees are healthy dogs that are available through local animal shelters. Be sure that you know the difference before opening your wallet.

CHAPTER 2

PUPPY'S FIRST DAYS AT HOME

Once you have found the perfect puppy, the real fun (and work!) begins. Transitioning to a new home can be confusing and disorienting for a baby dog. He may need a few hours, days, or weeks—depending on his temperament and personality—to adjust to his new life. By planning ahead, you can minimize the stress for both you and your puppy.

Your puppy is counting on you to provide him with a safe and healthy environment, which means puppy-proofing inside and outside. He also needs quality nutrition, regular training, and routine veterinary care. He needs hugs and kisses and cuddling and sweet nothings whispered in his ear. Equally important, you must provide him with guidance and direction, which means setting a regular schedule of eating, pottying, and sleeping. You will need to decide which behaviors are acceptable and which are not, such as jumping on the furniture, sleeping on the bed, begging at the table, snatching food, bolting out doors, and so forth. Household rules should be reinforced from day one to avoid confusing your puppy. Planning ahead will help you avoid the more common mistakes, thereby getting you and your puppy off to a positive start.

Puppy-Proofing and Boundaries

Your puppy is too young to understand that your expensive leather shoes are not for teething, your sofa pillows are not playthings, and your floors are not his personal bathroom. Therefore, puppy-proof your house *before* your puppy arrives. This point cannot be stressed enough. Like toddlers, puppies are curious and have an abundance of energy. They will want to explore their surroundings and try to put everything in their mouths—whether it fits or not.

Start by getting down on your puppy's level and taking a look around. What can your puppy get into? What can he eat? What can he climb on? Anything and everything that you think he won't eat or chew—he will! He is not being a naughty puppy: he is simply being a puppy. What do you see? Shoes, books, magazines lying around? What about a remote control, cell phone, iPad? Pick up or put away anything your puppy is likely to seek out and destroy. Electrical cords must be safely concealed behind furniture or under rugs or taped to baseboards because they can cause serious injury or death if a puppy chews on them. Prescription drugs, cleaning supplies, detergents, and poisonous houseplants

Americans Spend

The American Pet Products Association reports that pet owners spent an estimated $55.72 billion (yes, billion!) dollars on pet supplies in 2013—topping the $53.33 billion spent in 2012.

are a disaster waiting to happen if your puppy eats them. Shoelaces, buttons, socks, marbles, thumbtacks, and paper clips, if swallowed, can cause life-threatening intestinal blockages and may require emergency surgery to remove.

Puppy-proof your yard, garden, and other outdoor areas, too. Some puppies are climbers, others are diggers, and some are escape artists, eager to muscle their way through the tiniest openings. Make sure to secure all fencing and gates and make repairs if needed. Puppies are inquisitive, and if you think he can escape through it, then he will. Pick up hoses, sprinklers, and lawn ornaments that your puppy will likely try to chew. Be mindful of products, such as fertilizers, pesticides, rock salt, deicers, or slug bait. Many of these products are toxic and can seriously harm your puppy should he ingest them.

African violets, Christmas cactus, and calla lilies are a few of the countless plants that are toxic to dogs. Be sure to keep them far from your puppy's reach. Check your yard for mushrooms, too, because some of them are toxic if ingested.

You must carefully consider swimming pools, ponds, waterscapes, and so forth for your puppy's long-term safety. While many older puppies can swim, your youngster may not be able to find an easy means of escape should he climb or fall into a pool or pond.

While puppy-proofing may seem a bit overwhelming, it is a necessity. Keeping your puppy safe will save you a good deal of money and heartache down the road.

Start with the Right Stuff

Who doesn't love to shop? Ornamental beds, designer sweaters, doggie boots, IQ-boosting toys, automatic water dispensers, and custom crates that look like furniture—the list is endless, and with thousands of online vendors, you can shop 'til you drop without ever leaving your house!

Purchase puppy-sized bowls for your large-breed youngster. This Rottie puppy could take a bath in his future water bowl.

Basic essentials for your new puppy include a dog bed, collar and leash, crate, exercise pen, food and water bowls, identification, and an assortment of training toys and chew toys. You will also need a brush or two, nail clippers, shampoo, and conditioner; even if you choose to take your dog to a groomer, you should still have the basics on hand.

Food and Water Bowls

Owners often buy bowls that they like rather than what best suits their puppy. After all, who can resist the dog-bone-shaped bowl or the ceramic bowl with the decorative paws? You will need two bowls: one for water and one for food. Depending on the eventual size of the dog you have chosen, you may need to buy several sets of bowls as your puppy grows. What works for a ten-week-old puppy may not work for an 80-pound adult dog. Bowls should be easy to clean and made of material that is not potentially harmful; stainless steel fits these requirements. Ceramic can be toxic, and glass bowls can easily break. Plastic bowls are inexpensive but can harbor bacteria and are not as easily sanitized as stainless steel. Tenacious chewers could easily ingest or choke on shredded pieces from a plastic bowl. Choose bowls with nonslip bases so that they won't slide across the floor.

Gates

Few dog owners can live without baby (or puppy) gates. They are indispensible and ideal for corralling your puppy and keeping him safe when you cannot give him your undivided attention. Until he is thoroughly house-trained and well through the chewing stage, gates will restrict his access and prevent him from wandering the house, getting himself into trouble, and developing bad habits.

If you're prepared for the arrival of your new acquisition, you can savor and enjoy the first days of puppy ownership.

Crates

A crate is an absolute necessity because it serves so many purposes. It's a great house-training tool, the safest place for a dog to be while traveling, and a cozy den for sleeping, retreating, or relaxing. A crate placed in a quiet corner of the kitchen or family room will satisfy a puppy's natural instinct to seek a safe and secure environment. Your puppy should view the crate as a fun, positive, and inviting place—a quiet place all his own to sleep, eat, and retreat from the demands of being a puppy.

Crates come in different shapes, sizes, and materials. Consider how you will be using the crate and pick the best one for your puppy's needs. For example, folding wire crates provide good air circulation and help keep dogs cool when temperatures are high. Other crate types include heavy-duty, high-impact plastic kennels that meet requirements for airline travel.

Purchase a crate that is big enough to allow an adult dog of your breed to stand up, turn around, and stretch out while lying down. If the crate is too big, it defeats the purpose of providing the security of a den. If it is too small, your puppy will be cramped and uncomfortable.

Exercise Pens

An exercise pen (or ex-pen), which is a portable wire playpen for dogs, is another must-have for raising a well-behaved puppy. If you've been to a dog show, you've probably seen exhibitors using them. Available in varying heights—usually from 18 to 42 inches (46 to 107 cm)—ex-pens are ideal for placing anywhere you need a temporary kennel area. An ex-pen will safely confine your puppy when you cannot give him your undivided attention.

Beds

Puppies chew, and a tenacious puppy can turn a pricey canine bed into worthless confetti in the time it takes you to run outside and move the sprinkler. Your puppy needs a bed of his own, but it is best to hold off on anything too expensive until he is well through the chewing and pottying stages. A large blanket, folded towel, or cozy fleece pad placed in his crate will do the job for the first few months. A blanket, towel, or pad is easily cleaned in the washing machine and is therefore less likely to develop that distinctive doggy smell.

A simple dog bed that is washable is the best choice for a young puppy that's still undergoing house-training.

Collars, Leashes, and Harnesses

Ideally, your puppy should wear a lightweight nylon or leather buckle collar with proper identification attached. Nylon collars are inexpensive, which makes them a good choice for a puppy because you will need to replace the collar several times before the puppy is fully grown. Strong metal buckle fasteners may provide a slight advantage over plastic quick-release clips, which may break more easily. Again, much will depend on the type and size of your dog. Leather collars are more expensive than nylon, and while they are well worth the investment for adult dogs, they may not be feasible for puppies.

You'll need to check the collar size frequently—once a week or so. Ideally, the collar should fit around your puppy's neck with enough room for you to fit two fingers between his neck and the collar. It should not be so tight as to restrict his breathing or cause coughing, nor should it be so loose that it slips over his head. When too loose, the collar can easily snag on objects, causing the dog to panic and possibly hang himself.

A head halter goes over your dog's face and applies pressure to the back of the neck rather than the front of the throat. Many dogs object to head halters, so you may need to consult a trainer for alternative solutions.

You may decide to choose a harness for your new puppy. While a harness will take the pressure off a puppy's trachea, it will not keep him from pulling. In fact, harnesses can teach a dog to pull, which is the opposite of what you're trying to accomplish. A variety of models are available in different shapes, sizes, and materials.

Leashes

Countless choices exist when it comes to leashes. A lot will depend on the size and strength of the dog you have chosen, how much money you are willing to spend, and your personal preference. Ideally, you should have several leashes—at least one for home and a spare to keep in your car.

When a puppy enters your home, be ready for anything... and be ten giant steps ahead of your miniature new chum.

A good quality leather leash is expensive but well worth the investment. Leather leashes are gentler on your hands. The more you use a leather leash, the softer and more pliable it becomes. A well-cared-for leather leash will last a lifetime. Puppies love to chew leather, too, so be mindful of where you leave your leash lying around.

Nylon leashes are lightweight and relatively inexpensive, but they are not always the best choice for medium or large dogs because they are hard on your hands and can slice your fingers should your dog lunge or give a good pull.

Rope leashes made from recycled climbing rope are softer than nylon and have a smidge of elasticity to them. Ideal for most breeds, they are durable; come in a wide range of styles, lengths, and fashionable colors; and are gentle on your hands.

Retractable leashes are designed to extend and retract at the touch of a button. While some trainers use retractable leashes for teaching puppy recalls, many trainers recommend them only on well-behaved dogs that respond to voice commands. While a retractable leash allows your puppy more leeway, it can quickly become tangled around fence posts, bushes, and trees. If a strong or determined puppy gets too far out on the leash, you may have trouble reeling him in.

Newly Adopted Puppies

Depending on where and from whom you acquired your puppy, he may be a high flight risk. Maybe he has a history of escaping, which may be how he ended up at a shelter or rescue organization. Busy, excitable puppies that are too young or lack adequate recall or obedience training can easily escape and get lost. It can take a long time for some puppies and young dogs to get used to new homes, sounds, people, routines, and so forth. If you are uncertain about your puppy's history or training, you should always assume that he is at high risk of escaping and take precautions. Go beyond what you think is necessary, and the odds of keeping your pet off the "lost" list will increase greatly.

Puppy Brushes

Countless types of brushes—from slickers to boar hair to wire pin—are available, and the equipment you choose for grooming depends largely on your puppy's coat type and texture. A slicker works well for removing dead undercoat and debris from double-coated breeds; however, it will cause breakage on the long hair of drop-coated breeds. A brush with soft metal pins on a rubber-cushioned base, one in which the pins will give and not break the hair, are good for most breeds because they can work through the top coat and undercoat easily.

Metal combs can be used to help break up mats and remove stubborn undercoat. A curry comb, hound glove, and canine chamois work well on short- or smooth-coated breeds.

Identification

The importance of proper identification cannot be stressed enough. No one expects his or her dog to go missing, but accidents happen, and the nightmare of losing a dog happens to thousands of responsible owners every day. Taking preventive measures can save your dog's life.

ID Tags: Your puppy should have an ID tag with up-to-date information, including your name and telephone number. ID tags are your puppy's ticket home should he become lost or separated from you. Readily available at retail pet outlets and from mail-order catalogs and online vendors, tags come in a variety of shapes, sizes, colors, and materials and easily attach to your dog's buckle collar with an "S" clip or good-quality split ring. Nameplates that attach directly to your dog's collar are also available.

Check the collar and tag regularly for wear and tear, as collars often break or slip off a dog—leaving him with no identification. Some nylon collars have contact information embroidered right into them, so if the tags ever fall off, your contact information remains on the collar.

Microchips: A silicon microchip about the size of a grain of rice is painlessly inserted under a puppy's skin. It contains an unalterable identification number that is recorded in a central database along with your name, address, telephone number, and email address. The microchip is scanned and the identification number is read via a handheld electronic scanner. Most universal scanners can detect and read the frequencies of all major brands of microchips.

Once your puppy is microchipped, you will need to register the identification number. Most registries and pet-recovery assistance programs register all brands of microchips. AVID®, Home Again®, and AKC Reunite® are among the largest providers of microchip and pet-recovery services. It is important you understand the assistance provided and the costs associated with each brand of microchip. Get in the habit of asking your vet to scan your dog several times a year, or anytime you are at the vet's clinic, because microchips can migrate or stop functioning.

GPS Devices: You can track down a lost cell phone, computer, or car—so why not your dog? GPS provides this option, with several different brands available at reasonable prices. The GPS unit attaches to or is embedded in your dog's buckle collar and communicates with you via a smartphone, computer, or handheld device. The downside is that these units use GPS communication, so when GPS is not available, they don't work. Some services also require a monthly or yearly fee, which is a small price to pay for the safe return of a much-loved pet.

Toys and Treats

Puppies like and need to chew—especially during the teething phase, when their baby teeth erupt and fall out. Chewing makes their gums feel better, but puppies don't understand that they shouldn't chew on your purse, shoes, or chairs. Don't despair, though—you can seriously curb the destruction by providing your puppy with plenty of appropriate toys designed for chewing. Finding toys isn't difficult, but finding safe, healthy, nontoxic toys and treats takes a bit of effort. Some toys are virtually indestructible and designed for the most tenacious chewers. They exercise a puppy's teeth and gums, promoting oral health while relieving the need to chew. Some of these toys are hollow and specially designed for hiding treats, such as cheese or peanut butter, inside.

Be careful with vinyl or plush toys that contain squeakers or noisemakers. Puppies love them, but some puppies are four-legged destroying machines and will rip right through the material and even swallow the squeakers.

Rawhide chews are an alternative to nylon chews—provided your puppy chews them rather than swallows them whole. Stick with nonbleached chews, which won't stain your carpet, and beware of rawhide chews imported from other countries.

Rope toys and tugs are often made of 100-percent cotton and frequently are flavored to make them more attractive to dogs. Some rope tuggies do double duty because they have plaque-fighting fluoride floss woven into the rope to deep-clean your puppy's teeth and gums. Nylon tuggies are a haven for bacteria, so be sure to launder them regularly.

Welcome Home!

It seems like you have been waiting forever, but the day for picking up your puppy has finally arrived. It's an exciting time for you and your family, but it may be a scary, uncertain, and stressful time for your puppy. Remember, he is leaving the security of his mom and littermates and the only home he has known. Making the trip home and his first experience with his new family a positive and happy one will go a long way in helping reduce problems later on.

Ideally, you will want to pick up your puppy on a day when you're not working so you're not rushed. If possible, consider taking a few days off from work so you can be with your puppy to help him transition and to get started on the right foot.

On the ride home, your puppy should ride in a crate, not on someone's lap or loose in the car—and never in the back of an open pickup truck. These are accidents waiting to happen! A traumatic first car ride can make it more difficult to "car-train" your puppy later.

Get on your puppy's level to make his acquaintance. Puppy love begins with ticklish kisses.

Line the crate with a few towels in case the puppy has an accident. Your puppy may whine or cry because he is nervous or scared. Avoid yelling at him or telling him to be quiet. He won't understand, and you are likely to exacerbate the situation. Instead, be comforting and have a passenger come along who can sit near the crate or put his or her hand close to the crate.

Once home, allow your puppy plenty of time to freely explore his new yard and, if necessary, potty. If your yard is not fenced, keep him on a leash or long line at all times. Don't be surprised if he's nervous and just sits or lies in one spot. Give him plenty of time to explore at a pace comfortable for him.

Allow him to do his business, and calmly praise him when he's in the process of pottying. When he's finished exploring, and he's relieved himself, take him indoors. Have baby gates or an ex-pen in place to confine him to a certain room or area. Corralling him wherever the family tends to congregate will keep him from wandering around the house, where he can inadvertently learn bad habits and get himself into trouble. Also allow your puppy plenty of time to rest in his bed, crate, or ex-pen when he needs to escape the domestic hustle and bustle. Everyone—especially children—should understand that the puppy needs to be left alone while he is sleeping.

Parents need to teach children how to properly interact with young puppies that can be harmed by careless handling.

Children and the Pup

Children and puppies tend to go together, but too much "togetherness" all at one time can be overwhelming. Parents are the key figures when it comes to teaching children how to interact safely with a puppy, and vice versa. By setting a few ground rules, you can help ensure that your children and puppy develop a positive long-term friendship.

Young children are often boisterous, excitable, and inconsistent with their behaviors. Most puppies are excited by movement and like to chase and nip the legs of fleeing children. This is natural doggy behavior. However, reinforcing these behaviors means you will end up with an adult dog that sees no harm in chasing, jumping up, and nipping. Supervise your puppy and young children to discourage unwanted behaviors and create an environment of safe play.

Teach your children early on that your puppy is not a toy but a living animal that must be handled properly and treated respectfully. Never allow children to overwhelm your puppy or put him in a position where he can be bullied or frightened.

Children must also learn to approach the puppy quietly and slowly—no running, screaming, or grabbing. Teach older children how to properly pick up a puppy. For very young kids, do not allow them to pick up the puppy without your supervision. They can inadvertently hurt him or possibly even drop him should they try to pick him up by his ears or legs.

Introducing Dogs and Cats

Cats and dogs can and do live harmoniously when introduced in a positive manner. For the first introduction, keep your puppy on leash so he can't chase or harass your cat. You don't want your puppy's first introduction to the feline to result in a scratched nose! Some dogs like to stalk cats, so you'll want to be on the lookout for signs of this behavior and keep it under control. Allowing your puppy to harass a cat or any other animal is neither fair nor funny and should never be encouraged or tolerated. Provide your cat with plenty of escape routes. Cats like being up high, so provide plenty of access to countertops, furniture, and the like. Also, provide your cat with a room or area of his own—a spare room, office, den, the upstairs—so she can escape puppy antics and not be bothered.

If you live in a multiple-dog household, introduce your puppy to his canine housemates in a calm environment (one dog at a time). To be comfortable, your puppy needs to know that he is safe and that the other dog (or dogs) won't bully, intimidate, or hurt him. The same goes for the older dog. He needs to know that he can trust the puppy. It is your job to create an environment that is safe and comfortable for all dogs involved and promote a positive, tension-free friendship. If everything seems fine, let one dog interact but continue to supervise.

If your puppy is nervous, shy, or exceptionally outgoing, you will need to take the introductions slowly. Never force introductions because this may destroy any chance of the dogs' getting along—ever! Some dogs are naturally calm and

Supervise any interactions between the new puppy and the family cat. Puppies learn quickly that cats have claws that are as quick as they are sharp.

get along beautifully with other dogs from the get-go. In these instances, introductions may go off without a hitch, and your puppy and other dog will become fast friends. If your other dogs are pushy or bossy, put your puppy in his ex-pen and allow them to meet with a barrier between them. Sometimes learning simply to exist around each other is a huge step and a safe way for dogs to get comfortable in the same environment.

Most problems arise because a new puppy and another dog or dogs are allowed to run loose too quickly in a chaotic, stressful environment. When introductions do not go smoothly, and a squabble ensues, there is a good chance that the distrust will continue.

No one wants chaos and animosity between pets, so if you are uncertain, consult an experienced dog trainer or behaviorist. Investing the time and resources to establish a positive, stress-free environment from day one is preferable to trying to fix a bad situation later.

Puppy's Own Place

A puppy's first night in his new home—away from his canine mother and littermates—is usually stressful and difficult. Older puppies that have come from shelters or rescue can be equally stressed because of uncertainty and instability in their lives. Some puppies adjust more easily than others, but most will likely be feeling lonely and insecure and may whine and cry after being put in a crate. To help make the first night with your puppy more calm and stress-free, follow these tips:

- Before putting him to bed, be sure he has been outside to potty.
- Dogs are social animals who want to be part of a pack, which is your family. Isolating him in another room is likely to make him feel lonely and insecure.
- Place your puppy's crate next to your bed or that of another family member. Knowing that someone is near will help comfort him. During the night, you can reach down and reassure him that you are close by.
- Be sure to put some soft towels or a crate pad and a safe dog toy inside so he can curl up and be comfortable.

Once tucked into his new bed, your puppy may cry for a few minutes before dozing off. He might even scream and yowl for a while. Despite your best intentions, avoid taking him out of his crate and into your bed—unless that is where you want him to sleep for the rest of his life. Taking him out of his crate will reinforce in his mind: "When I cry, someone will rescue me."

Ideally, it is best to ignore your puppy's pitiful pleas, provided, of course, that you are certain he is safe and does not need to potty. Never scold or physically punish your puppy; this will only exacerbate the problem and may create a puppy that becomes fearful, anxious, or worried. Realize that this will pass. It's part and parcel of owning a puppy. It might take a few sleepless nights, but once the puppy settles down, he will become quite attached to his crate.

Bonding

The term "bonding" is tossed around a lot in the dog-training world, but what does it mean? The bond you form with your dog is what helps to cement the foundation of the human-canine relationship. Bonding is how you develop a meaningful, trusting, one-on-one rapport with your canine best friend.

Some experts dismiss the idea of making yourself the center of your puppy's world. But if you have ever been touched deeply by a dog, you know that bonding is real. The depth of emotion that owners have for their dogs is oftentimes inexplicable. Countless stories exist of people who are willing to risk their own lives to save their dogs.

Why is bonding important? In addition to the reciprocating human-canine friendship and all of the positives that come from such a relationship, research indicates that people who have an emotional attachment to or relationship with their dogs are more likely to stay committed for life.

Household Rules

Let's face it: unless you and your puppy live in a cave, he will need some manners. In other words, unless you want your puppy to grow into a hooligan, you will need to have household rules in place before he comes home. It does no good to establish puppy rules unless everyone in the family is following the same rules. Household rules help to teach your puppy that he cannot be cheeky, pushy, bossy, or obnoxious. He must learn to play nicely, act like a mannerly citizen, and not run wild.

The rules you establish and the behaviors you choose to accept are up to you. You should never feel guilty for allowing your puppy to jump up on you or sleep on the bed with you or beg for food at the dinner table—if those are behaviors you can happily live with for the next twelve to fifteen years.

White furniture is every puppy's favorite cozy retreat. Don't allow your puppy on the sofa if you're not going to permit him on the sofa when he's an adult.

On the other hand, if you decide to designate your bed and furniture as dog-free zones, then you must set a clear pattern of behavior by not allowing him on the furniture from day one. Avoid confusing your puppy by allowing him on the bed today but not tomorrow because you just changed the sheets. If you do not want a particular behavior, you should discourage the behavior when your puppy is young. You must manage his environment so he learns early on which behaviors are acceptable and which might preclude a long and mutually respectful human-canine relationship.

CHAPTER 3

DAILY ROUTINE

Your puppy may take a few days to a few weeks to settle in—depending on his age, temperament, and from where and whom you acquired him. No set time schedule exists for introducing him to his new home and environment. You will need to work with your puppy according to his individual temperament and personality—always progressing at a speed that is within his comfort zone.

Ideally, you will want to start right away establishing a daily routine. Dogs are creatures of habit and thrive on guidance, boundaries, and structure. Granted, some puppies are more challenging than others, and your puppy's first weeks home may not be the "honeymoon period" you had envisioned. Even so, he will adjust best if you provide some order to his life.

By setting a routine and sticking to it, you can begin instilling desired behaviors—such as eating and pottying at regular times, following you everywhere, walking politely on leash, and playing nicely—while simultaneously discouraging unwanted behaviors. What your puppy learns during this time will shape his character and ultimately enhance or impede the human-canine relationship. Puppy manners, such as waiting at doors and greeting people, allow your puppy to grow into a well-behaved adult dog that can coexist with your family.

An eight-week-old puppy is eight weeks old for exactly seven days. Your puppy needs to learn important puppy skills while he is young and impressionable, so get started right away. You will want to maximize the first four months of his life because you cannot afford to waste this formative period.

Make coming to you a game and practice it at home, in your backyard, and on every outing.

First and foremost, you should consider every moment spent with your puppy as a training session. Whether you are training, playing, or snuggling—your puppy will learn from every experience, be it positive or negative, and regardless of whether or not you're consciously teaching him.

Raising a puppy is a balancing act between being the "protective mama bear" and giving him freedom to make choices and work things out on his own. Like your puppy's canine mom, you will need to feed him and keep him safe, warm, and feeling loved. You need to know when to pick him up, put him down, ignore his whimpering, and gently nudge him in the direction of figuring it out on his own so he can build confidence.

You need to instill good behavior in a fun, playful way. You need to establish priorities so you don't overwhelm him by trying to teach everything at once. You need to decide what he needs to learn right away (such as feeding and pottying schedules) and what can wait. Only on rare occasions should you need to scold or correct a puppy.

"No" Is Not His Name

A puppy that hears "No!" enough times will think that it's his name! But "No!" is not the evil word many trainers make it out to be. That teeny-tiny word can save your dog's life, but it must be used appropriately. You want to keep all negative interactions to a minimum. The majority of your interactions should be fun and exciting as you mold his future character.

Puppies are smart and quick to learn when given the direction and guidance they need. Many of them are also sensitive, and they don't like to be wrong. If you are too harsh on your puppy, he may grow into a dog that is constantly worried or too afraid to try new things for fear of making a mistake. Rewarding the right behaviors—the behaviors you want—allows you to mold his personality into that of a happy, loving, fun dog.

"Dogs are a product of what we put into them" is advice that dog trainer Bobbie Anderson was fond of giving. If you are having problems with your puppy, always look to yourself first. Are you providing adequate training? Does he thoroughly understand the command? Did you teach it properly? Did you manage his environment sufficiently? For example, if your puppy is swiping food off the counter, barking incessantly, chewing, digging, or pottying all over your house, whose fault is that? (Hint: it's not your puppy's fault!)

You need to manage your puppy's environment on a minute-by-minute basis so he cannot get himself into trouble and develop bad habits. It is much easier and more effective to create and reward good habits than it is to try and fix unwanted behaviors. For example, it is normal for a puppy to chew, so why are you leaving your leather shoes out where he can get to them?

Puppy Meals and Potty Times

A puppy's daily routine goes something like this: play, potty, eat, play, potty, sleep, potty, eat, potty, play, play, potty, play, eat, sleep, potty—and then potty some more. This routine may vary slightly, but it's surprisingly accurate for most young puppies. Knowing this, it is not difficult to establish a daily schedule and routine. If you are constantly feeding him and taking him out to potty at different times, he will never get a sense of a routine, and house-training him will be much more difficult.

Right away, your puppy should learn where his food and water bowls are, and when and where he gets fed. A puppy's tummy is small, and it can't hold enough food at one time to meet his growth needs; therefore, he needs to be fed several small meals each day. Regular feeding times also help to facilitate house-training, because you know that he'll need to go out soon after eating.

Ideally, until he is about four months old, feed him three times a day. After that, feed him two times a day. Puppies also have small bladders with minimal bladder control until they are six months to one year of age. Therefore, your puppy will need to be taken outdoors regularly to eliminate. Depending on your puppy, it may not be necessary to take him outside every hour, but it is much safer to take him outside more often than necessary than to clean up accidents. Equally important, by taking him outside frequently, he will become house-trained in a much shorter time.

Play Time and Interaction

Puppies need plenty of physical and mental exercise as well as rest, so you will need to establish a regular routine and schedule for playing and resting. Puppies have a lot of energy, but they tire quickly. Of course, a tired puppy is a good puppy! A tired puppy is less likely to be bored and subsequently chew your shoes or table legs or otherwise misbehave.

Your schedule and work hours will dictate your puppy's schedule. The key is having a schedule that is flexible enough to suit your lifestyle yet still meet your puppy's daily needs. Ideally, you should play with your puppy multiple times a day, including in the morning—after

Make your puppy follow you! Never chase any puppy, especially one that will soon be able to outrun you.

he has pottied and before he has been fed—and five or six times throughout the day, and then a vigorous play session later in the evening before he goes to bed.

Most puppies tire after fifteen or twenty minutes of play. Much will depend on your puppy's breed and individual energy level and what and how you play with him. Puppies also have the attention span of gnats, so your playtime should be fun and productive.

Don't confuse interactive play with stimulating a puppy into hyperactive behavior; this encourages misbehavior. Instead, consider fun chase or wait games where you begin instilling the Come and Wait commands. Teach him to follow you everywhere, and make it fun and rewarding for him to be close to you. This is an important skill because Follow Me morphs into Walk Nicely on Leash and Come to Me.

Part of your daily routine should include handling your puppy at every opportunity. Put your hand in his collar, count his toes, check his ears, inspect his teeth, rub his tummy, and kiss his nose. Handling a puppy teaches him to accept being handled as an adult dog, which makes life easier when he needs to be groomed or examined by the veterinarian. Plenty of fun handling games help a puppy learn in a positive manner to enjoy being picked up and held.

Teach a Communication System

Developing a good communication system from day one is essential. Life is less stressful for dogs if we show them what we want and reward them for it, rather than let them guess what we want. "Down" should mean "lie down," and it should mean the same thing today as it does next week and next month. Of course, the words you choose are secondary. What's important is consistency. If you choose to use "Here" instead of "Come," that's OK, but be sure to use the same word every time.

You begin developing a communication system and building a puppy's vocabulary by associating a command (e.g., Sit) with the behavior. Remember, puppies do not come preprogrammed. Repeatedly saying, "Sit. Sit. Sit! I said SIT!" does nothing to expand your puppy's vocabulary. Until you show him what behavior goes with "Sit," and you reward him for the behavior over and over again, he does not know understand that "Sit" means "put your rear end on the ground."

Remember that puppies and adult dogs are not intentionally belligerent or naughty. If you are having a communication problem, you need to look at where your training went awry. What do you need to do to better explain what you want? How can you better show your puppy what you expect from him? Clear, consistent communication helps your puppy grow into a stress-free adult dog.

Communicating with your puppy is hands-on business.

PART II

TRAINING
YOUR
PUPPY

CHAPTER 4

HOUSE-TRAINING **PRIMER**

Despite the horror stories you might have heard, house-training your puppy is a relatively simple and painless process. It is the one area of puppy rearing that causes owners a great deal of angst, but honestly, it is very simple. Of course, few owners get through the house-training phase without an accident or five, but that is to be expected. More often than not, problems arise when owners complicate the matter by expecting too much from their puppy. An eight-week-old puppy is equivalent to a four- to six-month-old human baby. Would you expect a young baby to control his or her bladder? I think not. It is equally unfair to ask your baby puppy to exercise the control of an adult dog.

Good planning and preparation and your unwavering commitment to the process are the keys to success. Dogs are creatures of habit, and the house-training process will be more successful if you invest the time into teaching the appropriate behavior, which is pottying outside—not peeing from one end of your house to the other.

Crate or Paper?

First, you will need to decide which method—crate-training or paper-training—you will teach your puppy. Crate-training is by far the most efficient method of house-training. Years ago, owners did not capitalize on the fact that dogs are den animals that love having a place of their own to sleep and eat. Consider this: if your puppy were born in the wild, he would live in a cave or den, and most den animals have an instinctive desire to keep their dens clean. The fact that your puppy is now domesticated does not change one iota of his natural instinct to keep his sleeping area (i.e., his crate) clean.

Dogs will do just about anything to avoid eliminating where they sleep. A crate mimics a dog's den. By capitalizing on your puppy's deep-seated cleanliness instinct, you can teach him to control his bladder and bowels and to eliminate outdoors. Crate-training helps facilitate house-training and minimize accidents.

Paper-training (along with puppy pads and litterboxes), on the other hand, is an older yet still utilized method of house-training. It works well for people with tiny dogs or people who live in high-rise apartments and can't go down thirty floors every hour or whenever their puppy looks like he needs to do his business.

The concept of paper-training is that you teach your puppy to relieve himself on newspaper or absorbent pads that you have spread out on the floor. You place the paper in a convenient location, where the puppy can see it, but not too close to his crate. (Remember, he won't want to potty where he sleeps.) Over time, you gradually reduce the area of floor covered by newspaper until your puppy is pottying on just a small section of paper. Simultaneously, you begin moving the paper closer to the door. When you are home and able to supervise your puppy, you take him outdoors to potty—the theory being that by moving the paper closer to the door, and as the puppy develops more bladder control, he will eventually associate pottying with going outside rather than with the paper.

The downside to paper-training is that once you allow your puppy to potty indoors—even on paper—it creates the behavior of pottying in the house. Once this behavior becomes learned or ingrained, it is hard to untrain. Having a dog do his business indoors might not be a problem for Chihuahua owners, but it is not a pretty sight when an adult German Shepherd or Boxer relieves himself in the middle of your kitchen. Eventually, at some point, you'll need to backtrack and train your puppy to relieve himself outdoors. For small dogs, litterbox-training is a viable option if you do not mind having to clean litterboxes daily.

Set a Schedule

Despite what your friend tells you or what you read on the Internet, puppies have little or no bladder control until they are about five or six months old. Accepting this fact of puppyhood is the first step in any successful house-training program. Puppies mature at different rates, so your puppy's control may develop earlier or later. As he matures, he will gradually learn to hold his bladder for longer periods of time.

Your puppy must always have access to the "out" door. This smart Parson Russell Terrier is patiently waiting for his owner to take him for a walk.

What about Breed Size?

Experts disagree about whether small breeds, such as Chihuahuas and Yorkshire Terriers, are more difficult to house-train than large breeds. Some suggest that a small-breed's pea-sized bladder and not-yet-developed sphincter musculature are the likely cause. Small-breed house-training problems are often unnoticed if the puppy sneaks behind the couch or other furniture to do his business—unbeknownst to his owner. Having a small breed means that you will need to be as diligent—if not more so—as the big-breed dog owner.

Until your puppy begins developing some reliable bladder control, you must take him outdoors frequently. Yes, it is nearly a part-time job, but your 100-percent commitment to a regular schedule means that your puppy will learn quicker, which means fewer accidents in the house. The fewer accidents he has, the more reliable he will be as an adult dog. If you are inconsistent, your puppy will suffer in the long run because he will not understand the household rules.

Problems often arise when owners fail to recognize how frequently their puppy needs to relieve himself. As a general guideline, take your puppy outdoors at the following times:

- first thing in the morning when he wakes up, and at least every hour throughout the day
- about fifteen minutes after drinking water
- about thirty minutes after eating
- immediately after waking from a nap
- every time you arrive home
- anytime you take him out of his crate
- anytime he shows signs of having to go
- last thing at night

This guideline is for young puppies, which, of course, are unique and individual. You may need to tweak or adjust this schedule to fit your puppy's particular needs. Minimize accidents by providing your puppy with a regular schedule of eating, sleeping, and eliminating. When you are committed to a regular schedule, your puppy will learn that relieving himself occurs on schedule.

Set a Plan

Now that you have an idea of when and how often your puppy will need to potty, decide on a specific potty spot in your yard. If you don't have a fenced yard, or if you live in an apartment or condo, you will need to find a nearby grassy area (some people choose to use a piece of Astroturf on their deck). Wherever you choose, always use the same spot. You'll confuse your puppy by moving the spot daily or weekly.

Each time your puppy needs to potty, take him to his spot. Watch your puppy closely to be sure he relieves himself. Do not play with him yet—just stand around and pretend to ignore him until he goes. It may take a few minutes, so be patient. Just as he is finishing doing his business, calmly praise him with "Good potty" or "Good puppy."

You will need to repeat this routine many times throughout the day, beginning as soon as you wake up (or, more likely, when your puppy wakes you up) until just before you go to bed. If your puppy is younger than three months old, he will probably have to potty in the middle of the night, too.

Puppies are most active during the day—running, jumping, playing, exploring, and being puppies. Because of their small bladder size and lack of control, they need to relieve themselves many times during the day. During the night, however, they are usually exhausted from the activities of the day. As a result, many puppies can sleep five to eight hours without having to potty.

Some owners get lucky, and their puppy sleeps through the night. Others are relegated to months of sleeplessness. Remember, the puppy is not being naughty or willfully disobedient. He is a puppy. If your puppy wakes you in the middle of the night or early in the morning, it is best to get up with him and take him outside. The fewer accidents he has in his crate, the less stressful the house-training process will be, and the quicker he will learn to potty outside.

If you take your puppy outdoors and he gets sidetracked playing or sniffing bugs and does not relieve himself, you must put him in his crate for five or ten minutes and then try again. (If you are not using a crate, keep your puppy where you can watch him like a hawk for those five or ten minutes). Do this as many times as necessary until your puppy relives himself outdoors.

Never assume that your puppy has done his business. You must see him empty his bladder or bowels. Here is the reason why: If your puppy gets distracted outdoors and forgets to potty, and then you bring him back indoors and give him free run of the house, guess where he is going to potty when he is no longer distracted and has a sudden urge to go? It's a safe bet he will potty on your carpet. Be upset with yourself, not with your puppy, because it is not his fault. Chalk up the situation to experience, and endeavor to be more observant in the future.

Grass is the most popular choice for dogs: it's soft, squishy, and always smells inviting.

Another important reason for going with the puppy when he potties is the foundation of the Come command. When he is finished doing his business, calmly praise him with "Good potty" or "Good puppy," and then make a game of having him chase you back to the house. Tell him, "Good boy!" and then run toward the house while you clap and cheer him on. When you get to the house, offer verbal praise and reward him with a yummy tidbit. Remember, young puppies are eager to follow you anywhere and everywhere. Plus, you are inciting his natural chase instinct. So by going with him to potty and then having him chase you back to the house, you maximize every opportunity to begin to instill desired behaviors.

Adding a Verbal Cue

Even when your puppy knows to go to his designated spot and can successfully make the journey, you should still go with him. By doing so, you can begin instilling a verbal cue for the command, such as "Go pee" or "Go potty." Some owners use "Wee wee" or "Poo poo." You can choose a separate word for urinating and defecating. A word of caution: choose your words carefully. What might be cute or silly in your yard could be embarrassing or downright inappropriate in public.

Give the verbal cue each time your puppy is in the process of doing his business so he begins to associate the cue words with the appropriate action. It won't take long, and you will be able to prompt your dog to go potty on command, which is very helpful in bad weather or when you are traveling. No one wants to stand around at a rest area for twenty minutes, waiting for a puppy. Give the cue word(s) in a calm but encouraging tone of voice. If your voice is too enthusiastic, your puppy is likely to be distracted and forget what he is doing.

Is My Puppy Trained Yet?

Owners run into trouble when they think too soon that their puppy is house-trained. Some puppies are harder to house-train than others, and success is hugely dependent on owner commitment and compliance. Chances are, your puppy will not be reliably house-trained until he is *at least* six months old.

It's worth mentioning that puppies that have spent all of their time outdoors or in kennels or on the streets may take longer to house-train because they have never had to learn bladder control. A four- or six-month-old puppy, for instance, that has lived his life in a kennel simply potties whenever and wherever he felt like it. He has never had a reason to control his bladder. The kennel was his bathroom. That's not to say that these puppies can't be house-trained—they can, but it may take longer and require extra diligence and commitment on the part of owners.

Puppies between the ages of eight and ten weeks do not show signs of having to urinate. When a puppy of that age has to go, he goes right away—often stopping to urinate in the middle of a play session. It is unrealistic to expect an eight-week-old puppy to stop what he is doing and tell you that he needs to go outside. More often than not, your puppy will not realize he has to go until he is already going. Around ten or twelve weeks of age, a puppy will start to exhibit signs—warning signals that he is about to urinate or defecate—by circling, making crying noises, sniffing the floor, or standing by the door. Don't get overconfident and think you are home free. These are signs that your puppy is learning, not that he is fully house-trained. You mustn't become complacent. Now more than ever, you need to remain diligent and stick to the program. Puppies are either house-trained or they are not. Any wavering on your part will only set your puppy up for problems.

When Accidents Happen

Ideally, you should do everything possible to prevent accidents or at least keep them to a minimum. If an accident does happen, resign yourself to being more observant and diligent in the future. Did you miss the prepotty signals? Did you keep to his regular feeding and pottying schedule?

Never scold or hit your puppy and never, ever rub his nose in the mess. This is not dog training, and it injures the relationship you're forming with your puppy. Successful house-training is your responsibility. Your puppy won't understand why you are angry or why he is being scolded. Punishing, yelling, or otherwise berating your puppy will only confuse him and prolong the house-training process. At worst, it teaches your puppy to be afraid of you. A puppy that lives in fear of you is likely to grow into an adult dog that is anxious and frequently worried, which can exacerbate urinating in the house or cause him to develop all sorts of unwanted behaviors.

Instead, calmly and completely clean up the mess, using a product designed to eradicate pet stains and odors. This is doubly important if the accident is on your carpet; otherwise, your puppy will continue returning to the scene of the crime.

As your puppy becomes more reliable indoors, you can give him greater access to other rooms. Don't let him wander around unsupervised until he's completely house-trained.

CHAPTER 5

FIRST LESSONS FOR THE NEW PUPPY

Your puppy will grow into an adult dog that is a reflection of what you put into him. The time and effort you invest today in bonding and instilling life skills, as well as in teaching basic obedience, will reap plenty of rewards down the road as your puppy grows into a well-mannered adult dog that is fun to be with.

Socialization includes growing your puppy's confidence and teaching him to be handled, which are big parts of the many life lessons he will learn. But your puppy must also learn how to learn, listen, and be calm and not zoom around like a four-legged monster. He needs to learn how to make the right choices, such as not whining, pestering you, demanding your attention, snatching food or toys from your hand, and fighting with other animals. He needs to learn how to handle stress and to figure out some things on his own. He needs to learn patience and that it's OK to be left alone for short periods of time.

As you can see, there is a lot that your puppy needs to learn in a short period of time. While dogs continue to learn throughout their lives, their first experiences are very powerful. If your puppy is on the shy or timid side, you will need to work on bolstering his confidence while providing comfortable learning situations.

Bonding Games

Simple everyday tasks and positive interactions with your dog—feeding, walking, bathing, brushing, playing, exercising, snuggling, and whispering sweet nothings in his ear—are great ways to strengthen your bond with your pup; so are fun games that help to instill basic obedience behaviors.

How much time is required for bonding? Much depends on you and your puppy, and how much time and energy you are willing to invest. Each puppy is unique and must be treated as such. Some puppies are more independent and will take more time and coaching to bond closely with their owners.

Leash Training Your Puppy

Teaching your puppy to walk nicely on leash isn't terribly difficult if you start while he is young. To begin, you will want to accustom your puppy to wearing a buckle collar. Attach a

6-foot leash or long line to his collar and allow him to drag it around the house or yard. This serves two purposes. First, if your puppy begins to wander off, you can step on the leash and reel him in, thus eliminating the counterproductive need for grabbing at or chasing your puppy. Second, dragging a leash accustoms the puppy to following you and being close to you, thus providing a foundation for walking on a leash.

It won't take more than a few sessions to teach the puppy to stay close to you while he is attached to his leash. Eventually, that behavior morphs into walking nicely on leash at your side. Your puppy learns from day one that being close to you is fun and highly rewarding.

Follow Me!

Most puppies between eight and twelve weeks of age will follow you pretty much everywhere, which makes teaching the Follow Me exercise rather easy. Your puppy's mother and siblings are gone, and you are now his security. Teach your puppy to follow you everywhere you go by rewarding him for staying close to your side.

To start, your puppy should be dragging his leash attached to his buckle collar. Get your puppy's attention by using tasty tidbits. In the beginning, lure and reward your puppy by holding the treat near your side. Be generous with your treats and your verbal praise so that he learns that being close to you is rewarding and a fun place to be. Use a cue such as "Stay close" and praise him with "Good boy!" or whatever words you choose to use.

If your puppy is toy-crazy, you can use a toy and reward him with a fun game of tug while he is close to you. Do this multiple times throughout the day in as many different places as possible, such as your kitchen, living room, backyard, and so forth. It won't be long before your puppy wants to be by your side all the time, which makes it much easier for you to teach him how to walk nicely on leash.

Many puppies will try to pick up their leashes and carry them around. Don't worry about this. In fact, put a command to the behavior. "Have you got your leash?" eventually becomes "Get your leash!"

By fourteen or fifteen weeks of age, most puppies have been out and about, socializing and exploring new surroundings. They are more confident and secure and don't need you as much as they did when they were eight to twelve weeks old. Around this time, most puppies will begin testing to see if

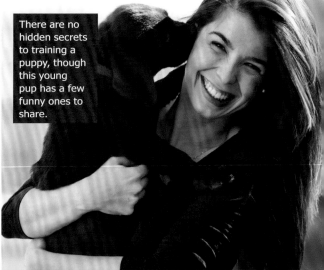

There are no hidden secrets to training a puppy, though this young pup has a few funny ones to share.

their owners are really going to enforce the rules. You may need to work extra hard to keep your puppy's attention, but by continuing to reinforce the desired behaviors, you continue to reinforce a strong bond. Also, you establish in your puppy's mind that you are the boss. If your puppy thinks he can ignore you today, he will think he can ignore you when he is older, too. Then, when you encounter a critical situation, such as when you need him to come to you or lie down, he will ignore you because he has been allowed to ignore you in the past.

Walk Nicely on Leash

Once your puppy is used to dragging his leash around and being close to you, teaching the Walk Nicely on Leash exercise is pretty simple. While your puppy is dragging his leash and following you around, simply pick up the leash and start walking. Depending on your puppy, you may be able to walk two steps or ten steps or more. Only keep walking if your puppy is walking with you; if he refuses to walk or starts to pull or walk off in another direction, stop in your tracks and try again.

Avoid pulling or jerking the leash to get him to follow. A puppy should never associate his leash and collar with a barrage of corrections or nagging. You want him to view walking on leash as something fun that the two of you do together. Remember that his reward for doing his job (i.e., following closely and staying by your side) is yummy treats or his favorite toy. Praise and reward only polite walking. Remember: the behavior you reward is the behavior you want. By rewarding your puppy while he is jumping, lunging, or bucking, he will think that those behaviors are what you expect. In his mind, he is thinking, "I get cookies when I jump and thrash around, so that's what I'm supposed to do."

Progress a few steps at a time, gradually increasing the distance that your puppy can walk nicely on leash by your side. Practice four or five times a day, first around the house and yard and then eventually on safe, quiet sidewalks in areas with few distractions.

Teaching this exercise is much easier if you keep the puppy on your left side until he understands the exercise. Once your puppy masters walking on leash, there will be times when you won't care whether he is on your left or your right.

And away we go...

Handling Games

Handling your puppy at every opportunity is a great way to build a strong bond. Handling is a fun way for a puppy to learn that being picked up or held is safe. We know that not all puppies or adult dogs enjoy handling. Some puppies have trust issues. Teaching them to accept being touched and handled can take a long time and may require intervention by an experienced trainer or behaviorist. Some dogs dislike handling but learn to tolerate it without much of a fuss.

Teaching your puppy to accept handling is well worth it. Think of all of the times that safe handling is necessary—a trip to the veterinarian, grooming, putting on a collar, checking a paw for thorns, and so forth. Gently handle your puppy multiple times daily. Count his toes and teeth, check his ears, and rub his tummy. This type of handling increases the odds that your puppy will grow into an adult dog that enjoys human contact.

Hand in the Collar

Think of how many times you might need to put your hand in your puppy's collar: snatching him out of danger, during grooming, when attaching his leash, and, of course, for simply putting on or taking off his collar. Your puppy should learn that your hand in his collar means that good things will happen. A puppy should never think that a hand in his collar means he is bad or in trouble.

Umbilical Cord

Another technique that works with some puppies is to tether your puppy to you. This method is referred to as the *umbilical cord method* because the puppy is attached to you with his leash (or a 6-foot cord). You praise and reward your puppy when he is close to you, but not when he is straining at the end of the leash. When carried out properly, this method can produce excellent results. One drawback is that some toy-breed puppies may be in danger of getting trampled underfoot, and some particularly unruly puppies may pull you around.

Again, depending on your puppy's personality and temperament, teaching this game may take some time and patience. You may need to employ the help of a trainer or behaviorist to help your puppy if he seriously objects to handling and touching.

Ideally, you should start handling your puppy's collar from day one. At every opportunity, nonchalantly slip your hand in your puppy's buckle collar and then praise, reward with a tasty tidbit, and release. It is that simple! Think of all the times you can practice this behavior—when you are brushing him, placing down his feeding bowl, petting him, talking to him, and on and on.

If your puppy panics or objects, you will need to progress in small steps. Start with just touching the collar, followed by plenty of yummy tidbits and verbal praise. Gradually advance to putting your hand in the collar. Always praise and reward him for small increments of progress. Let your puppy come to you. Never grab your puppy or his collar because this will exacerbate the problem and make him hand-shy.

The No-Wiggle Game

Just as your puppy should accept handling and touching, he should learn to sit and accept verbal and physical praise while you check his ears, teeth, and feet. Ideally, your puppy should be wearing his buckle collar and his leash. With your puppy sitting, kneel on the ground with the leash tucked under your knee to prevent him from wandering off. Have a handful of tidbits nearby.

With your puppy sitting, use your right hand to gently hold his collar while you use your left hand to gently pet his back for three or four seconds. Praise with a calm "Good boy." Be sure to praise him only while he is sitting and not wiggling. The praise reinforces the behavior you want, which is sitting still. If you praise while he is wiggling, you are telling your puppy that wiggling is what you want. If your praise is too wild, excited, or animated, it will cause the puppy to become excited—and thus wiggle—thereby defeating the purpose of the exercise. Switch hands: place your left hand in the collar and gently stroke him with your right hand. Praise, reward, and then switch hands again.

Teach your puppy to accept physical and verbal praise while he is standing and lying down, too. Some puppies find the mere anticipation of physical praise too stimulating; therefore, always progress at a speed that is within your puppy's physical and mental capabilities.

Fetch

Fetching is a great way to tire out a puppy while simultaneously building a strong bond. Retrieving games are the foundation of many obedience skills and other games that you can play with your puppy. By capitalizing on your puppy's natural instinct to retrieve, you can get toys back easily and stay in control of the games.

Some dogs are more eager to retrieve, even at a young age. Most, but certainly not all, retrievers and other sporting dogs, as well as many herding breeds, are natural retrievers, whether retrieving a stick, tug toy, ball, or flying disc. If your puppy is not, don't despair. Some puppies need a bit of encouragement to flourish at retrieving. This fun game is sure to teach even the most reluctant puppy how to retrieve and, more importantly, to love retrieving.

Hunting breeds, whether gundogs, sighthounds, or scenthounds, live to chase.

As with nearly everything associated with puppies, you make retrieving a fun game. To generate excitement, tie a long line on your puppy's toy and drag and wiggle it around on the ground. Drag the toy around until your puppy shows excitement. Put a command to it, such as "Fetch" or "Get it" so that he begins to associate the command with running and picking up things. When he gets the toy, reward with "Good boy" or "Good fetch." Let him strut around with the toy in his mouth as he savors his mammoth achievement.

Continue playing and dragging the toy but don't let him get it every time. The excitement comes from the chase and capture. Make him work a little harder each time for the toy. If he is reluctant to pick the toy up, drag or wiggle it some more to generate more movement to encourage him to get it. If necessary, sit on the floor and drag the toy around your legs and behind your back as you bolster his interest in the toy.

Once the puppy masters this game, you can incorporate the fun recall game by tossing the toy across the room, sending your puppy for it, and then running to the other side of the room or yard so he chases you with his toy. This begins instilling the behavior of bringing the toy back. When he gets to you, praise and reward but don't take the toy right away. Let him savor the moment.

Retrieving Games

Keep in mind that retrieving games should be avoided while your puppy is teething. A teething puppy's mouth will be tender, and vigorous games can harm his emerging teeth and developing jaw bones. During these tender-tooth times, spend time working on other games and come back to retrieving when your puppy is done teething.

Tugging

Tugging is a game that has fallen out of favor with some trainers because they consider it a test of strength. The theory is that a puppy that wins strength games often assumes that he is stronger than his owner, both physically and mentally, which leads him to naturally assume he is better suited to be the pack leader. Some dogs may see this as an opportunity to exploit the situation and take control.

Tugging does stimulate or create arousal in some dogs, especially high-drive-type dogs such as terriers and herding breeds. When a puppy gets too wound up or overly excited, his owners usually lose control of the game, and that's when trouble happens.

That said, tugging is a great interactive game that you can play with your puppy, provided you set some ground rules from day one. First, you must win as often as your puppy wins. If you win all the time, your puppy will get bored and lose interest. If your puppy wins all the time, he may think he doesn't need to share with you. As dog trainer Sylvia Bishop likes to say, "You win, he wins, you both win." This gives him the right message regarding his status in the pack.

You must control all the games, including tugging. You determine when the two of you tug, how hard you tug, how long each of you will tug, when your puppy is to release the toy, and when the game is over. If your puppy becomes too stimulated or out of control or begins snatching the toy from your hand or showing any aggression (other than normal puppy play-growling), stop the game immediately. Resume the game once he has calmed down and you have regained control of the situation.

When positive play and training are used to teach your puppy's first lessons, including games and basic obedience skills, he will grow into an adult dog that is fun to be with all of the time.

CHAPTER 6

SOCIALIZATION

How well your dog gets along with other dogs and people has a lot to do with how he is socialized as a puppy. Behavior comes from a combination of genetics *and* environment, so a lot will depend on his breeding. Even so, a combination of good genetics and proper socialization is critical when it comes to raising a puppy to become a well-adjusted, confident adult dog that is friendly toward people and other animals.

So what is socialization? Trainers have all sorts of definitions, but in the simplest of terms, it is about classical conditioning: creating an association between two stimuli. It is a learning process in which your puppy is exposed—in a safe, positive, and nonthreatening way—to all of the things he is likely to encounter as an adult dog, such as other animals, people clapping, elevators, stairs, vacuums, trash cans, kids on bicycles, women in floppy hats, and so forth. Introducing your pup to these things and more, without causing him trauma, helps him develop the coping skills necessary to grow into a mentally sound, confident adult dog.

Critical Periods

We know from the pioneering work of behavioral scientists John Paul Scott and John L. Fuller that both genetic and environmental influences impact the development of canine behavior. One of their most important contributions is the description of sensitive periods in the social

Socialization means getting kisses from kids and adults alike!

development of dogs, with the *socialization period* being the critical time between three and twelve weeks of age (some experts extend this to fourteen to sixteen weeks). This is the time frame in a puppy's life during which a small amount of experience will produce a great effect on later behavior. This is a critical period because once the window of opportunity closes, you will never get it back. Of course, puppies grow into adult dogs that continue to learn throughout their lives, but the positive experiences during these early weeks are critical for development.

If a puppy is properly socialized during this period, chances are good that he will grow up thinking the world is a wonderful, safe, and positive place—and that is what you want. Socialization experiences strongly influence what kind of dog he will grow up to be and how he will react to the world.

Puppies that lack socialization during this critical time are more likely to develop fearful reactions to people, noises, and unfamiliar locations. They tend to grow into adult dogs that are more cautious, shy, fearful, and nervous and that avoid or retreat from unfamiliar objects or situations. As adult dogs, they usually find it more difficult to cope with new or stressful situations.

Birth to Eight Weeks

From birth to three weeks of age, your puppy is helpless. Puppies are born deaf and blind, but their sense of touch is fully developed at birth. A good canine mother, with little interference from people, will provide everything for her puppies, including food, warmth, and security. Many breeders begin gently handling and weighing their puppies from day one, which helps with the developmental process and, as some suggest, to kick-start some aspects of neurological development.

Even at this young age, a puppy is learning important lessons through his experiences with the world around him, such as snuggling with his canine mom and littermates and gentle handling from the breeder. These encounters, while seemingly insignificant, are beginning to shape and form the personality and social skills he will possess throughout his life.

Around fourteen days of age, a puppy's ears and eyes are functioning, and puppies need continued handling and exposure to help process sight and sound. Like human babies, puppies need plenty of rest and quiet time, but when the puppies are awake, most savvy breeders will expose them to adequate visual and audio stimulation to help with neurological development.

Around four weeks of age, a puppy's needs are still provided by his canine mom, but as he and his littermates grow and become stronger and more adventurous, they begin playing and tussling. At this stage, the breeder can

Young puppies are impressionable and receptive to new experiences. Before the days fly by, take advantage by introducing your blue-eyed baby to as many fun and positive experiences as possible.

provide safe toys and "obstacles," such as tunnels, boxes, and wobble boards, for the puppies to figure out, climb on and through, and investigate. Such activities help provide environmental enrichment, which, again, help puppies learn to cope with stress as they develop.

During the fifth through seventh weeks, a puppy is growing rapidly and becoming more coordinated and adept at walking, running, playing, and escaping his puppy pen. At forty-nine days of age, a puppy's brain is neurologically complete: he emits the brain waves of an adult dog, yet his brain is still a blank slate, minimally affected by experience and learning.

By the time your puppy is ready to begin his new life at your home, usually between seven and ten weeks, the process of socialization has already begun. A responsible breeder will have seen your puppy through the neonatal period (approximately zero to thirteen days) and transitional period (approximately thirteen to twenty days), and halfway through the critical socialization period (approximately three to twelve to sixteen weeks).

Eight Weeks and Beyond

Once your puppy comes to live with you, it is your job to keep up the breeder's good work. Your puppy must keep learning important socialization skills until he is sixteen weeks of age. Your window of opportunity is small, so you will need to use your time wisely.

You want your puppy's association with his world—everything and anything he is likely to encounter as an adult dog—to be positive so that he grows up thinking that life is good and safe. This point cannot be stressed enough. Taking your puppy to the park and allowing him to be bombarded by other animals, strange sights, weird noises, and screaming, rambunctious kids is *not* a positive experience. Likewise, taking him to a puppy class and allowing him to be mauled, bullied, or sent yelping by bigger, bossier, more dominant puppies is *not* a positive experience, either. These types of negative experiences can permanently traumatize a puppy.

This Frenchie puppy is looking to make new friends at the beach. Socializing your puppy in new places can help to make your puppy more well rounded. (Don't forget the sunscreen and umbrella!)

As soon as your puppy is fully vaccinated, you should take your puppy for plenty of introductions and treats everywhere that is safe and dog-friendly, such as:

- parks and recreation sites
- outdoor cafés
- shopping centers

- hardware stores
- pet-supply stores
- farmers' markets
- the veterinarian's office

Expose him to a wide variety of people, including toddlers, teenagers, people in wheelchairs, and people in uniform. Expose him to other animals, such as cats, birds, horses, goats, and chickens. Let him hear the clapping of hands, the jingling of keys, and the clatter of dog bowls. Let him walk and play on different surfaces, such as gravelly driveways, grassy lawns, sandy beaches, and vinyl and tile floors. Walk across bridges with planks of wood or metal.

Puppies should be exposed to open stairs, closed stairs, steep stairs, narrow stairs, wooden stairs, and grated stairs (watch his toes and be careful that he doesn't fall). Expose him to elevators, honking horns, garden hoses, sprinklers, and wind chimes. Let your puppy play in and around empty boxes and buckets. Allow him to investigate trees, rocks, bushes, branches, leaves, and acorns. Take him to the beach and let him climb on driftwood and dig in the sand. Go for a hike in the woods and let him climb on and over fallen trees. Take him to a farm where he can sniff all of the animal odors. Walk him on city sidewalks so he can see and hear the hustle and bustle.

Attend a small puppy class—preferably with no more than three or four other puppies—or invite friends and neighborhood kids over for supervised play. Remember, *positive* is the key to success.

Socialization and Vaccinations

While vaccinations are important to your puppy, so too is socialization. A hotly debated topic is the perceived risk of exposing a puppy to other dogs prior to completing the puppy's full complement of vaccinations at around sixteen weeks. Some veterinarians adamantly oppose socialization to other dogs and in public places before sixteen weeks of age due to the puppy's risk of contracting an infectious disease, such as parvovirus. A 2013 study published in the *Journal of the American Animal Hospital Association* (JAAHA) indicated that "vaccinated puppies attending socialization classes were at no greater risk of CPV infection than vaccinated puppies that did not attend those classes."

The decision is a personal one and should always be made in conjunction with your veterinarian. Plenty of opportunities exist to safely socialize your puppy, but until he is fully vaccinated, avoid those public places where the risk of encountering infected dogs is high, such as dog parks, pet-supply stores, and crowded puppy or obedience classes.

A Puppy's Temperament and Limitations

Puppies are unique individuals and must be treated as such. By understanding as much as possible about the breed you have chosen, you will have an easier time understanding how best to manage your puppy's behavior during the socialization process.

Some dogs are prone to developing obsessive-compulsive behaviors, so it is important during the socialization process that you do your to best to prevent these behaviors from

Balancing Act

Socializing your puppy is a balancing act. You must expose him to the world around him while protecting him from potentially harmful or fearful situations and never encouraging or rewarding fearful behavior. You want to find the right amount of exposure and stimulation while still providing a safe, stress-free environment. Understanding canine body language is especially handy during this time. You will need to read his signs by observing his reactions to different situations. Here are a few examples:

- If your puppy is afraid of the vacuum cleaner, remove the vacuum and turn it on in another room. If possible, have someone turn it on in another room while you praise and reward your pup with plenty of yummy treats.
- If your puppy is afraid of a particular person, do not force him to engage. Have the person sit on the floor, which is less intimidating than having him or her stand over the puppy, and reward the puppy with treats when the pup approaches.
- If your puppy is not used to children, restrict his exposure to just one quiet, well-behaved child until your puppy is confident enough to handle more.
- If your puppy yelps because someone accidently stepped on his foot, avoid coddling him. Instead, immediately play with him and talk to him in a happy voice.

developing or continuing. Some puppies can be prone to spookiness, so you will want to discourage that behavior by exposing your puppy to lots of different sights, sounds, and people. If your dog tends to be aloof, you will want to socialize him to all types of situations so he does not develop fearful or aggressive reactions to people. Once behaviors such as fear or aggression become ingrained, they are more difficult to eliminate. The socialization period is the best time to address any perceived problems. If your puppy is showing signs of anything other than normal puppy behaviors, this is the time to seek advice from a behaviorist who can help fix the problem.

Many dogs recognize their mortal enemies in vacuum cleaners. This Bulldog puppy is finally making friends with this bad-mannered sweeper.

Flight Instinct

A primitive yet important trait to recognize is a dog's natural *fight or flight reflex*. Think of it

Little-Dog Syndrome

There is a difference between a well-behaved puppy that you indulge from time to time and a spoiled ruffian that bites and snaps at people. Labeled "little-dog syndrome," this spoiled behavior tends to be seen more often in small or toy dogs. People tend to be amused by snarky behaviors in little dogs, such as a pampered Pomeranian sitting on his owner's lap and growling at passersby or a 4-pound Chihuahua sprinting to attack someone's shin bone. Some owners think this behavior is comical, so they reward it, whether intentionally or not. Sadly, these behaviors are dangerous because they become ingrained, and these puppies grow into adult dogs that think they are invincible. It is nearly impossible to turn these half-pint hooligans into nice, happy dogs. Instead, these puppies grow into dogs that can't be trusted and really aren't fun to be around. Look ahead to your puppy's future and recognize what behaviors you want to encourage and discourage so that you instill and reward those behaviors that foster a happy, healthy puppy.

as a survival and self-preservation behavior. In the simplest of terms, a wild animal's fight or flight reflex almost always triggers his flight from something threatening his existence, such as becoming another animal's supper. Rarely do wild animals choose to stand and fight if other paths to safety (i.e., flight) exist. Only when they feel cornered, with no way to escape, will they stand their ground and fight.

Despite thousands of years of domestication, dogs still maintain their wild ancestors' fight or flight reflex. However, flight is not always an option for puppies or adult dogs. As a result, many dogs turn their fear into fighting or aggressive actions. These dogs may growl or bite when pushed to the point of feeling cornered.

How close a fearful dog allows you to get to him before he moves away is called the *flight zone.* The more fearful the dog, the larger his flight zone tends to be. Fearful dogs tend to be less sure of themselves and will likely flee rather than stand their ground. When cornered, they usually, but not always, bite.

Your Puppy's Future

Evidence clearly shows that early socialization can prevent the onset of serious canine problems, such as fear, aggression, avoidance, and so forth. If you do nothing else for your puppy, you owe it to him to take the time to properly and adequately socialize him during this critical life stage. Doing so is time consuming and takes a lot of energy. However, it is a necessary and obligatory investment if you want your puppy to grow into a happy, confident dog. His future will be shaped by how much you do—or fail to do—during the critical socialization period.

CHAPTER 7

PUPPY SCHOOL

Training puppies is great fun because they are cute, irresistible, and free (for now) of any bad habits; they are clean slates that you can mold into astonishing canine companions. All puppies need and deserve basic obedience training and puppy manners, as well as direction and guidance. Of course, all puppies have different temperaments and personalities and must be treated as such. So how do you choose the best training method for your puppy?

Myriad training methods exist, and it is safe to say that no one training technique works for every dog. Some puppies are confident, bold, cheeky, tenacious, or determined. They challenge their owners at every opportunity and can take a lot of energy to train. Other puppies are fearful, shy, timid, or uncertain, and they challenge you in different ways.

Sometimes, a puppy needs his owners to be calm because too much excitement may stimulate a puppy and stir up frenzied energy beyond his capacity to learn. Other puppies have a "must I wag my tail today?" attitude and need upbeat, energetic owners who can motivate them and pump them full of enthusiasm. Some puppies need their egos stroked to build confidence and encouragement so they can make decisions without constant handholding.

Before jumping into training, it is important to recognize that puppies and adult dogs learn through repetition, consistency, reinforcement, and, of course, their successes and failures. That almost sounds simplistic, doesn't it? Yet, with dog training, you will find countless methods of getting from point A to point B.

This chapter is not intended to present you with one absolute method of training because many effective training methods exist. Rather, it is intended to point out the general principles that form the cornerstone of all good training.

Learning Theory Basics

Canine learning theory is multifaceted and certainly goes well beyond the scope of this chapter. Consider that some behaviorists have PhDs in animal behavior! That said, understanding the basics and having an overview of how dogs learn will help you make smart decisions about your puppy's training and future behavior.

Two theories govern the scientific principles of learning: classical conditioning and operant conditioning. Without delving too deeply into the complexities of each, here are the basics.

Classical Conditioning

Classical conditioning is creating an association between two stimuli. Russian scientist Ivan Pavlov first described the most notable example of classical conditioning in the early 1900s, when he discovered that a dog salivates at the anticipation of food. In his experiment, Pavlov rang a bell immediately before feeding a dog and found that, in time, the dog would salivate at the sound of the bell alone. The dog had no control over this reflex. Salivating at the sound of the bell became a conditioned reflex.

In retrospect, Pavlov's thesis seems so simple. He took something that had absolutely no meaning to the dog (the bell ringing) and paired it with something good and desirable (the food) over and over again until the dog began to equate the meaningless thing (the bell) to the really good thing (the food).

If your puppy has already learned different behaviors, maybe you are connecting the dots, seeing the connection, and realizing how simple behaviors, be they wanted or unwanted, can be trained. For instance, does your dog go crazy when you put on your shoes or coat? If so, he has no doubt associated your shoes or jacket with something fun—maybe a hike in the woods, a game of fetch, or a ride in the car.

Classical conditioning works both ways. It can work against you and your puppy because it is not exclusive to positive behaviors; in fact, research indicates that unpleasant experiences are conditioned much more quickly than pleasant ones. A dog may become conditioned to react fearfully after just one exposure. For instance, a puppy that has had a bad experience following a ride in the car, such as being abandoned at a shelter or experiencing a painful event at the veterinarian's office, may run and hide when you grab your car keys. The sound of thunder may paralyze a dog with fear or send him into a frenzy of barking, cowering, pacing, or destructive behavior. A noise-phobic dog may start to shake long before he hears the thunder.

The dog's fear response prevents him from thinking or performing a previously learned behavior, such as Sit, Down, or Come. Think of something that terrifies you. Maybe it is snakes or spiders or flying in an airplane or getting an injection. The presence of a snake, for example,

If you reward your dog for a behavior, he will repeat it. This Chinese Crested stands for tasty treats.

Some trainers still employ archaic training methods—the old pop-and-jerk training that involved a choke chain, force, and total domination of the dog. While these methods appear to provide a quick resolution of "bad" behaviors, they often come at a hefty price that includes stifling a puppy's personality as well as his willingness and desire to please. Be smart. Stick with positive-training methods. You and your puppy will be a lot happier!

may be so terrifying to you that you are paralyzed by fear, unable to remember something as simple as your telephone number. Your fear overrides your ability to think.

The same concept applies to dogs. A dog that is fearful is not in a state to learn anything or even remember previously learned behaviors. It is important to recognize that the dog is not dumb, willfully disobedient, or stubborn. Regardless of how much you sweet-talk him or how many treats you offer, the conditioned fear response will override any previously learned behavior.

Operant Conditioning

In contrast to classical conditioning, operant conditioning capitalizes on the principle that a dog (or any animal) is likely to repeat a behavior that is reinforced. Think of it as a cause and effect relationship in which the dog performs a behavior, such as sitting, on his own and is rewarded with something positive, usually a tasty tidbit. The dog quickly learns that his own behavior (e.g., sitting) causes a reward (tasty treat or favorite toy) to appear. If a dog jumps on his owner and is ignored (e.g., no treats, no physical or verbal reward), the dog quickly learns that that behavior (jumping) pays no dividends.

Dogs, at least the really smart ones, tend to drop a behavior that reaps them no reward. Remember, dogs do what is most reinforcing. Why would a dog waste his time on something that gains him nothing? Here's another example: you are eating dinner while your dog sits patiently with pleading eyes. You ignore him. He sits up on his hind legs. You ignore him. He starts whining. You cave and give him a tidbit of food. Your dog just learned that he could offer behaviors (sitting, sitting up, whining) until he hit on the behavior that paid off in treats (this is called being "operant.")

The basic principles of operant conditioning are:

- A behavior that is rewarded will repeat itself.
- A behavior that is ignored will go away.

The behavior you reward is the behavior you get, which is not necessarily the behavior you want.

Operant conditioning presents consequences for a dog's actions, teaching him to think about his choices and choose the one that gets him a reward (e.g., treats). In the simplest of terms, the essence of operant conditioning is that a dog (or any animal) is required to perform a behavior to receive a reward.

The principle that behavior is driven by consequences was first described by Edward Thorndike in the early 1900s. The basic notion is that a behavior that is reinforced will increase in frequency, while a behavior that results in an unpleasant outcome will be avoided by the animal in the future.

The Tricky Part

Here is where it can get a bit confusing because in almost every situation, classical conditioning will override operant conditioning. When a dog is stressed from fear, for example, classical conditioning will have a more powerful influence over his behavior than anything he learned through operant conditioning. If a dog is truly terrified, you can dangle a chunk of steak in front of his nose and it won't make one bit of difference. The conditioned fear response will overpower any previously learned operant conditioning. A dog can't eat and digest and have adrenalin coursing through his system at the same time.

That said, classical conditioning can be used to treat an existing fear or phobia, such as fear of entering a new building, riding in a car, coming into contact with strange people, thunderstorms, and so forth. Many trainers use a combination of classical and operant conditioning. Effective training isn't about one training strategy versus another. The approach that works best depends on the type of behavior that you are trying to teach or reinforce. It is about what works and doesn't work for you, your puppy, and his individual temperament and personality.

Positive and Reward-Based Training

Dog training has come a long way in the last twenty years. The talk these days is all about positive (and purely positive) motivation. Ideally, all of your puppy training should be through positive motivation and rewards. The goal is to instill all of the behaviors you want your puppy to have as an adult dog in a fun and humane manner. Unless your puppy is biting you or another animal, there should be no need for corrections. The golden rule of dog training is that you never, ever correct a puppy or adult dog that has not yet learned a behavior (e.g., Sit, Down, etc.). Correcting him for something he has not yet learned is unfair and will damage the human-canine bond.

Positive reinforcement simply means adding something positive, such as a treat or praise, to increase

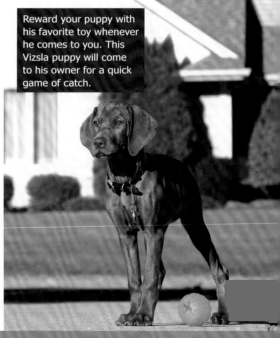

Reward your puppy with his favorite toy whenever he comes to you. This Vizsla puppy will come to his owner for a quick game of catch.

the likelihood that a behavior will reoccur. For instance, if you reward your puppy with a favorite treat each and every time he comes to you, you greatly increase the odds of his repeating that particular behavior. If you repeat this routine 7,200 times in your puppy's first year of life, he will grow into an adult dog that views coming to you as a positive experience. This is the essence of positive reinforcement: when a dog does something that you like, he instantly should get something that he likes (treat, toy, game of tug) so he will want to repeat the behavior.

If, on the other hand, your puppy comes to you when called, and you then correct him for something he did ten minutes ago, it will not be a positive experience for him. Your dog will be thinking, "She yelled at me the last time she called me, so I don't think I'll do that again!"

Dogs are learning every single minute of the day, whether you pay attention to them or not. If allowed to do so, they will always choose what is most rewarding to them. For some dogs, chasing a cat or squirrel (or digging, chewing, barking, jumping on people, or chasing a delivery person) is inherently self-rewarding. Managing your puppy's environment and not allowing him to get himself into trouble will help you reinforce the behaviors that you want while minimizing his opportunities to engage in self-reinforcing behaviors.

Purely Positive Training

The essence behind purely positive training is that everything is positive and a dog is never, ever corrected, regardless of the circumstances. We all want our puppies to grow into adult dogs that never misbehave or get into trouble or embarrass us in public. Alas, if you are looking to avoid public humiliation, you should have invested in an aquarium, not gotten a dog.

A purely positive trainer never use corrections. If he or she tells a trained dog (emphasis on *trained*) to come, and the dog chooses to ignore the command, the trainer waits until the dog does the command or any other command that he or she can reward, or the trainer distracts the dog with a different command.

You'll feel very proud every time your puppy runs to you when he hears you say, "Ringo, come!"

Purely positive training has been compared to raising kids without ever telling them "No" or setting any boundaries. We all know what that looks and sounds like in the grocery store!

The flaw in this type of dog training is that dogs need boundaries. They are happy when they have rules. Rules give a dog freedom— freedom to be off leash in a safe situation, freedom to be loose in the house, freedom to play with his canine buddies.

On the other hand, purely positive training is great for puppies or adult dogs that have been trained harshly in the past because it provides a safe way to let them know that the rules have changed and that training is fun and, more importantly, safe.

The key difference between purely positive and reward-based training is the corrections, or the lack of corrections. This is why and where many trainers part company.

The philosophy behind most positive motivation/reinforcement training is that when a trained dog (again, emphasis on *trained*) thoroughly understands a command, such as Down, and chooses to ignore the command, the trainer feels that a correction is warranted. Rules are black and white, and if a trained dog willfully ignores a command, there are consequences.

A Few Words about Corrections

Corrections are not the evil affair that many trainers and owners make them out to be. A correction is simply taking an incorrect behavior and making it right. A correction should never mean that a dog is bad—only that he made the wrong choice. Again, it does not matter if you have a six-month-old puppy or a five-year-old dog—if you have not thoroughly taught a behavior, such as Come, then you cannot correct him for not coming. This point cannot be overemphasized. Unfair corrections can ruin a good puppy or adult dog and, in some instances, create aggression.

Problems arise with purely positive training because a lot of dogs have their own agendas, which don't necessarily include their owners. As a result, purely positive training, while handy in many situations, may not serve you well in all instances. For example, most hounds will find chasing a rabbit more rewarding than any treat you can offer. So if you ask your dog to sit but he decides instead to chase a rabbit, purely positive training provides no consequences for his actions.

Clicker Training

Operant conditioning is closely associated with clicker training, which starts by first using classical conditioning to the sound of a clicker. The clicker, like Pavlov's bell, must mean something to the dog before you can begin clicker training. Typically, a trainer clicks and then immediately delivers a tasty tidbit to the dog, and then repeats the process again and again—perhaps twenty-five or thirty times in rapid succession. Click, feed, wait a beat, click, feed, wait a beat, click, feed—always in that order. The click always comes first because you are classically conditioning the dog to respond to the sound of the clicker—just as Pavlov conditioned his dogs to respond to the bell. The technical term is *creating a conditioned reinforcer by using classical conditioning.*

In a relatively short time, the dog makes the positive association between the sound of the click and a yummy treat. The dog figures out that the clicking sound *always* means that a tasty tidbit is coming. In training terminology, this process is known as *loading the clicker* or *powering up the clicker.*

A Pinch of Both Methods

It is perfectly acceptable to use any combination of training that works for you and your dog, provided, of course, that the methods you choose are fun, fair, and humane. You can train by luring a dog into a Down, or you can strictly go the route of clicker training and operant conditioning. You can use food and toys along with physical and verbal praise. You can try purely positive training if that better suits you and your puppy. The bottom line is that the training method you choose—whether classical or operant conditioning, positive reinforcement or purely positive—is less important than consistency and balance.

Once a dog connects the clicking noise (the conditioned reinforcer) with a food reward, you can use operant conditioning to teach everything from basic obedience commands to fun tricks by reinforcing any desired response that the dog offers.

This type of training has big advantages because the dog gets rewarded incrementally for figuring out what you want. In other words, the dog's behavior makes the reward appear. Many dogs quickly become obsessed with trying to figure out what behavior will produce the click and subsequent tidbit of food. Eventually, the dog fires off a bunch of behaviors, and you mark (by clicking) and reinforce the behaviors you want. (Remember the begging dog at the table that offered behaviors until he found the behavior that paid off?)

Operant conditioning requires spot-on timing because the behavior you click is the behavior you teach, which, of course, requires you to pay close attention to what your dog is doing. If your timing is off, you are likely to click and inadvertently reward undesired behaviors. For instance, if you are teaching your puppy to sit and you click at the moment he paws your leg, you just taught him that pawing your leg is the behavior you want.

In the beginning, until you get the mechanics of clicking and treating in sync, you might find it easier to start with teaching your puppy fun games, such as touching your hand, kissing your nose, or standing on a box. This helps you get the hang of clicking and rewarding and also helps teach your puppy that learning is fun.

Shaping

Shaping and clicker training, for the most part, go hand in hand, and shaping is another concept you are likely to encounter with operant conditioning. Key components of operant conditioning are *shaping* and *marking* behaviors by rewarding small increments of a behavior that put the dog on the path to the desired behavior, without luring. The key to operant conditioning is that the dog must think that performing a behavior is *his* idea—not yours—because the behavior must be spontaneously expressed and not elicited by a stimulus, as in classical conditioning. This creates a thinking dog: "what do I have to do to get my owner to click and give me a yummy reward?"

Shaping can be a chore for some dogs—occasionally even a stressful chore. You can almost see some dogs thinking, "Just show me what the heck you want!" Many trainers use shaping along with some luring and showing the dog what is expected of him. Once the dog catches on, it is important to drop the luring as soon as possible.

Motivating Your Puppy

Everything in dog training comes down to motivation, and motivation is all about finding the reinforcer/reward that your puppy wants. Like people, dogs need motivation and reinforcement. Think of it this way: would you clock eight hours a day at work if you didn't get paid? If you stopped getting paid at noon, would you go back to work after lunch? If someone offered you five dollars to wash his or her car, would you do it? What if the person offered you one thousand dollars?

The same concept applies to puppies and adult dogs. To simplify, think of motivators as *primary* and *secondary*. A puppy's primary motivator should always be you—pleasing you and working for you, for verbal and physical praise, for play, for fun, and for the love of working. He must enjoy being with you, and vice versa. He should see you as his leader. He should respect you but not fear you and see you as someone who is important enough to issue commands.

Secondary motivators are simply extensions of yourself. They put a little extra "oomph" into training. Most often, but not always, food is an excellent motivator because most dogs will do backflips for chicken, steak, or cheese. Some dogs, however, aren't all that turned on by food, so their owners will need to find the toy or activity that flips their switch.

Some owners go wrong by allowing the food (or toy) to become the primary motivator. Your puppy should come when called because he thinks you are the most fantastic and captivating person, not because you're bribing him with a chunk of food or a favorite toy. The problem with luring and bribing is that when the food or toy is not forthcoming, many dogs have little or no interest in coming when called, sitting, lying down, walking nicely on leash, or anything whatsoever. That is why you must work hard to establish yourself as his primary motivator—to enthrall him with your voice and mannerisms, to be the most exciting person in his world.

Once you have found what motivates your pup, use that toy or treat *only* for playing and

While owners of small dogs tend to be more lax about training, owners of large, powerful breeds must recognize that training is mandatory.

It's a Treat, Not a Meal

Soft foods work better as treats than hard, crunchy dog bones do. Ideally, the treat should be so tiny that the dog can just swallow it without chewing (or chew just once or twice). Standing around for twenty seconds crunching on a bone only serves to disrupt the dog's focus and the momentum of fun and excitement. Use tiny pieces of food—about the size of a small pea. The goal is to motivate, engage, and reward your puppy—not fill him up with treats.

training. You can even put a name to it, such as "Where's your tuggie?" or "Get your Frisbee."

Keep Sessions Short

Puppies are individuals, and they learn at different rates. Some puppies become bored after a few repetitions. Others get frustrated because they are too young mentally to play certain games or learn specific exercises, such as the Stay command. Almost all puppies have short attention spans and tire quickly, both physically and mentally. Always play and train within your puppy's individual physical and mental capabilities.

When playing and training basic obedience commands or fun tricks, it does not take long for your puppy to learn. Work for five minutes at a time, several times a day, and you will be surprised how much your puppy absorbs and learns in a short period of time. One trainer calls it "string cheese" training because multiple times a day she will take one piece of string cheese and cut it into small pieces. Then, she will do as many Sits or Downs or Recalls as possible using that one stick of cheese. When that stick of cheese is gone, you are done training for that session. Do this three or four times a day, and it won't be long until your puppy will be able to do all kinds of fun tricks and commands.

The goal is to always quit while your puppy is still craving more playing and training. If you train for too long, your puppy is likely to shut down and will not be as eager to participate the next time.

Attention

If you do not have your puppy's attention, you cannot teach him anything. Start right away by making yourself your puppy's primary motivator. Without your puppy's attention, he is likely to wander off and find his own fun.

Attention is a learned behavior, and teaching it is like teaching any other command, be it Sit, Down, Stay, or Come. You are not going to teach an attention cue or command. Instead, the goal is to keep your puppy's attention on you, which means that you must be more exciting and stimulating than his surroundings—and there is a lot of competition out there. Focusing on you (i.e., paying attention) is going to become your puppy's default behavior. If your puppy is with you, he should pay attention to you. Everywhere you go and in everything you do, your puppy should be conditioned to look to you for direction and guidance—as well as fun! As he grows and matures, you begin asking for longer periods of continuous attention. Doing so requires him to learn to ignore distractions.

In the beginning, when first working on attention, choose a place where there are few or no distractions, such as your backyard or living room. As your puppy progresses, you can include some minor distractions, such as placing a toy on the floor or having a friend or family member nearby. Gradually increase the number of distractions while you play games with the puppy, always encouraging the puppy to focus on you. Don't be afraid to be silly or creative in finding ways to keep the puppy's two eyes and nose on you.

The Handy Treat

Stash tasty treats or your puppy's favorite toy in your pocket, or have containers of food or toys strategically placed around the house or yard. This way, you always have a reward handy when your puppy does something clever. Surprise him by "finding" a tidbit or toy on a shelf or behind a planter. Ask him, "What's this?" Have him do a quick Sit for a treat or a quick game of tug or retrieve.

The more you reinforce your puppy's attention, the faster he will learn. Eventually, he will focus on you despite other dogs and people, noises, smells, and, yes, even squirrels scurrying up trees.

Tone of Voice and Verbal Praise

Your tone of voice is your greatest motivator and training tool—more so than any treat or toy. What you say and how you say it can make all the difference. For example, if you say, "Bad dog!" in a stern voice, your puppy will most likely cower and run for cover. But if you say, "Who's a *baaaddd* dog?" in a fun, happy, upbeat, you're-my-crazy-little-puppy kind of way, the reaction will be much different.

Some dogs become happy and wag their tails when you speak to them in a normal tone of voice. Other dogs get excited or cock their heads at the sound of a high-pitched voice. Some dogs are more responsive to low, soothing tones—staring adoringly at you as they wait to see what's going to happen next.

No two puppies are alike. The type and quantity of praise required depend on the individual puppy's personality and temperament. Generally speaking, calm verbal praise works well for a high-energy dog because just the tiniest bit of excitement in their owner's voice causes them to become too revved up to concentrate on the task at hand.

Pay attention to the sound of your voice and how your puppy reacts. Is your voice happy or flat and dull? When dogs hear a boring, repetitive tone of voice for every cue and all verbal praise, all of the words run together, and the dog isn't able to decipher between commands, praise, and his owner's tedious drone. Unless the owner animates his voice to motivate the dog, the dog will never get a sense of what behaviors his owner really likes.

Physical Praise

Physical praise is a personal thing with dogs. Yes, it is a reward for a job well done, and it is also a great motivator, especially when combined with verbal praise. How much physical praise a puppy likes, needs, or can handle will vary from puppy to puppy. Some dogs enjoy physical interaction if they have a toy but dislike being stroked, patted, petted, or otherwise touched when they are working because it annoys them or distracts them. Such a dog usually just wants an enthusiastic "Good boy!" and a chance to get his toy or get on with his duties.

As with verbal praise, finding out what type of physical praise works best for your puppy involves reading his body language—and a bit of trial and error. How does he react when you pat him on the shoulder and tell him he's a rock star? Does he lean into you—happy, relaxed, panting, eyes open? Or does he lean away, trying to avoid physical contact?

If you want to teach your dog to enjoy physical contact, teach it as a separate exercise and do it in a fun and humane manner. Proceed slowly and always work within your puppy's threshold.

Timing Is Everything

Dog training is all about timing. Correct timing tells your puppy exactly which behavior you are rewarding. Poor timing—praise that is given too soon or too late—confuses puppies. Good timing can be a bit tricky, but with a bit of practice, it is a skill anyone can learn.

It also helps to look at it from your puppy's perspective. What is he doing at the exact moment you are telling him he's a good boy? Is it a behavior you want to reinforce? Remember, the behavior you reward is the behavior you reinforce, which may not necessarily be the behavior you want.

If, for example, you verbally reward your dog with "Good boy!" as he charges out the door, he will think that charging out the door is what you like, and he will keep doing it. If you give

Physical praise isn't as tasty as liver, but it's close.

him a tasty tidbit each time he barks, he is pretty much guaranteed to bark all the time. Try to really pay attention to when you are praising (or clicking) and what behaviors you are intentionally or inadvertently reinforcing.

On the other hand, if your puppy comes tearing over to you, his tail and ears up, with an attitude that screams, "Here I am!" and you lavish him with kisses, treats, and praise, he will think coming to you is fun, and that is definitely a behavior you want to reinforce.

Release Cue for Tugging

A separate type of release cue should be taught for tugging games. When your puppy is tugging, tell him, "Good tugging!" or "Pull" or "Get it." This teaches him to associate the behavior with the command. By teaching him to tug, you can teach him to stop tugging with a "Give" or "Out" or "Drop it" or whatever words you choose.

Some tenacious puppies are more reluctant to give up a toy, and getting such a puppy to release it may take a bit of finesse on your part. If this is the case, do not continue tugging! This only encourages more tugging on the dog's part.

For young puppies, you can (carefully!) stick your index finger between his cheek and molars and encourage him to open his mouth and give the cue. If you are uncomfortable with this method, simply show him a different toy and encourage him to get it. When he lets go of the first toy, put your command to the behavior of releasing the toy.

Build a Foundation

Now that you understand the basics of how dogs learn and how to motivate your puppy to learn, you need to keep adding to your puppy's foundation so he can grow into an adult dog that is well behaved and fun to be around.

Release Cue

Early on in your foundation work, you need to teach your puppy a release cue, such as "OK" or "Free." A release cue tells your puppy that the training session or the behavior you are working on is over, and he can do as he likes. If you teach your puppy from day one to continue doing what you ask him to do, such as a Sit, until you give him a release cue, he will grow into an adult dog that is clear about his job. If you fail to teach him a release cue, and you allow him to get up from a Sit or Down anytime he feels like it, he will not understand why you are annoyed at him when he breaks his Stay.

Teaching a release cue is not difficult. First, pick the cue you want to use. A lot of people use "OK," while others prefer "Free" because "OK" is used so frequently in day-to-day conversations. Have your puppy do a Sit or Down, and when you are ready to release him, tell him "OK."

Teaching the Basic Commands

Basic obedience commands include Sit, Down, Come, and Stay. Ideally, all puppies should grow into well-mannered adult dogs that are able to perform these commands without fail and without a lot of fuss. Using what you have learned so far, teaching the basic commands is a piece of cake!

Sit

Three options exist for teaching the Sit. The first is through strict operant conditioning, which says that you do not do anything to initiate the behavior. You shape the behavior, meaning that you can click for just a little movement toward a Sit, and you keep clicking for more progression toward a Sit, and then finally click for actually sitting. This is time consuming and frequently frustrating for owners (and puppies!) who have limited patience and just want to teach their puppies to sit.

The second option is that you can reward your puppy for sitting on his own. For instance, when you are playing, strolling around the yard, or just hanging out, and the puppy sits on his own, tell him "Good sit!" (or click) and reward. You praise and reward every behavior you want to reinforce. This works well for some owners, especially those who are super observant and have good timing.

In the interest of expediency, a third option is to lure your puppy into a Sit using a treat in the following manner:

- Begin with your puppy on leash. This is especially helpful if your puppy, like most puppies, is easily distracted or tends to wander off.
- Start with your leash in one hand and a tasty tidbit in the other hand, with your puppy standing in front of or close to you, facing you.
- Hold the treat between your thumb and index finger.

There are many possible methods to teach your puppy to sit. While you choose the one that best suits your puppy, he'll likely just sit and wait.

- Show your puppy the treat, holding it close to and slightly above his nose.

As he raises his nose to take the treat, slowly move the treat in slightly upward and backward toward his tail, keeping the treat directly above his nose as he moves his head to follow the treat. (If he jumps up, the treat is too high. If he walks backward, the treat is too low.) When you do this correctly, a puppy has no choice but to lower his rear end toward the ground. As his bottom touches the ground, tell him, "Good sit!" (or click) and reward with the treat. Release with your chosen release cue.

Repeat this exercise three or four times in succession, three or four times a day.

Once your puppy begins to understand the behavior, make the treat a reward rather than a lure. The puppy should now associate the cue "Sit" with the action of putting his bottom on the ground, so all you should have to do to get him to sit is use the verbal cue. As soon as he sits, give him his reward.

Down

The same options that exist for teaching the Sit exist for teaching the Down: you can shape small behaviors that move your dog closer to the final Down position, you can praise and reward your puppy each and every time he lies down on his own with "Good down!" (or click) and then reward, or you can show him what you want by luring him into a Down.

Hold a treat in one hand and kneel on the floor so that you are eye level with your puppy, with your puppy standing in front of you. Let him sniff the treat. Move the treat toward the floor, between his front feet. When done correctly, your puppy will plant his front feet and follow his body into the Down position as he follows the treat to the ground.

When his elbows and tummy are on the ground, calmly praise him with "Good down" (or click) and reward with the treat.

Be sure your puppy is completely in the Down position while you praise and reward, or you will be teaching him to associate the wrong behavior with the verbal cue. Release with your chosen release cue. Repeat the exercise three or four times in succession, three or four times a day.

The Wait Game

The Stay command is considered a static exercise, which is challenging for many dogs—especially young puppies—because they can quickly become bored or anxious. Most puppies are not physically or emotionally mature enough to handle a Stay command until they are about five to seven months old. Instead of starting too soon, begin playing a fun version of the Stay, which is the Wait command.

Keep the Down lesson positive and reassuring. This position is less natural to most dogs and may require some calm coaching.

This game to teach Wait was adapted from an exercise used by trainer Bobbie Anderson. Start by playing in an enclosed area, such as your living room, patio, or small fenced yard.

Stand next to your puppy (he can be sitting or standing) and hold his leash in one hand. (Always use a buckle collar, never a pinch collar or choke chain.)

Have tasty treats handy in your pocket or a bait bag, or have his favorite toy ready. Tell your puppy in a nice, fun voice, "Wait." With your free hand, toss his toy (or a treat) about 5 or 6 feet in front of him.

If he strains or jumps at the leash, which is highly probable, remind him in a nice, fun, playful voice "You have to wait! Don't you cheat!" Be proactive and try to remind him before he starts pulling or straining on the leash (or at least pulling or straining uncontrollably). When he is standing or sitting still (waiting) nicely for a few seconds, tell him "Get it" and give him some slack in the leash. Hold on to the leash and walk with him to prevent him from wandering or running off.

Once he gets the treat, back up so that you encourage him to come back to you. If you are using a toy, encourage him to bring the toy back so that you can repeat the game by putting a command to it, such as "Bring it here." Tap your legs or chest while giving the verbal cue to encourage the puppy to come back; moving backward will also help.

It won't take long before your puppy realizes that bringing the toy back means he gets to continue playing. When you do the exercise properly, your puppy will soon think that waiting is a fun game. Eventually, the command morphs into Stay as your puppy matures physically and mentally and is able to hold his Wait for longer periods of time with low-level (and then high-level) distractions.

Come to Me

Coming when called is a simple exercise to teach, yet it is the one behavior that seems to cause owners a good deal of difficulty. Where owners often make mistakes is by assuming that a puppy comes preprogrammed with a Come command. Unfortunately, you cannot simply say "Come" and expect a ten-week-old puppy, or any dog, to come to you. You first need to teach him that the Come cue means "Stop what you are doing and run back to me as fast as you can—*right now*!"

Another common error that owners make is to yell "Come" louder and louder when the puppy doesn't respond. When that doesn't work—and it never does—owners resort to chasing their puppy while still yelling "Come!" The puppy starts to think that "Come" means "You chase me and I run. Yeah! Fun game!"

The following fun recall games will show you how to achieve a reliable recall with your puppy—but first, some ground rules.

Call him to come to you for good things, never for reprimands. If you call your puppy to you and then scold him, he will not want to come to you the next time you call him. If you call your puppy to you and he comes, you must always, always praise and reward. If you cannot do that, do not call your puppy. It is that basic, and there are no exceptions. If your puppy doesn't come to you, do not chase him—your puppy must always chase you.

If you want a strong, reliable Come command, you need to instill the behavior when he is young and impressionable. A puppy that learns early on that Come is a fun game is more likely to develop a reliable response to the command. If he stays reliable with this behavior throughout his puppyhood, and you remain positive and enthusiastic each and every time he comes to you, you will have a strong and positive response to the command as he matures into an adult dog.

Find Me!

The Find Me game is a modified version of hide and seek that capitalizes on a puppy's natural chase instinct. Start with a handful of tasty treats. Show your puppy the food and then toss a tidbit down the hall or across the room.

As your puppy runs to get the food, run in the opposite direction and either go into another room or hide behind a chair or a door.

Call your puppy's name enthusiastically: "Ringo! Ringo! Ringo!"

When he finds you, shower him with praise—"Aren't you smart! You found me!"—and a generous smattering of kisses and a tasty tidbit or a tug on his favorite toy.

In the beginning, your hiding spot should be somewhat obvious, making it easy for your puppy to succeed. As he becomes more enthusiastic and proficient, make your hiding spots more challenging.

When playing outdoors, wait until your puppy is distracted—sniffing the grass, eyeing a bird—and then take off running or duck behind a tree, shed, or whatever is nearby while saying your puppy's name in a happy, enthusiastic tone. When he finds you, always shower him with praise and enthusiasm.

This puppy is expecting the usual good stuff when he gets to his owner—treats, praise, a fun game, and maybe even a hug.

If your puppy is reluctant to run and find you, make your voice more inviting and exciting, make it easier for him to find you by letting him see you, or have the person holding your puppy run with him to find you.

Playing this fun, interactive game builds enthusiasm, develops your puppy's personality, and builds an intense eagerness and desire for him to be with you. Remember to always progress at a rate that is comfortable for your puppy and his individual temperament.

PART III

CARE
OF YOUR
PUPPY

CHAPTER 8

GROOMING

For your puppy to look and feel his best—and not to mention strut his stuff as the most eye-catching pup on the block—he needs regular grooming of his coat, nails, teeth, and skin. A well-conditioned and coiffed coat is a beautiful sight. No doubt it makes a puppy feel more comfortable, and it is less prone to mats, rashes, skin infections, and external parasites.

Grooming should be a regular part of your puppy's routine, and puppyhood presents the perfect opportunity to introduce and establish that routine. If started early, when your puppy is still young and receptive to new experiences, grooming becomes an enjoyable part of his routine—just like eating, sleeping, and playing.

Grooming goes beyond just keeping your puppy's skin and coat in tip-top condition. Grooming allows you to spend quality time with your puppy, which helps the natural bonding process and fosters a strong human-canine relationship.

Coat Types and Textures

Just as the size and structure of dogs vary drastically, so too do their coats. A dog's original function—the job for which he was originally bred—could dictate his coat color, length, abundance, and texture. Coat type is an essential element of "breed type" in many dogs. A Curly-Coated Retriever, for example, has a mass of small, thick, tight curls that are water resistant and protect him in the "heaviest of cover and the iciest of waters," according to the American Kennel Club's breed standard. Can you imagine a dog with long, silky hair surviving the harsh, icy waters? Or an Alaskan Malamute with no undercoat surviving the freezing Arctic environment?

Some breeds have several coat varieties. The Dachshund, for example, is seen in three varieties—smooth, wirehaired, and longhaired—while the Chihuahua has two varieties—long coated and smooth coated. A few breeds have grooming requirements that are dictated by the breed standard, the most notable being the Poodle's Continental clip, which comes from early attempts to protect the breed's "action parts" from freezing waters. You are not likely to see this type of grooming on dogs other than show dogs, as it is labor intensive.

Long- or Drop-Coated Breeds

Long- or drop-coated breeds, such as the Maltese, Yorkshire Terrier, and Afghan Hound, require special attention because their hair drapes down their bodies nearly or all the way to the ground. Keeping up appearances with this type of breed requires extra commitment. The hair is highly susceptible to damage and breakage caused by harsh shampoos, excessive blow drying, and exposure to environmental elements. Every aspect of care, from brushing and bathing to housing, requires special attention in order to maintain these sensitive yet exquisite coats, which is the primary reason that many owners opt to pay professional groomers.

Smooth-Coated Breeds

A smooth coat tends to lie flat and close to the body. Smooth-coated breeds can be either single coated or double coated. The smooth-coated Border Collie, smooth Collie, and Smooth Coat Chihuahua, for example, have undercoats, while the Vizsla and the Boxer have no undercoats. Smooth-coated breeds are often referred to as "wash and wear" breeds, but they too require bathing and grooming to remove dead hair and debris.

Double-Coated Breeds

Most breeds are double-coated, consisting of an undercoat that is usually short, soft, and dense—acting as a protective blanket against water and the elements—and an outer coat or top coat that is generally longer. The undercoat sometimes acts as a support for the top coat, which varies in texture depending on the breed. The corded coat of the Hungarian Puli, the shaggy coat of the Old English Sheepdog, and the wiry coat of the Sealyham Terrier are just a few of the distinctive yet different double coats. If not regularly groomed out, the undercoat gets thick and matted and can be extremely uncomfortable for the dog. Double-coated dogs shed—often a lot. The amount of shedding, which is a natural process in which strands of hair die, fall out, and are replaced by new hairs, varies according to the dog, the season, and the climatic conditions.

The Maltese always has a single coat, except when he's wearing a jacket!

Single-Coated Breeds

Single-coated breeds have no undercoat, but they still require regular grooming to keep their coats in tip-top condition. Interestingly, it is not only smooth-coated breeds, such as the Italian Greyhound, that have single coats. The long, silky coat of the Maltese and the thickly planted coat of

Mixed-Breed Coats

Mixed breeds (and so-called "designer dogs") often have combination-type coats. The Goldendoodle, for example, which can be a groomer's nightmare, has a soft undercoat similar to that of the Golden Retriever and a soft Poodle top coat, which is not unlike trying to comb through cotton. These coats require regular care and maintenance to prevent painful mats.

the Portuguese Water Dog are both single coats, yet they could not be more different.

Rough-Coated Breeds

Some breeds are considered rough coated, but that is a bit misleading because they are not always rough or harsh to the touch. The Border Collie's rough coat variety, for example, is medium to long with a flat to slightly wavy texture. Likewise, the Chow Chow and the Collie, both double-coated, thick-coated breeds, have rough-coated varieties.

The term *rough,* however, is more commonly used to describe the harsh, wiry coats of some terriers, such as the Wire Fox Terrier and Scottish Terrier, as well as the coats of some gun dogs, such as the Wirehaired Pointing Griffon and Spinone Italiano.

Hairless Breeds

A few hairless breeds exist, including the Chinese Crested and Xoloitzcuintli, both recognized by the American Kennel Club, as well the lesser known Peruvian Inca Orchid and American Hairless Terrier. Both the Chinese Crested and Xolo are bred in hairless and coated varieties; in the Chinese Crested, the coated variety is called the Powderpuff.

Good Equipment Is Worth the Money

Grooming your puppy, like anything else, is always easier when you have the proper equipment. Investing in good professional equipment will cost a bit more up front but will pay off in the long run. When properly cared for, quality grooming tools will last your dog's lifetime. Grooming is quicker and easier when you have the right equipment handy.

The equipment you purchase will depend on your puppy's breed as well as your budget. Grooming equipment is available at most pet-supply stores, at feed stores, and from online vendors. Dog-show vendors are an excellent source of good-quality equipment, and most are knowledgeable about the various breeds, coat types, and textures. A few of the must-haves for any dog include brushes, combs, nail clippers, and shampoos.

Brushes

Countless types of brushes—from boar bristle to pin to slicker—are available, and the equipment you choose depends largely on your dog's coat type. Using the proper brush for your puppy's coat means that your job will be much easier, and you will produce top-notch results.

If you decide to have your puppy professionally groomed, you will still want a brush or two to maintain your dog's coat between visits.

Boar bristle brushes are specialty brushes that are made from the hair of an adult boar. The quality of a brush depends on the quality of the natural bristle and which cut of bristle is used (first, second, or third cut). Boar bristle brushes are ideal for stimulating hair and skin follicles, distributing natural oils, and removing dander on smooth-coated or flat-coated breeds.

Pin brushes have metal pins in a rubber-cushioned base. The pins vary in their stiffness, flexibility, and length and are tailored to suit various canine coat types. Pin brushes work well on medium- to long-coated breeds, such as German Shepherds and Golden Retrievers.

Flexible pins are less likely to break the hair and are good for daily grooming. Some are better than others at removing undercoat. Brushes can range from five to more than sixty dollars. Top-quality pin brushes have stainless steel pins, gold-plated stainless steel pins, or brass tips for static-free brushing. Some pin brushes have wooden pins, which are the softest and gentlest for detangling hair. Run the brush down your bare arm, if it scratches you—it will scratch your puppy's skin, too. Be sure to buy a quality brush with a pin length suited to your dog's coat length.

Square or rectangular slicker brushes have fine, closely spaced metal bristles that work well for removing dead undercoat and debris from double-coated breeds. Many groomers discourage their use on the long hair of drop-coated breeds because they can cause breakage. Be careful not to brush the skin itself with a slicker brush because this can create nicks, scratches, and even welts—often referred to as "slicker burn."

A rubber curry brush is ideal for smooth-coated breeds. It consists of a rubber pad with soft nubs that stimulate your puppy's coat and skin and remove dirt, loose hair, and undercoat. It is ideal for use during bathing, too, because it helps distribute the shampoo deeply. When you use a curry, your puppy will think he is getting a massage!

Combs and Rakes

Combs are often used for "finishing" a coat but can also be used for removing undercoat and detangling knots. Combs come in a variety of sizes and types—single- or double-sided—and have teeth of varying length and spacing for different coat types and textures.

The slicker brush is ideal for removing dead undercoat from double-coated breeds.

Flea combs have teeth that are positioned very close together to remove fleas and dander from a dog's coat. They come in metal or plastic with various handle sizes. They are designed for smooth-coated breeds but are not as efficient on medium- or long-coated breeds.

Grooming or undercoat rakes look somewhat like miniature stiff-tined garden rakes. They are ideal for stripping out a dog's undercoat. The newer versions have an anti-static coating on the pins to help them easily glide through a dog's coat. Look for a rake that has pins long enough for your dog's coat. Pins that are too short won't reach the undercoat, and pins that are too long may scratch your puppy's skin.

Nail-Care Equipment

Nail clippers are used to clip a dog's nails, and they come in several styles, the most popular being the guillotine and scissors styles. The guillotine style cuts from only one direction and has a replaceable blade. The scissors-type nail trimmer comes in sizes for small and large dogs. Replacing nail scissors from time to time may be necessary because they cannot be sharpened effectively, but you can usually get several years of use out of this type of clipper. The type of clippers you use comes down to your personal preference and which type your puppy will tolerate.

Canine nail files are not unlike nail files you would use on your own nails—only larger and quite a bit stronger. Some groomers will file nails, as opposed to clipping them, because some dogs—especially those who have not been conditioned at an early age—find nail clipping too stressful. Files are also used to smooth the rough nail edges left after clipping.

A grinder grinds your dog's nails down instead of clipping them. Grinders are readily available at most pet-supply stores or online. They come in a variety of models, including corded and cordless. Most grinders have two speeds, with the top speed being about 13,000 rpm. If you go this route, invest in a good-quality grinder; they are well worth the extra money.

A puppy that is accustomed to hands-on affection will more readily accept grooming.

Shampoos and Conditioners

A huge variety of shampoos and conditioners for dogs is available, ranging from all-breed products to coat-specific care to medicating, herbal, and color enhancing. The shampoo and conditioner you choose will depend on your puppy's coat and skin. Shampoos and conditioners can either enhance and complement coats or damage them by stripping them of natural oils, weighing them down, or gumming them up.

While dogs benefit from a good shampooing, not all dogs need a conditioner. Unless your dog has a specific skin condition, such as dry, flaky, itchy skin, choose a good-quality shampoo and conditioner designed specifically for dogs—something nontoxic and not detergent-based so as not to strip the hair of its natural oils. The pH balance of human shampoos is different than those for dogs, so it is best to stick with doggy shampoos.

Important but Optional Products

Some items are not necessarily essential but they do make grooming easier and more enjoyable.

Grooming Table: A grooming table can be a costly but worthwhile investment because it will save your back! It is convenient because you can stand comfortably while you groom your dog. Tables run the gamut in size, price, and quality. Some tables are height adjustable, and the surfaces vary from rubber matting to waterproof coatings. Sturdy construction is paramount with any grooming table. Most fold down for portability and storage, and some have wheels for easy maneuverability.

Blow Dryer: Depending on your dog's coat, a blow dryer designed specifically for dogs may well be a necessity as opposed to a luxury. For medium- or long-coated adult dogs, a forced-air dog dryer will cut your drying time in half. Dog dryers differ from human dryers in a number of important ways. The least expensive dog dryers are like handheld dryers made for humans, though these are not recommended. Forced-air dryers are what most breeders and groomers use. They are the most efficient for drying thick-, medium-, and long-coated breeds because they literally blow the water off the dog. Most forced-air dryers rely on high-velocity airflow rather than heat to efficiently penetrate and remove the water from a dog's coat. Most have variable speeds, with the low speed being ideal for drying a dog's sensitive parts, such as his feet, ears, and face. Although these are more expensive, they can cut your drying time in half (or better!) and they will not burn your dog's coat or skin.

Introducing Grooming Basics

A puppy's coat differs from the coat of an adult dog. It is usually softer, fluffier, and

Giving your puppy an occasional quick bath will help make him more accepting of the routine when he's an adult.

shorter. That's why puppies are called little bundles of fur! Still, it is important that your puppy becomes accustomed to handling and grooming at a young age—even if he doesn't need a lot of brushing and grooming just yet. A well-trained dog is always easier to groom than an unruly one. Set aside some time every day for the first five or six months. You can do this while you are watching television or just sitting on the sofa. This helps your puppy to learn that handling is a necessary habit of daily life rather than something to dread.

Start by having your puppy sit in your lap (if he is small enough) or sit or stand next to you on the floor. Gently massage and stroke his body, rub his ears, count his toes, check his mouth, and so forth. Exposing your puppy to positive, calm, and delightful handling experiences sets up the whole grooming process. This is doubly important if you have a grooming-intensive breed, such as a Maltese or Yorkshire Terrier.

Once he is accustomed to handling, you can then gently introduce a brush in a soothing, calm manner. Most puppies readily learn to love the experience and interaction. Some dogs never learn to like grooming, but they should learn to at least accept the necessary chore. Puppies have limited attention spans, and some are more agreeable than others when it comes to remaining still for more than a few seconds. In the beginning, you want progress—not perfection. Your goal is for your puppy to stand or lie still for a few minutes while you brush him.

If your handling is too rough or animated, your puppy may become anxious and squirm to get away. Try to be more gentle, calm, and slow with your movements. Don't be surprised if your puppy is frightened, nervous, or unsure at first. Patience, gentle handling, and plenty of hugs and kisses will help build his confidence and teach him to accept and even enjoy the grooming process.

In order to preserve the naturally harsh texture of the terrier's coat, the groomer must pluck the coat by hand or use a stripping knife to remove the dead top coat.

Brushing and Daily Care

Establish a routine of brushing your puppy for a few minutes each day. In addition to allowing you to bond with your puppy, this time enables you to check his entire body for lumps, bumps, cuts, rashes, dry skin, fleas, ticks, and debris. You can check his feet for cuts, torn pads, or broken nails and examine his mouth for signs of trouble, including redness, broken teeth, or discolored gums.

As your puppy grows and matures, depending on his breed and coat type, once- or twice-weekly brushings may suffice, though most plushly coated breeds benefit from daily grooming.

Some groomers recommend starting at the dog's head, brushing the top of the head and around the ears, and then proceeding down the neck, chest, and front legs. Continue in one long stroke from the head toward the tail, then brush down the sides, and then finish with the rear legs. Others begin by brushing the legs, then working up to the body, and then finishing with the head. With puppies, some days you have to be satisfied with just getting them brushed—no matter which part comes first.

Shaving a Dog's Coat

As your puppy grows into an adult dog, you may be tempted to shave his long locks as a way of keeping him cool in hot weather. This is a controversial topic, and you will want to speak to your veterinarian before doing so. A normal, healthy coat helps protect a dog from the sun. When shaved, your dog is more susceptible to sunburn. If you want to keep your dog cool in the summer, be sure his coat is clean and free of mats and dead undercoat.

Many groomers discourage backward brushing—brushing against the direction of hair growth—because it can damage the coat, and some dogs find the process uncomfortable and irritating.

For dogs with short, straight coats, a rubber curry brush to pull out the dead hair and a boar bristle brush to shine the coat a few times a week is usually sufficient. Rubbing down your puppy with a hound glove, chamois, or soft towel and applying coat oil will add shine to his coat.

Medium-length coats require about ten minutes of regular brushing several times a week to keep up their appearances. A pin brush, slicker brush, or comb works well on these types of coats. The pin or slicker brush (or even a curry brush) helps to remove the dead hair and undercoat. Running the comb through the coat after you are finished brushing will help remove any remaining dead coat.

Long- or drop-coated breeds require significantly more maintenance than their short- or medium-coated counterparts. Some pet owners opt to keep these breeds in short clips or puppy cuts, which are less troublesome.

Puppies differ in their sensitivities. Always work within your puppy's comfort zone, being careful not to tug or brush too hard. Keep coat damage to a minimum by brushing gently. Part the hair with one hand and work from the skin out, brushing only in the direction of the hair growth, and continue right to the ends. Avoid "flicking" the ends of the hair, which can lead to breakage.

Never brush a dry or dirty coat, as this will cause the ends to break. Instead, mist or spray the hair first with a cream rinse diluted with water or a coat conditioner to help control static and prevent breakage.

For double-coated breeds, be sure to brush down to the skin, brushing both the top coat and undercoat. Brushing only the top coat can result in painful mats and tangles underneath that are difficult, if not impossible, to comb out. When a matted coat gets wet, the moisture is trapped near the skin, causing hot spots—circular lesions that are inflamed, raw, moist, and very painful. Be sure to check hidden spots, including the puppy's "armpits," chin, belly, and groin area, which are havens for mats.

Bathing and Drying

Bathing your puppy may seem like a daunting task, but it really is quite easy once you get the hang of it. When introduced correctly, most puppies grow into adult dogs that enjoy the process. Bathing and grooming also help with the bonding process because you are spending valuable time loving your puppy.

One key to success is having all of your supplies handy before you start running the water. You do not want your puppy jumping out of the sink or tub or off the grooming table while you are searching for shampoo or towels.

How often your puppy requires bathing depends on where you live, how much time he spends outside, and how dirty he gets. Some puppies—like some kids—have a knack for getting dirtier than others, so you will need to be the judge.

In warmer climates, you may be able to bathe your dog outdoors with a garden hose, provided the water is not too cold. If your puppy is small enough, you can bathe him in the sink. For larger puppies, a bathtub or shower stall works well, and be sure to use a rubber mat to provide secure footing and prevent your dog from slipping. Do not forget about slippery floors, either. A rubber mat or plenty of dry towels on the bathroom floor will prevent your puppy from slipping and injuring himself. Have plenty of towels on hand for cleaning up and drying off.

A sprayer attached to the faucet works well, and no doubt you will need to accustom your puppy to the sprayer's sound and the sensation of water soaking his body. Saturate your puppy's coat and skin with lukewarm water. Apply a dab or two of shampoo and gently scrub. Work the shampoo into the coat with your fingers or a rubber curry brush or massaging glove designed specifically for dogs. Massage the shampoo into his coat from head to toe, being careful to avoid the eye area. Don't overlook his belly, the inside of his hind legs, under his arms, and behind his ears.

To clean around a puppy's eyes, wipe the eye area with a damp cloth. Tearless shampoos are available for washing around the head and eye area, but you still want to avoid getting any in your puppy's eyes.

Rinse his entire body with lukewarm water until the water runs clear. Some coats can hold a lot of suds, and residual shampoo can irritate the skin and leave a dull film on the coat, so be sure that his coat is thoroughly rinsed. If necessary, shampoo and rinse again to be sure that your puppy is squeaky clean. If you are using a coat conditioner or skin moisturizer, follow the directions carefully.

Use your hands or a highly absorbent towel or chamois cloth to squeeze out excess water from your puppy's coat and then wrap him in a warm, dry towel before lifting him out of the sink or tub. A lot of puppies love to shake immediately after their baths. You might want to encourage this behavior while he is still in the tub or sink; otherwise, your wet puppy is likely to make a mad dash around the house!

If you live where temperatures are warm, and your puppy is likely to air-dry quickly, blow drying may not be necessary. Otherwise, to prevent him from getting chilled, blow-dry him with a dryer designed for dogs or, if necessary, a human blow dryer. If your dryer has a heating element, be sure to use the lowest or cool setting—never hot. Hold the dryer at least 6 inches away from the coat and keep the dryer in motion to avoid damaging the coat or burning your puppy's skin.

Most puppies and adult dogs dislike having air blowing into their faces, and for good reason. The face is sensitive, and the eyes, nose, and mouth can easily be injured with excessive heat or air pressure. Angle the dryer away from his face or simply allow his face to air dry.

You will need to accustom your puppy to the noise and sensation of the blow dryer. Start with a low speed and gradually work up to a higher speed, if necessary, always using cool air.

Foot and Nail Care

To keep your puppy's feet in tip-top shape, you will need to inspect and trim his

Whether using a blow dryer or warm towels, be sure to remove as much water as possible from the puppy's coat.

nails on a regular basis. If you are the slightest bit lazy about nail care, you run the risk of your puppy's nails growing too long, making walking awkward and painful for him. Long nails can break, tear, or snag, and they can scratch furniture, hardwood floors, and skin. Torn or broken nails can cause a puppy a great deal of pain and discomfort, and they may become infected, which can require veterinary attention. Nails that are not regularly trimmed and are allowed to grow too long put undue stress on the paw by forcing weight on the backs of the foot pads, which can, over time, break down the foot.

How often a puppy's nails need to be trimmed depends a good deal on the individual dog. Some puppies and adult dogs seem to require little nail trimming, while others need their nails trimmed weekly or at least several times a month. Also, much depends on the ground surface on which a puppy or adult dog spends most of his time. A puppy that spends the majority of his time indoors or running on grass will likely require more frequent nail trimming than his canine counterpart that spends a good deal of time walking on asphalt or concrete. While walking on hard surfaces, such as pavement, may help naturally wear down a dog's nails, few puppies or adult dogs wear down their nails naturally to the point that they never require trimming.

Guillotine-style nail clippers are preferred by most groomers and owners.

Dogs have a blood vessel called the "quick" that travels approximately three-quarters of the way through the nail. Regular nail trimmings will keep the quick from growing too close to the end of the nail. If the nails are neglected and they grow too long, it becomes more difficult to cut them back to the appropriate length because as the nail grows, so too does the quick. For that reason, it is better to get in the habit of trimming tiny bits of nail on a regular basis rather than waiting for the nails to get too long and then expecting to cut them back easily.

Your puppy may have white nails, black nails, or a combination of both. White nails make it easier to see the quick, which looks like a pink line extending through the nail toward the tip. Black nails make it difficult to see where the quick ends and the hook—the dead section of nail that extends beyond the quick—begins.

You want to trim only the dead section of nail. Clipping a dog's nails too short can cut the quick and cause bleeding. It's pretty darn painful for a puppy, too, and he will likely be hesitant to allow you to continue. One nip of the quick can lead to a lifelong aversion to nail clipping. A number of blood-clotting products are available through retail stores, such as powdered alum, styptic powder, or styptic pencil. Some breeders also recommend cornstarch in a pinch. Having one of these products in your doggy first aid kit is always a good idea.

Before clipping, examine the underside of the nail. You will see that the section closest to the paw is solid, while the tip (or hook) of the nail looks hollow, like a shell. You may be able to see or feel the slightest groove on the underside of the hook portion of the nail. Trim only the thinner hollow part, just nipping it where it curves slightly downward.

If you use a grinder, do not hold it in one spot for more than a second or two because it has an abrasive tip (similar to sandpaper) that spins at a high speed. The easiest way to use a grinder is to lightly touch the nail, release, and then repeat. Applying too much pressure or filing too close to the quick can cause a puppy a lot of discomfort. Nail grinders make whirling noises, and the vibration on the dog's nails can take some getting used to. If started at a young age, though, many puppies learn to accept the nail grinder as part of the routine grooming process. At first, until your puppy is comfortable with the process, it's safest to grind only half as much of the nail as is necessary. Also, be sure that your puppy's hair doesn't get caught in the rotating grinder head—be ever alert about keeping the hair away from the rotating head.

In no time, with practice and patience, you will discover that trimming nails is not as hard as it may seem. Ideally, you should have a veterinarian or experienced groomer show you how

If your puppy has dewclaws, be sure to trim them regularly. Certain breeds, such as the Beauceron (pictured), Briard, and Great Pyrenees, retain their dewclaws.

to do it correctly. Learning how to do it properly, using the correct equipment, and having a dog that accepts having his feet handled will make this necessary task easier and go a long way in reducing the odds of inadvertently nipping the quick.

You will need to find what works best for you and your puppy. If your puppy never grows to tolerate the procedure, you can always take him to the groomer or veterinarian's office for nail clipping.

Dewclaws are the fifth digits on the inside of the front and rear legs, usually an inch or so above the feet. In some puppies, the rear dewclaws are absent at birth. When present, some breeders choose to leave them on, while others have them removed shortly after birth. If your puppy has dewclaws, you will want to make sure that you include them in your regular nail care. If left unattended, they can curl around and grow into the soft tissue, not unlike an ingrown toenail on a human.

Ear Care

Routine ear cleanings are a necessary part of puppy and adult care and will help to reduce ear infections, which top the list of reasons that owners take their dogs to the veterinarian.

First a quick anatomy lesson: a dog's ear has three major parts:

- the outer ear, which consists of the ear flap (also called the "pinna")
- the middle ear, which is separated from the outer ear by the eardrum
- the inner ear, which connects to the brain and contains nerves and the circuit board for balance and hearing

Unlike a human's ear canal, which lies basically in a horizontal line from the side of the head inward to the eardrum, a dog's ear canal is L-shaped. The internal ear canal descends vertically before making almost a 90-degree bend and terminating in a horizontal stretch to the eardrum, also known as the tympanic membrane. A major benefit of the dog's two-directional ear canal structure is protection of the eardrum, which is vulnerable to injury. The downside is that gravity encourages wax, dirt, and other debris to collect in the ear canal's bend. Dogs can shake out some of the material, but the gunk that remains sets up a haven for infection.

Compounding the problem is the thick hair that grows in the ears of some breeds, which prevents proper aeration of the ear canal and contributes to ear infections. Dogs that swim or are bathed frequently may have water left in their ears, which is another potential source of ear problems. Recurrent ear infections are a common clinical sign of dogs with allergies. Parasites, foreign bodies, trauma, tumors of the ear canal, ruptured eardrums, and certain skin disorders, such as seborrhea, all can contribute to ear problems as well.

At least once a week, check the inside of your puppy's ears. The L-shaped canal means you can't see everything, but what you can see should be clean and light pink in color. It should have a clean, healthy doggy smell. Honey-colored wax in the ear is normal, but a dark crusty substance may indicate problems, such as ear

Keep your puppy's smile shining.

mites. If your puppy's ears have a discharge or smell bad, or if the canals look abnormal, red, or inflamed, do not clean the ears; instead seek veterinary attention right away.

Symptoms of an ear infection typically include signs of discomfort, such as depression or irritability, scratching or rubbing of the ears or head, shaking the head, or tilting the head to one side. The problem might be a foxtail or burr in his ear, ear mites, or the start of an infection. The longer an ear infection goes untreated, the harder it is to get rid of, and your puppy will be in a lot of pain. Left untreated, ear infections may cause permanent damage to your puppy's hearing, so do not procrastinate in getting your puppy to the veterinarian.

Cleaning Your Puppy's Ears

When cleaning your dog's ears with an ear-cleaning solution, do not place or force the tip of the bottle into the ear canal, as you run the risk of rupturing the eardrum. Massage the base of the ear to distribute the wash, and then gently wipe the inside of your puppy's ear leather (ear flap) using a cotton ball or a strip of gauze wrapped around your finger. If necessary, dampen the cotton or gauze with a bit of ear-wash solution or witch hazel.

Only clean the section of ear flap that you can see. Never stick cotton swabs or pointed objects into the ear canal because this tends to pack the debris in rather than remove it. Most important, you risk injuring your puppy's eardrum should you probe too deeply.

Eye Care

Your puppy's eyes should be clear and bright. You can easily clean your pup's eyes by saturating a gauze pad or soft washcloth with warm water and then, starting at the inside of the eye, gently wiping toward the outside corner of the eye. Excessive tearing, redness, swelling, discoloration, or discharge may be signs of an infection. If you suspect that something is wrong, do not hesitate to call your veterinarian.

Anal Glands

In the simplest of terms, anal glands are scent glands located around a dog's anus, which produce a strong-smelling, oily secretion. When dogs greet each other with their familiar rear-end sniffing, they are smelling the secretion from each other's anal glands.

When viewing a dog from behind, the sacs are located at approximately the 4 o'clock and 8 o'clock positions. The glands are emptied naturally during bowel movements. If not emptied regularly, the liquid contents become thick and plug the openings of the anal sacs. If the impacted (clogged) glands are not cleared, they can become abscessed. If you notice your dog scooting his rear on the floor or licking or biting the anal area excessively, chances are his anal sacs may be full or clogged. Abscessed or infected glands can be very painful, and a dog may be hesitant to allow you to touch around the area. Abscessed anal glands require veterinary attention, as do impacted or clogged glands.

Dental Care

As with other aspects of grooming, you should begin exposing your puppy to regular toothbrushing at an early age. If you have not started yet, do not worry. It is never too late to begin. Puppies often struggle with having their mouths examined because their mouth and gums can be super sensitive, especially when they are teething.

It is much easier to brush a puppy's teeth than you think. You can begin conditioning him to the process at the same time you are introducing grooming basics and handling. Calm handling and touching your puppy's mouth and teeth set the foundation for regular oral hygiene.

You will need a pet toothbrush or a finger toothbrush (a rubber cap that fits over your finger) and toothpaste made specifically for dogs. Most canine toothpastes are formulated with poultry- or malt-flavored enhancers for easier acceptance. Never ever use human toothpaste because it can upset your puppy's stomach.

Start by using your finger to massage your puppy's gums. Put a small dab of doggy toothpaste on your index finger and let your puppy lick it. Praise him for being brave. Apply another dab on your finger, gently lift up his outer lips and massage his gums.

Ideally, it is best to massage in a circular motion but, in the beginning, you may need to be satisfied with simply getting your finger in your puppy's mouth—without getting nipped by those razor-sharp baby teeth. Try to massage top and bottom, and the front gums, too. Keep a positive attitude, praising and reassuring your puppy throughout the process. Try to avoid wrestling with your puppy or restraining him too tightly. This will only hamper the process and make him resistant to the task.

Once your puppy is comfortable, try using the toothbrush or finger toothbrush. Let your puppy lick some toothpaste off the toothbrush and, again, praise him. You may find it easier to start with the canine teeth—the big fanglike teeth in the front of the mouth. They are the easiest to reach, and with any luck you should be able to brush them with little interference or objection from your puppy. In time, you can progress to a few more teeth, and then a few more, until you have brushed all twenty-eight puppy teeth. Remember to always progress at a pace that is suitable for your puppy.

Choose safe chew toys for your puppy. The raised nubs on a nylon or resin bone can help remove plaque buildup on your dog's teeth.

CHAPTER 9

FEEDING AND NUTRITION

Nutrition is one of those tricky canine topics where you ask six people a question and you get seven different answers. What you feed can have a significant impact on your puppy's future development. Sorting nutritional fact from fiction is a daunting task for many owners. Doubly frustrating is that canine nutritionists don't always agree on what types of foods are best for dogs or even how much fat, protein, and carbohydrates your puppy should eat. So how do you know what is best for your puppy? Let's start with the basics.

The Importance of Good Nutrition

Good nutrition, along with exercise, helps prevent disease, promote healthy skin, build strong bones and ligaments, and provide your puppy with the best opportunity to grow into a healthy adult dog. Everything a puppy does requires energy, including everyday activities such as drinking, eating, running, jumping, and retrieving, of course, as well as such functions as breathing, stretching, yawning, and even maintaining blood chemistry, blood pressure, and body temperature.

Overall energy requirements are affected by variables that include anxiety or stress related to his transition to a new home, learning new behaviors, and experiencing new things every day. Fluctuations in weather also affect his energy requirements.

Puppies grow at an astonishing rate, and you can practically see their size and weight increasing daily—especially the larger breeds. In order to grow into a healthy adult dog, your puppy needs about twice as many calories per pound of body weight as an adult dog of the same breed. He also needs all of the nutrients—protein, fat, carbohydrates, vitamins, and minerals—in the proper amounts, because too much or too little of some nutrients can cause growth issues. Puppies that grow too slowly may not be getting proper nutrition. Puppies that grow too quickly run the risk of bone and joint problems as they mature. Whether you own a Chihuahua or a Great Dane, your puppy needs to grow at the correct rate so he can reach his genetically programmed adult size, be it 2 pounds or 200 pounds.

It's important for you to look at your puppy's individual nutritional needs and then feed a diet that provides the correct combination of nutrients. What works for one puppy may not work for another because a puppy's nutritional needs will change depending on his age, environment, housing conditions, exposure to heat or cold, and overall health, and the emotional and physical demands placed upon him.

Some puppies are constantly in motion, and the more active the puppy, the more energy he burns. As a result, some puppies require a higher intake of nutrients to fuel their bodies. As your puppy grows into an adult dog, his dietary needs will change many times. To help your puppy's complex system run efficiently, it is important to find the diet that provides the correct balance of nutrients for his individual requirements.

Know Your Dietary Components

Research indicates that owners are becoming increasingly savvier about canine nutrition—and that is a good thing. Whether your choose grain or no-grain, age-specific, or organic food, the nuts and bolts of nutrition remain the same. The six basic elements of nutrition are carbohydrates, fats, proteins, vitamins, minerals, and water.

A puppy's energy is derived from the metabolism of energy-yielding nutrients—carbohydrates, fats, and proteins. During digestion, the body breaks down these three nutrients into four basic units that can be absorbed into the blood: carbohydrates are broken down into glucose, fats into glycerol and fatty acids, and protein into amino acids.

Carbohydrates

Carbohydrates are complicated because they come in many different forms, which a dog's body deals with differently. Dogs are classified as omnivorous—consumers of the primary sources of carbohydrates: meats and vegetables. Interestingly, carbohydrates are not an essential part of a dog's diet because his body can get its energy from protein. However, carbohydrates provide an excellent, cost-effective, and readily available source of dietary energy, which explains why many commercial dog foods contain somewhere between 46 and 74 percent carbohydrates.

Carbohydrates are often referred to as protein-sparing nutrients because the action of carbohydrates (and fats) in providing energy allows proteins to be used for its own unique roles. Without adequate carbohydrates, a dog's body can use protein for energy. Protein, however, is less efficient as an energy source because its primary functions are building muscle and regulating body functions. A dog's body must dismantle its valuable tissue proteins and use them for energy.

Whether you're feeding a Border Collie or a Bulldog puppy, the amount of food required will depend on your puppy's activity level.

Carbohydrates are introduced to the diet primarily through vegetable matter, legumes, and cereal grains, such as rice, wheat, corn, barley, and oats. (Carbohydrates in commercial dog foods are usually cereals, legumes, and other plant foods.) A dog's body breaks down carbohydrates into glucose and then into long glucose chains called starches. Glucose is the primary energy used to fuel a dog's body. It is readily absorbed in the small intestine and is transported via blood tissues for fuel. Unused carbohydrates are stored in the body as converted fat and as glycogen in the muscles and liver.

Carbohydrates are divided into two categories: simple and complex carbohydrates. Simple carbohydrates, also known as "simple sugars," include fructose (fruit sugar), sucrose (table sugar), and lactose (milk sugar). Simple carbohydrates require little or no digestive breakdown and are readily absorbed in the small intestine. Complex carbohydrates, which include potatoes, yams, legumes, and whole-grain flours (e.g., wheat and rye), are longer and more complex chains of simple sugars that require additional breakdown by the intestinal enzymes before they are absorbed and utilized as energy.

Fats

Fats get a bad rap even when it comes to canine nutrition. Granted, too much fat can be the culprit of some health issues, such as obesity or acute and/or chronic pancreatitis, but fats are not the dietary bad guys that some experts make them out to be. Fats are derived from animal fats and the seed oils of various plants, and they are the most concentrated sources of food energy in your puppy's diet. Fats account for approximately 2.25 times more metabolizable energy—the amount of energy in the food that is available to the dog—than carbohydrates or proteins.

Fats play an important role in contributing to your dog's healthy skin and coat and aiding in the absorption, transport, and storage of the fat-soluble vitamins A, D, E, and K. Fats also increase the palatability of foods, but they contain more than twice the calories of proteins and carbohydrates. While dogs can digest fats with great efficiency—an estimated 90 to 95 percent of the fats they eat gets metabolized—fats in your puppy's diet should be regulated. Too much fat can result in excess calorie intake, which is not good for your puppy's health or waistline.

Canines require meat as well as greens and grains to thrive.

Fat also serves as a source of essential fatty acids (EFAs), which are specific types of polyunsaturated fats that are essential to your dog's diet. Dogs can produce some, but not all, fatty acids, and the ones they can't produce must be obtained through their food. For instance, two essential fatty acids—omega-3 and omega-6—are important to the health of your puppy because they have anti-inflammatory properties and help regulate blood pressure, blood clotting, and other body functions. They also contribute to your dog's lustrous coat and help combat allergies, autoimmune conditions, arthritis, inflammatory bowel disease, and cancer-related issues, to name a few.

Proteins

A protein is a compound of carbon, hydrogen, oxygen, and nitrogen atoms arranged into a string of amino acids—much like the pearls on a necklace. Amino acids are the building blocks of vital proteins that promote the development of muscles, ligaments, organs, bones, teeth, and coat. Protein also defends the body against disease and is critical when it comes to the repair and maintenance of all of the body's tissues, hormones, enzymes, electrolyte balances, and antibodies.

There are ten essential amino acids that your puppy's body either cannot make on its own or cannot make in sufficient quantities. These amino acids must be obtained through his diet. To make protein, a cell must have all of the requisite amino acids available simultaneously because the body makes complete proteins only. (A complete protein provides all of the essential amino acids.) If one amino acid is missing, the other amino acids cannot form a partial protein. If complete proteins are not formed, the body's ability to grow and repair tissue is limited. Each protein is different in its ability to be broken down into amino acids.

Complete proteins, often referred to as *high-quality proteins*, are found in sources such as meat, poultry, fish, milk, eggs, cheese, certain grains and legumes (e.g., quinoa, lentils, and buckwheat), and some veggies and fruits (e.g., peaches, figs, and beets). An *incomplete protein* source, such as beans, peas, some grains, and corn, is one that is low in one or more of the essential amino acids. *Complementary proteins* are two or more incomplete protein sources that together provide adequate amounts of all essential amino acids. For example, soybean meal is not an ideal protein, and neither is corn. However, combining them forms a complementary protein because the amino acids that are deficient in one are present in the other.

Not all proteins are created equal. The higher the biological value of protein—meaning how efficiently your puppy utilizes the protein—the

A balanced diet contributes to a dog's overall health and a lustrous coat.

less protein he needs in his diet. For instance, eggs have the highest biological value of 94. Fish meal and milk have a value of 92. Beef is around 78, and soybean meal is 67. Meat and bone meal and wheat are around 50, and corn is 45. The percentage of protein noted on a bag of dog food indicates the protein content, not the digestibility, of the protein. You can see why it's important to find out from where your puppy's protein comes. Most experts agree that the best protein sources come from animal products.

Vitamins

A dog's body does not extract usable energy from vitamins, but vitamins are essential as helpers in metabolic processes. Vitamins are required in only small amounts, but they are vital to your puppy's health. Antioxidants such as vitamin C, vitamin E, and zinc help neutralize the effects of stress and environmental irritants. Vitamins are available in food sources, but they can be easily destroyed in the cooking and processing of commercial dog foods.

Certain vitamins are dependent on one another, with nearly every action in a dog's body requiring the assistance of vitamins. Vitamin deficiencies or excesses can lead to serious health problems, such as anorexia, artery and vein degeneration, dehydration, muscle weakness, and impairment of motor control and balance.

Vitamins fall into two categories: water-soluble (B-complex and C) and fat-soluble (A, D, E, and K). Unlike humans, dogs can manufacture vitamin C from glucose, so they do not need to acquire it in their food, which means that you should never need to supplement your dog's food with it. All other water-soluble vitamins must be replenished on a regular basis through diet. Any excesses in water-soluble vitamins are excreted in the urine.

Fat-soluble vitamins are absorbed and stored in the body's fat cells until they're needed, which can make oversupplementation potentially dangerous. Seek your veterinarian's advice and read as much as you can before supplementing your dog's food.

If you're fortunate to have a puppy with a hearty appetite, your task of feeding him is greatly simplified.

Minerals

Minerals do not yield sources of energy, but they are important in the overall nutritional equation because they help regulate your puppy's complex system and are crucial components in energy metabolism. They're also essential for strong, healthy teeth and bones, which are super important for growing puppies.

Minerals are classified as macrominerals or microminerals depending on how much of them the body needs. Microminerals, or trace elements, include iodine, iron, copper, cobalt, zinc, manganese, molybdenum, fluorine, and chromium; dogs need microminerals in very small amounts. Macrominerals, such as sodium, potassium, magnesium, calcium, and phosphorous, are needed in larger quantities.

Like essential fatty acids, essential nutrients are those that your puppy must obtain from his diet because his body cannot make them in sufficient quantity to meet his physiological needs. Commercial dog-food manufacturers add minerals and vitamins to their recipes, so it should not be necessary to supplement your puppy's diet. Doing so can upset the delicate balance and cause serious health problems, including tissue damage, convulsions, increased heart rate, and anemia. Always consult with your veterinarian before attempting to supplement your puppy's diet with minerals.

That's Billion with a "B"

It is important for savvy dog owners to keep in mind that the pet-food industry is a multi*billion*-dollar business. From the large corporations to the small private-label companies, they are in business to make money, as well as feed as many pets as possible. According to the American Pet Products Association (APPA), pet owners spend over $22 billion on pet food annually. Advertising experts spend a significant amount of time and money researching, developing, and marketing products to convince you to buy particular brands. This is not necessarily bad, but it is important to keep in mind if you are choosing a food because of the creative advertisements and fancy packaging rather than nutritional requirements of your dog.

Water

Don't overlook the importance of water because it is the single most important nutrient needed to sustain your puppy's health. Water regulates a dog's body temperature, plays an important part in supporting metabolic reactions, acts as the transportation system that allows blood to carry vital nutritional materials to the cells, and removes waste products from your dog's system.

The amount of water a puppy or adult dog needs to consume daily varies depending on growth, stress, environment, activity, and age. Your puppy will need more water when he expends more energy while working, exercising, playing, or training because dissipation of excess heat from his body is accomplished largely by the evaporation of water through panting. Plus, dogs generally require and need to consume more water as the temperature rises. Puppies that eat primarily dry dog food will also need access to fresh water to help with digestion.

The best way to be ensure that your puppy drinks enough water is to provide him with access to an abundant supply of fresh, cool drinking water at all times. (Don't forget to change it at least daily.) When dogs have free access to water, they will normally drink enough to maintain the proper balance of body fluids.

What Type of Food?

No shortage of options (or opinions) exists when it comes to feeding your new four-legged friend. Do you go with the convenient commercial foods (of which there are hundreds!) or the more time-consuming homemade meals? What about raw? The most important things to remember is to find a diet that works for you and your puppy. When in doubt, speak with your veterinarian—especially before making drastic changes to his diet.

Commercial Foods

Commercial foods have come a long way since James Spratt invented the first "dog cake"—a combination of wheat meal, vegetables, beetroot, and meat—in London more than 150 years ago. Commercial foods are undoubtedly the most convenient to buy, store, and use. They are readily available and, when compared to homemade diets, they are definitely less time-consuming.

Several major dog-food manufacturers and a number of veterinary universities have invested enormous sums of money into researching and studying the nutritional requirements of dogs in different stages of life. Experts say that commercial foods are balanced for vitamins and minerals, which is often difficult in homemade diets. Certain commercial foods have unique protein sources, such as bison, duck, and rabbit, and unique carbohydrates, including sweet potatoes and brown rice.

There is no denying that commercial foods are convenient. Who doesn't like one-stop shopping for the family's groceries and the dog's food. Commercial pet foods are readily available, and while premium foods were at one time stocked mainly at feed stores, they are beginning to show up at natural or specialty grocery stores as well. Many commercial foods are now formulated for puppies and senior dogs, tiny dogs and giant breeds—and everything in between.

Dry dog food, or kibble, is the most popular choice of dog owners.

Commercial foods tend to be classified into three main food types: canned, dry, and semimoist.

Canned Foods: Designed to be fed alone as a complete diet, quality canned foods are highly palatable, and most dogs love them. They are approximately 75 percent water and usually contain higher protein levels than dry food, depending on the brand/recipe. Look for meat as the first two ingredients, followed by veggies and fruits. The high-heat pressure-canning process kills harmful bacteria, which can be found in raw diets, but some destruction of critical nutrients is possible. Some canned foods contain textured protein (either soy or wheat-gluten based). The downside is that they are more expensive than dry foods, making them cost-prohibitive for many owners with multiple dogs or medium- or large-breed dogs. Canned foods provide little or no abrasion from chewing, which allows faster plaque and tartar buildup on your dog's teeth.

Dry Foods: Commonly called "kibble," dry food is one of the more commonly purchased pet-food types. Dry food is also among the most highly processed diets and contain about 10 to 12 percent moisture. Hundreds of brands and options are readily available, and formulas range from puppy growth and pregnancy formulas to breed-specific formulas and formulas geared toward special

Storing Dog Food

Storing dry food can be a bit challenging because the food is attractive not only to enterprising puppies but also to bugs, mice, roaches, raccoons, and any number of hungry critters. Other sources of damage to dog foods are oxygen, heat, humidity, and light. Foods with natural preservatives may have a shorter shelf life because natural preservatives, such as vitamin E, tend to break down quicker than artificial preservatives. Dry foods usually have a shelf life of one year, and canned foods are normally good for two years, but always double check the "best if used by" date on the bag or can. Follow these tips for proper storage of foods:

- Store opened bags of food in a plastic or rubber-type container (intended specifically for storing food) with a tight-fitting lid to preserve freshness, maintain palatability, and minimize the food's exposure to environmental factors.
- Keep dry food in its original bag, placing the opened bag inside the storage container.
- Store both dry and canned foods at room temperature, never above 90°F (32°C). Storing foods below 50°F (10°C) may change the consistency and palatability of the food but should not alter the nutritional value.
- Avoid storing dry foods in basements and bathrooms, as moisture encourages the growth of mold.

concerns (such as healthy joints, digestion, or weight management). Gluten-free formulas, no-grain formulas, and formulas with meat sources from poultry to bison to venison are available at most pet-supply outlets. Although dry foods tend to be easier on the pocketbook than canned foods, some high-end premium foods are quite expensive.

Semimoist Foods: Often shaped into patties and prepackaged for convenient feeding, semimoist foods have fallen out of favor as savvy consumers have become more educated. Semimoist foods are the poster-food for processed pet foods—containing fresh or frozen animal tissues, cereal grains, fats, artificial food colorings, flavorings, sugars, and even propylene glycol, an odorless, tasteless, slightly syrupy liquid used to make antifreeze and deicing products. Propylene glycol is recognized as generally safe by the US Food and Drug Administration for use in dog food and other animal feeds (up to 5 percent of the total food intake); it is used to absorb extra water and maintain moisture, and as a solvent for food coloring and flavor. But who wants to feed a puppy that stuff?

The Raw-Food Alternatives

Raw-food diets are becoming increasingly popular because many owners are looking to feed more natural foods. Poor nutrition has been linked to many canine health issues, and in humans, disease prevention through proper nutrition is a widely accepted philosophy. Diet as a preventive measure against canine disease is becoming an accepted path in dogs, too.

Raw feeding has its share of opponents, who cite parasites and salmonella poisoning as the primary concerns. Veterinarians also have concerns about bacterial or parasitic infections, or punctured organs or gastrointestinal blockages from bone shards. Dogs that are immune-compromised may experience health issues if fed raw foods.

Owners are also concerned with whether raw-food diets are balanced and whether they should be adding calcium or other vitamin/mineral supplements. These are legitimate concerns that owners should address with their veterinarians before beginning to feed raw diets. On the flip side, proponents say that feeding a more natural diet is paramount, and they rave about their pets' health, alertness, energy level, and skin and coat condition.

Freezing keeps raw foods from spoiling, and experts recommend that it stay frozen for at least three days prior to being served. Not all raw-food diets are balanced and may or may not have been tested in food trials, so be sure to check the package for American Association of Feed Control Officials (AAFCO) compliance, which means that the food has been approved by the AAFCO as "nutritionally balanced for all life stages." Equally important, look for raw foods that are "products" of the United States, not simply "packaged" in the United States; the latter means that ingredients can be imported from other countries and then packaged in the United States.

The popularity of dehydrated raw food is increasing with dog owners looking for an alternative—and a happy medium—to raw or commercial dry foods. Dehydrating is one of the oldest and most gentle forms of food preservation. By maintaining a consistent dehydration temperature, the water is removed, which inhibits the growth of bacteria without destroying sensitive nutrients. Nutritional

Determining the best diet for your puppy may take some experimentation.

loss is minimal—about 3 to 5 percent. Dehydration suspends the activity of enzymes in the ingredients until the food is rehydrated. Dehydrated foods must be rehydrated prior to serving to your puppy.

Two Australian veterinarians, Ian Billinghurst and Tom Lonsdale, are the gurus of raw food diets. Billinghurst introduced the Biologically Appropriate Raw Foods (BARF) diet, which many people refer to as "Bones and Raw Foods." His diet emphasizes that dog foods be prepared from raw meats, muscle meats, organ meat, bone, fat, raw fruits, and raw vegetables, but never grains. The philosophy behind BARF is that the diet a dog evolved to eat—over many millions of years of evolution—is the best way to feed it. And that means not feeding your dog cooked or processed food. Lonsdale also promotes raw foods, but he recommends that dogs regularly get raw meaty bones and whole carcasses as part of their diets.

Feeding any type of raw diet should be undertaken only after a great deal of research, and it is highly recommended that you work closely with a veterinarian or certified canine nutritionist to provide a diet that is balanced and meets your puppy's individual nutritional needs.

Homemade Diets

Years ago, people employed the "leftover" method of feeding dogs: whatever was left over from family meals was given to the dog. Of course, experts tell you that table scraps are the worst possible food source for dogs. Maybe that is true, but most of us probably know dogs that were fed home-cooked "leftover" diets and lived to be fifteen years old or even older.

Presently, home-cooked diets are making a comeback. Preparing a canine diet that is complete and balanced and that contains the proper ratio of nutrients on a routine daily basis takes some effort and research. It is also tricky, time-consuming, and a bit pricey. Not only do you need to shop for the ingredients, you need to prepare, cook, and store the food. The nutritional value of ingredients will fluctuate depending on their sources, and supplementing with vitamins and minerals is usually necessary.

Plenty of dog-friendly recipes can be found online and even include convenient slow-cooker options. Many of these recipes can be made ahead of time and stored in the refrigerator for three or four days. However, many of the recipes are not nutritionally complete or balanced.

Active breeds and working dogs, like the Sheltie, will require more food than normal pet dogs.

For the first few days after bringing your puppy home, continue feeding the same type and brand of puppy food that he has been eating, provided he has been eating a well-balanced, good-quality puppy food. If you intend to switch foods, it is best to do so slowly to prevent diarrhea and gastrointestinal upset. Veterinarians recommend increasing the amount of the new diet and decreasing the amount of the old diet by one-fourth every three days.

- For the first three days, feed ¼ cup new food and ¾ cup old food.
- For the next three days, feed ½ cup new food and ½ cup old food.
- For the next three days, feed ¾ cup new food and ¼ cup old food.
- On the tenth day, feed only the new food.

If your puppy experiences diarrhea or an upset tummy, go back to the previous mixture for two or three days, or longer, and then try again. If the diarrhea worsens, consult your veterinarian.

Your best bet is to work with an experienced canine nutritionist who can develop a diet especially for your puppy's nutritional needs.

How Much to Feed?

Once you choose the right food, you will need to feed the correct amount, which can be a bit tricky. A growing puppy needs about twice as many calories per pound of body weight as an adult dog. A busy, active puppy will require more calories than a more sedate one. Keep in mind that the feeding guidelines on puppy-growth food packages are just that—*guidelines*. A good rule of thumb is to use the manufacturer's guidelines, which are listed on the food package, as a starting point to help you estimate your puppy's needs for his age and weight.

Watch your puppy carefully to see if he is gaining too much weight or not enough weight. If he is getting pudgy, you know to decrease his food a teeny bit. If he's too thin, you can add a teeny bit more. Always use a standard 8-ounce measuring cup for accuracy, which better helps to control body weight and growth rate. When in doubt, always consult your veterinarian, who can help you determine the proper food and the correct amount to feed.

Nutraceuticals

Nutraceuticals is a fancy word for nutritional supplements and all dietary supplements, including vitamins, vitaminlike substances, minerals, amino acids, dietary fiber, botanicals, and other substances. The Nutraceutical Institute defines these supplements as "natural, bioactive chemical compounds that have health-promoting, disease-preventing, or medicinal properties." Some veterinarians go so far as to say that anything added to your puppy's food, be it yogurt, brewer's yeast, fish oil, vegetables, broth, and so forth, are supplements.

Nutraceuticals are often called *phytochemicals* or *functional foods*. The terms *nutraceuticals* and *supplements* are often used interchangeably, but their meanings do differ. All nutraceuticals are supplements, but not all supplements are nutraceuticals.

The most popular supplement group continues to be joint-health products. Glucosamine and chondroitin, with or without methylsulfonylmethane (MSM), are two of the most popular supplements. Glucosamine and chondroitin are critical components of cartilage and are typically used to help diminish the symptoms of osteoarthritis. Glucosamine used for supplementation is typically derived from the shells of shrimp or crab or, more recently, corn. Chondroitin sulfate is usually derived from pig or cow cartilage, but shark and chicken cartilage have also been used. MSM, which is synthetically produced, is used primarily for treating pain associated with osteoarthritis.

Omega-3 fatty acids are also popular, and there is increasing evidence that they are beneficial in mediating and regulating inflammation and immune response within the body. Omega-6 fatty acids are helpful for maintaining a dog's skin and coat and aiding in tissue repair.

Probiotics are becoming increasingly popular supplements because they are friendly bacteria that help a dog's body fight disease and illness and keep harmful bacteria from colonizing and creating digestive problems.

Despite their popularity, nutraceuticals are not regulated by the FDA and are not endorsed by all veterinarians. Many question the possible side effects from the prolonged and continuous use of untested alternative therapies. Supplements can cause side effects or result in cross-reactions if combined with other supplements or medications. Always consult your veterinarian before using supplements.

Feeding Schedule

Many breeders will send their puppies to their new homes with information that includes the type of food that the puppy has been eating, when he eats, how much he eats at each feeding, and how to gradually increase his food portion. If not, don't be shy about asking for this information. Most breeders will usually give you enough puppy food to get you through a few days. If possible, you should follow your puppy's normal

The first lesson in sharing occurs at the puppy feeding station.

routine and use the same brand of food. If you plan to switch foods, do so gradually by mixing the old food with the new food over a ten-day period to avoid stomach upset or diarrhea.

If no prior feeding information is available for your puppy, you will need to choose a puppy food that best suits your puppy. If you are unsure, ask your veterinarian, a canine nutritionist, or a knowledgeable breeder for a recommendation.

Ideally, puppies under four months of age should be fed three times a day because they have tiny tummies and can't consume their daily caloric intake all in one feeding. From four months on, you should be able to feed two times a day—once in the morning and again in the evening. Some veterinarians recommend feeding a puppy three meals a day until six months of age.

Feed your puppy at regular times. If there is food left in his bowl after fifteen minutes, pick it up and either throw it away or refrigerate it for his next feeding. This is called *scheduled feeding,* and it is your puppy's best bet. Yes, it's a teeny bit less convenient than free-feeding, but the benefits are abundant. This regimen will help your puppy establish a regular routine of eating and eliminating, which will help speed up the house-training process. What goes in on a regular basis comes out on a regular basis.

Free-feeding means putting the food out, leaving it out all day, and allowing your puppy to eat at his leisure. This doesn't establish a set schedule for feeding and eliminating, so it's not recommended for puppies. Plus, if your puppy is nibbling all day long, it's difficult, if not impossible, to establish a regular routine of eating and eliminating. It is also much harder to determine your puppy's "normal" eating habits, which could be important information if your puppy gets sick.

Breeders often feed puppies individually to monitor their intake (and avoid certain puppies pigging out).

Some puppies are able to regulate their food intake, but most puppies (and adult dogs) will eat and eat and eat until they make themselves sick, and then happily start all over again. When food is perpetually available, some dogs will develop the potential dangerous habit of food-bowl guarding (also called *resource guarding*).

Dangerous for Dogs

Dogs have different metabolisms, and some human foods (and nonfood items) can cause serious health problems, ranging from a mild upset stomach to death. The list below is a *sampling* of some of the most common foods that can cause your puppy serious health problems if ingested. If you suspect that your puppy has ingested a toxic substance, it is always better to err on the side of caution and seek veterinary attention immediately.

Alcohol. Never give your dog alcoholic drinks; alcohol can cause intoxication, coma, and, in some instances, death.

Cat food, while not fatal, is high in protein and fat and particularly appetizing for enterprising puppies. Too much can cause intestinal upset, vomiting, diarrhea, and unnecessary weight gain.

Chocolate—who doesn't love it? A lot of dogs love it, too, but it can be deadly. It contains theobromine, which, even in small amounts, can cause serious health issues. Depending on your puppy's size and how much he consumes, it can increase his heart rate and breathing, resulting in serious illness and death.

Grapes and raisins contain an unknown toxin that can damage your puppy's kidneys. Stories have been told of dogs' becoming seriously ill after eating only a few grapes.

Mushrooms contain toxins that vary depending on the species. They affect multiple systems, resulting in shock and death.

Onions contain sulfoxides and disulfides, which can be toxic to dogs, damaging red blood cells and causing anemia.

Tobacco contains nicotine and can cause increased heartbeat, collapse, coma, and death.

Xylitol is widely used as a sugar substitute and in sugar-free chewing gums, mints, and other candies. Even in small amounts, it can be toxic to dogs, causing a sudden and life-threatening drop in blood sugar (hypoglycemia), seizures, and liver failure.

A puppy's first meal was provided by his dam. There was only one flavor of milk available in Mom's kitchen.

CHAPTER 10

THE VETERINARIAN AND YOUR PUPPY

One of the more important responsibilities of puppy ownership is providing your puppy with excellent and regular veterinary care. Puppy vaccinations, spaying or neutering, teeth cleaning, wellness checks, and flea and tick preventives should be on your must-do list. He may also need veterinary attention for any number of injuries or ailments, such as a cut, dog bite, cat scratch, diarrhea, or gastrointestinal obstruction. Hopefully, he will never need a specialist, but if he does, many veterinarians are board-certified in fields such as radiology, endoscopy, neurology, cardiology, and oncology, as well as orthopedic surgery and canine sports medicine.

Compared to human medicine, veterinary care is reasonably priced though certainly not cheap. Consider, for example, that out-of-pocket expenses for canine cranial cruciate ligament surgery can run from three thousand to five thousand dollars or more, which does not include any postsurgical physical rehabilitation. Canine health insurance might be something to seriously consider.

The good news is that today's veterinarians have the training and expertise to help prevent, reduce, or treat any number of canine ailments, be it inherited conditions such as hip or elbow problems or infectious diseases such as parvovirus or kennel cough.

Selecting a Veterinarian

Ideally, you will want to select a veterinarian before your puppy comes to live with you. Would you scan the Yellow Pages for a pediatrician if your toddler were sick? Likely not. Scanning the telephone book or Internet once your puppy is sick or injured is not a good idea, either. Without a designated veterinarian, the alternative becomes a trip to an emergency veterinary hospital, which is neither cheap nor convenient.

Where to Start

The best way to find a good veterinarian is to ask your pet-owning friends, neighbors, or coworkers. Your puppy's breeder may know of local veterinarians, as may trainers at local dog clubs and obedience schools. Ask where they go and why. What do they like or dislike about their veterinarians? For clinics with multiple veterinarians, do they like all of the doctors in the practice? Can they request a specific veterinarian or must they see whoever is available? What about the front desk people, vet techs, and assistants? Are they knowledgeable and easy to deal with?

From these recommendations, cull your list to those clinics that best meet your requirements. The veterinary clinic down the street from your house may be conveniently located, but have you gotten positive feedback about the veterinarians there? Likewise, the vet clinic three towns over may be your favorite, but is it realistic to travel that far? That is not to say you should choose based solely on location, but if you are wavering between several excellent clinics, location may be the deciding factor, which is a particularly smart choice if you're ever dealing with emergencies.

The Clinic

Visiting clinics is time-consuming but necessary when it comes to picking the right facility. Again, the time you invest today will pay off down the road when you need to put your puppy's health and well-being in the hands of a veterinarian and his or her staff.

When visiting clinics, observe how the staff interacts with their clients and animals. What does your gut tell you? The waiting room should be organized and run smoothly. Is the waiting area large enough to separate large dogs from small ones, and unruly dogs from nervous ones?

Most importantly, you have to trust that the veterinarian you choose is the right person to put in charge of the long-term care of your best friend.

Let the staff know that you are shopping for a new veterinarian. Ask to see their exam rooms, X-ray rooms, operating and recovering rooms, boarding areas, and so forth. The clinic should be spotless, and the exam rooms should be modern, clean, and always disinfected between animals. Is there adequate parking and a fenced or designated (preferably grassy) area to potty your puppy?

If the clinic is busy, you may need to make an appointment to visit, which is a reasonable request. If the staff balks or makes excuses about your touring the facility, run, don't walk, to the nearest exit.

The Veterinarian

Like human doctors, veterinarians differ in their bedside (tableside) manners. Some are personable, outgoing, chatty, caring, compassionate, and understanding. Others are more businesslike. If possible, ask to meet the veterinarian. Again, if you catch the clinic on a busy day, you may need to make an appointment.

Establishing a good working relationship with the veterinarian and his or her staff is paramount. Chances are you will be seeing a lot of the clinic over the next ten or more years (more than you probably think!). So it is important to be comfortable with the clinic, its people, and its practices. If you sense a clashing of personalities, it is probably best if you look at other clinics. If you are not comfortable talking to the veterinarian and asking questions, your puppy's long-term care may suffer.

Veterinarians are understandably busy, but you should never feel rushed. The vet and his or her staff should be patient, knowledgeable, and friendly. They should be willing to explain the diagnosis, treatment, and expected outcome in layman's terms.

Ask about the clinic's regular office hours, holiday and weekend hours, and how emergencies or urgent care are handled. Will you be referred to an emergency clinic after hours, or will someone meet you at the clinic? What type of services do they offer—surgeries, hip or elbow X-rays, ultrasound, dentistry, eye exams? Do they have specialists on staff? If not, do they have a network of specialists to whom they refer patients? If your puppy must stay overnight, is the clinic staffed 24/7 with a veterinarian or licensed veterinary technician?

Does the veterinarian offer you the kind of care you're hoping to offer your puppy?

Most veterinarians are in business because they love animals, but they also need to make money. What different clinics charge for the same service— say, a routine spay or neuter—can vary wildly depending on the facility and its location. However, low cost does not necessarily equate to low quality, and an expensive clinic is not necessarily the best clinic. Policies and procedures, as well as available equipment, factor into what clinics charge. Many clinics have access to high-tech gadgetry, including 3-D imaging scanners and ultrasounds, as well as magnetic resonance imaging (MRI) equipment. Veterinary medicine has come a long way in the last few decades, and many of today's owners are willing to pay for state-of-the art, top-notch medicine.

Philosophies

An important part of choosing a veterinarian will depend on your personal preference and philosophy. Humans have been helping sick and injured animals for thousands of years, but veterinarians today have differing approaches, and you will want to find one who meshes with your philosophy (assuming you have one). Most, although certainly not all, veterinarians who practice conventional medicine—also referred to as Western medicine—tend to view disease as a set of signs and symptoms. Their primary concern is the treatment of sick animals. Their philosophy is rooted in science, research, data, and double-blind studies. They tend to prescribe conventional medicines as opposed to herbal remedies or supplements. Most also practice preventive care in terms of regular vaccinations, dewormings, dental care, and so forth.

Some veterinarians adhere strictly to the tenets of holistic medicine, often referred to as Eastern medicine, by treating the body as a *whole*—mind, body, spirit—in harmony with the environment. Holistic practitioners may use treatments that are not documented or rooted in science but have nonetheless been used for hundreds or thousands of years. Veterinarians who combine conventional and holistic or alternative medicine are practicing what is called *integrative medicine*. They incorporate conventional and alternative therapies ranging from supplements and nutrition to acupuncture and homeopathy. Again, the route you take will depend on your personal philosophy and what is best for your puppy.

Puppy's First Vet Visit

Once you have selected a veterinarian, you will want to get your puppy checked out. Regardless of where and from whom you acquired your puppy, you want to establish a record of health. Therefore, it is important to have your puppy checked by your veterinarian within forty-eight to seventy-two hours after bringing him home. To the untrained eye, a puppy that appears healthy can still have health problems that may or may not be immediately apparent.

At the first visit, your veterinarian will check your puppy's overall health, which includes inspecting his skin and coat, examining his eyes, and checking his

A puppy's first visit to the vet's office can be stressful for the new patient (and new owner).

What Is Your Dog's True Age?

Someone once said that a dog's only fault is that he does not live long enough. That is true, but calculating a dog's age is no easy task. The old adage of multiplying a dog's age by seven to calculate his "human" age is a bit deceiving because dogs age at different rates depending on their size, breed, health care, and breeding.

Dogs are the most diverse mammal species on the planet. Their weight when fully grown can vary from less than 4 pounds to more than 200 pounds, with vastly different body shapes. Small dogs reach adulthood—skeletal and reproductive maturity—faster than large dogs. Many large dogs take two years to fully mature. Experts do not yet fully understand why dogs age at very different rates.

No one knows for certain where the 7:1 ratio came from, but it has been around for a long time. While it is not a bad estimate, it's not that simple. Experts suggest that one human year can be equivalent to six to ten dog years. For the super inquisitive owner, online calculators can help you estimate your dog's age.

mouth for broken or retained baby teeth as well as plaque buildup. The vet will check his gums and gum color, take his temperature, and examine his ears for any signs of infection or ear mites. The vet will listen to your puppy's heart and lungs and feel his abdomen, muscles, and joints. The vet should also ask about your puppy's daily routine, including his eating and elimination habits.

Ideally, you should bring along any relevant information provided to you by the breeder, such as his current vaccination and worming schedule, and so forth. Prior to the appointment, the clinic may ask you to bring along a stool sample. You will be surprised how often you are asked about your puppy's poop. It won't take long to become an expert on the topic, and by understanding what normal stool looks like, you will quickly be able to tell when something is amiss.

Preventive Care

Ask the veterinarian about setting up a preventative healthcare plan that includes vaccinations, worming, spaying or neutering, and dental care. At the minimum, your puppy will need one or two annual checkups to be sure he is healthy. Granted, when your growing puppy is happy and healthy and full of energy, it is easy to put regular checkups on the back burner. Yearly checkups make it more likely that your veterinarian will be able to diagnosis, treat, and perhaps prevent problems early on before they become serious.

Common Puppy Ailments

Puppies are susceptible to any number of illnesses and diseases, some of which can be prevented with a proper vaccination protocol. Chances are your puppy will grow into a happy, healthy adult dog. However, understanding what can go wrong before anything does go wrong is an important part of canine ownership. Here are a few of the more common puppy ailments.

Demodicosis

A noncontagious skin disease, demodicosis is caused by an excessive or abnormal infestation with the microscopic mite *Demodex canis*. (*Demodex canis* is the most commonly recognized Demodex mite, but two other species, *Demodex injai* and *Demodex cornei*, have been reported.)

Clinically, canine demodicosis, also known as demodectic mange, is complex, and the pathogenesis is not completely understood. Small numbers of Demodex mites normally inhabit the hair follicles and sebaceous glands of dogs and are passed from a mother to a puppy in the first week of life. Veterinarians believe that some puppies may have ineffective or sensitive immune systems that interfere with their ability to keep the mites under control and, as a result, they develop demodicosis. The tendency to develop demodicosis may have a genetic component, as well, as some breeds appear to have an increased incidence. Factors such as stress, poor nutrition, unsanitary conditions, and/or intestinal parasites may favor the overgrowth of mites and cause localized forms of the disease in puppies.

Canine demodicosis can be divided into the more common canine localized demodicosis (CLD) and the less common canine generalized demodicosis (CGD). Both forms usually occur in puppies, and there is also an adult-onset form of CGD, which is difficult to treat.

CLD represents approximately 90 percent of all cases of demodicosis and occurs in dogs under one year of age. A self-limiting disease, it involves five or fewer lesions that can appear as crusty, red skin with hair loss and may have a greasy or moist appearance. Most lesions are confined to the face, around the eyes or the corners of the mouth, and occasionally the forelimbs. Prognosis is good, with an estimated 90 percent of dogs recovering without treatment because it tends to heal spontaneously in about two months, or at least by one year of age. In some cases, topical antiseptic shampoos or lotions such as benzoyl peroxide may be recommended. Approximately 10 percent of the affected puppies develop the more severe generalized form.

Your puppy should have had his first vaccinations while he was with the breeder. Be sure to bring all of the information provided by the breeder to your first veterinary visit.

Like localized demodicosis, CGD usually develops in young dogs less than twelve months of age. Affected dogs usually have a history of prior localized demodicosis from which the generalized form evolves. Characterized by the presence of five or more lesions, generalized demodicosis typically causes hair loss over the entire body, red skin, and lesions on the head, neck, stomach, legs, and feet. In severe cases, dogs may become quite ill, developing lethargy, fever, and loss of appetite. Diagnosis is based primarily on the dog's history, clinical findings, and the identification of Demodex mites in skin scrapings.

Treatment for CGD almost always requires administration of miticidal medications (substances that kill mites) as well as antibiotics because it is usually associated with secondary bacterial infections. Shaving the dog is sometimes recommended as well. The prognosis is uncertain, depending on the dog's age at the time he develops the disease, but as many as 90 percent of cases can be successfully managed, according to some experts. Many dogs require long-term monitoring because any stressor may trigger a relapse.

Adult-onset canine demodicosis is not common but does occur—most often in dogs three to four years of age or older. Experts note that it can be triggered by certain drugs or diseases that alter immune suppression, with 25 percent of cases being idiopathic (of unknown cause). Some dogs may recover without miticidal treatment if the demodicosis is associated with a systemic disease that is treated successfully.

Shetland Sheepdogs and other herding dogs are sensitive to ivermectin, commonly used to treat scabies and as a heartworm preventative. Discuss this with your vet.

Scabies

Canine scabies, also known as sarcoptic mange, is a highly contagious, intensely itchy skin disease caused by the burrowing epidermal mite—*Sarcoptes scabiei* var. *canis*. Restricted almost exclusively to canines, this particular mite prefers dogs but will infect other animals, including cats, ferrets, foxes, and even humans. These microscopic mites invade the skin of healthy puppies or adult dogs and lay their eggs, and the emergent mites start the process all over again. The life cycle is completed in ten to twenty-one days. Transmission is usually, but not always, via direct contact with an infected dog.

Clinical symptoms are characterized by

Retained Baby Teeth

Puppies are born without any teeth. Their baby teeth, also referred to as temporary, deciduous, or milk teeth, begin to erupt around three weeks of age. By eight weeks of age, most puppies will have all twenty-eight of their baby teeth. Although razor-sharp, these baby teeth are not as strong as permanent teeth and can easily break. Around three to four months of age, most puppies start losing their baby teeth as the corresponding permanent teeth begin to come in. By six months of age, most puppies have shed all of their baby teeth and should have a full complement of forty-two permanent teeth in place.

More often than not, nothing goes wrong, but retained deciduous teeth can be an issue with puppies between four and seven months of age. A retained tooth is a baby tooth that hasn't fallen out after its adult-tooth replacement has erupted. Overcrowding results when both the baby and adult teeth remain in the mouth. Misaligned teeth can also rub against other teeth, wearing away the enamel. Doubly important, if a retained baby tooth is blocking a permanent tooth, it is unlikely that the permanent tooth will be able to move into the correct position possibly causing malocclusion problems.

itching, itching, and more itching. The intense itching, experts believe, results from the mites as they burrow into the skin and from their production of allergy-inducing compounds (or toxic allergens). These mites generally prefer to live on the areas of the skin that have the least amount of hair. Small red pustules, scaling, crusting, and hair loss develop typically on the belly, elbows, armpits, hocks, face, and pinnae (ear leathers). As the condition worsens, it can spread to the entire body.

Diagnosis is based on the history and clinical symptoms as well as a superficial skin scraping with the identification of mites under a microscope. A positive skin scraping confirms the diagnosis. Unfortunately, on average, 20 to 50 percent of infected dogs will test negative for these mites, but a negative scraping does not rule out scabies. Therefore, some veterinarians recommend treating for mange and observing for signs of resolution within two to four weeks.

Several treatment options are available, with ivermectin and ivermectin-derivative products being among the more common treatments. Certain dog breeds, including Collies, Australian Shepherds, Shetland Sheepdogs, and other herding dogs, are potentially more sensitive to ivermectin due to the multidrug resistance (MDR1) gene, which diminishes the functionality of the blood-brain barrier. Always consult your veterinarian before using these products. Antibiotics to control secondary infections and a cortisone derivative to control itching may also be recommended.

The prognosis for scabies is good, but all canine housemates of an affected dog should be treated because they may be harboring sarcoptic mites with or without accompanying symptoms.

Protozoal Intestinal Infections

Protozoa are not worms—they are one-celled microscopic organisms that infect the intestinal tracts of dogs. Many protozoa are free-living in the environment and beneficial. Only parasitic protozoa are of concern to veterinarians and owners. Two of the most common protozoal infections that can affect your puppy are coccidiosis and giardiasis.

Coccidia: Spread in the feces of carrier animals, Coccidia are a group of intracellular parasites that invade the cells of a dog's small intestine, where they multiply, rapidly destroying tissue. At least six different genera of *Coccidia* can infect dogs, the most common belonging to the genus *Isospora*.

Here's how it works: an infected dog passes oocysts (immature *Coccidia*) in his feces. When a susceptible dog ingests the active oocysts, the oocysts will release sporozoites that invade the intestinal-lining cells and set up a cycle of infection in neighboring cells. Thousands of intestinal cells can become infected and destroyed as a result of your dog's swallowing a single oocyst. Once infected, the disease is referred to as coccidiosis.

It is most common in puppies less than six months of age, adult dogs with suppressed immune systems, and dogs that have other diseases or that are under physiological stress, such as change of ownership, shipping, weaning, fatigue, and dietary changes. Coccidiosis can also occur to dogs living in crowded environments where an increased chance of infection exists through contaminated water or food. Young puppies exposed to their mother's infected feces or to infected feces in the environment are common victims of coccidiosis. Also, a dog that eats a mouse or another animal infected with *Coccidia* can become infected.

Puppies can become infected by *Giardia* by digging in sand or contaminated soil.

Young dogs may experience diarrhea streaked with blood, weight loss, diminished appetite, and, in some instances, even death. Coccidiosis is highly contagious, and any infected puppy is contagious to other puppies. A stool sample is the most common method of diagnosis. *Coccidia* aren't worms, so dewormers will not work. The good news is that it is treatable with prescription drugs. Controlling the spread of coccidiosis requires strict sanitary practices. You must clean up fecal matter right away and keep your dog's water and food where it cannot become contaminated with feces. Cleaning the environment with a disinfectant helps, but ask your veterinarian for recommendations because *Coccidia* are resistant to most common disinfectants. Heat treatment of surfaces with steam or a flame gun may be necessary. While this helps reduce the potential for infection, it does not guarantee that infections will not occur.

Giardia: Nicknamed the "backpacker's disease" because it is commonly acquired by people (and dogs) who drink infected water in high mountain lakes and streams, giardiasis is an infestation of microscopic parasites (*Giardia*) that live in the small intestine of dogs. (The human version is also called "traveler's diarrhea.") Giardia infections are usually acquired by ingestion of the cyst form of the parasite. The microscopic parasites reproduce by dividing in half many times. After an unknown number of divisions, they are passed in the stool.

Giardia prevent proper absorption of nutrients, damage the intestinal lining, and interfere with digestion. In many cases involving adult dogs, there are few symptoms. Younger dogs may develop acute foul-smelling diarrhea or abnormal, soft, or light-colored stools that have a greasy or excess mucousy appearance. Abdominal discomfort, nausea, and vomiting may occur. Some dogs will not lose their appetites, but they may lose weight.

While beavers are most often blamed for contaminating the water by passing the intestinal organism in their feces, dogs can become infected if they come in contact with infected feces from another dog or cat or if they roll or play in contaminated soil. A dog that licks his body after contact with a contaminated source, such as a dirty litterbox or dog crate, can become infected.

Diagnosis is confirmed by identification of trophozoites (motile feeding forms) or cysts in a puppy's feces. Antibiotics and/or antiprotozoal medications are the most common treatments. Supportive fluids may be needed when dehydration or severe diarrhea is present. No over-the-counter treatment is available for *Giardia* infection. Prognosis in most cases is good.

Despite your best efforts at prevention, *Giardia* can persist in outdoor spaces, with reinfection being a vicious cycle. To reduce incidences of reinfection, remove fecal matter from the dog's area daily, and regularly disinfect household surfaces as well as dog bowls, toys, and bedding. Don't forget to wash your hands frequently.

Spaying/Neutering

To spay or neuter is the best health-insurance policy you can give your dog. Although there are various studies about when is the best age to spay or neuter your dog, there is no doubt that altered dogs gain some health benefits. Females spayed before their first estrus or heat cycle have 90 percent less risk of several common female cancers and other serious female health problems. Males neutered before their male hormones kick in, usually before six months of age, enjoy greatly reduced risk of testicular and prostate cancer. Many breeders include mandatory spay/neuter clauses in their pet buyers' contract. By altering your pet dog, you not only will make a positive impact on your dog's long-term health but also do your part for the pet overpopulation crisis in the country.

CHAPTER 11

EXERCISE

All dogs—big and small—need daily physical and mental exercise. In humans, the benefits of exercise are widely recognized, with one physiological impact being a beneficial change in the brain's neurochemical levels. While the same is probably true for dogs, experts recognize that exercise burns calories, stimulates circulation, builds strong bones and muscles, and maintains flexible joints, keeping a puppy fit and trim as he grows and matures. Exercise strengthens a puppy's respiratory system, aids in digestion, and helps get oxygen to the body's tissues. It nourishes and energizes a puppy's mind, keeping it active, healthy, and alert.

Exercise also can help eliminate loneliness, stress, and boredom, which are primary causes of unwanted behaviors such as barking, digging, chewing, and ransacking trash cans. Exercise, along with play, also establishes and builds a strong bond and a mutually trusting relationship between you and your puppy.

Puppies Are Not Adult Dogs

Puppies are not scaled-down versions of adult dogs. Puppies are markedly different from adults in strength, stamina, and physical and mental coordination, and their exercise, play, and training should reflect those differences. If you have access to a securely fenced area, allow your puppy to run freely off leash; this is excellent exercise. When he is older and reliably comes to you when called, you can take long off-leash walks in the woods, where he can run and jump over branches and logs. Romping and playing with you is fun exercise, helps increase your puppy's coordination, and tires him out.

Exercise helps puppies grow into active, trim adult dogs with strong muscles, good bone, and overall good health.

Many dogs love—or can be taught to love—fetching and retrieving. While this can certainly raise a dog's heart rate and give him a good workout, be careful not to excessively stress your young dog's joints with tight turns or jumping.

It is worth noting that some dogs simply cannot be allowed off leash unless they're in a triple-secured environment rivaling any maximum-security prison. Siberian Huskies, for example, are born to run and run and run. Let one off leash, and he is guaranteed to run off—kicking up a cloud of dust (or snow) in his wake. Some dogs, regardless of their breed, simply lack a strong and reliable recall outside of a controlled environment. A Pharaoh Hound's chase instinct, for instance, is so strong that the sight of a rabbit, squirrel, or other type of prey instinctively sends him into chase-and-hunt mode. He may hear you calling him, but chances are his prey drive will override any training.

Dogs that cannot be trusted off leash need other alternatives in addition to leash walks and mental stimulation. Thankfully, plenty of options are available.

How Much Exercise?

Trainers and behaviorists will tell you that a puppy needs daily exercise, but what type and how much? No set formula or rules exist for how much exercise a dog needs on a daily basis. Much will depend on your dog's age, breed, and physical capabilities, as well as your own level of fitness. Many working dogs—herders, retrievers, pointers, and terriers—require exercise in units of hours, not minutes. Burning off their abundant energy can seem like a full-time job. A 3-mile hike may be a respectable outing for an adult Labrador Retriever, but is it enough to tire him out? Most fit and trim Labs won't even be breathing hard. On the flip side, a thirty-minute stroll around the block may tucker out a Bulldog or Pug, who has to work harder to cover less ground. Likewise, a young puppy will tire more quickly than an adult dog. Therefore, a puppy will require multiple short exercise periods spaced throughout the day.

More relevant, perhaps, is the type of exercise, be it physical or mental, on or off leash, and so forth. Consider, for example, a Border Collie that spends part of his day herding, which requires the dog to listen, think, react, and control the sheep, duck, or cattle. It stands to reason that herding may require more brain cells than simply running wildly around a pasture, hiking, or fetching a ball. Similarly, a 10-mile horseback

A working herding dog requires hours of daily activity to keep fit, busy, and sane.

Growth-Plate Injuries

Growth-plate injuries have long been a concern for owners and trainers of performance dogs, and for good reason. These soft plates are susceptible to injuries or fractures, especially in dogs younger than twelve to fourteen months of age, and can lead to lifelong problems.

In the simplest of terms, all bones have growth plates. These growth plates, or epiphyseal plates, are rich in immature noncalcified cells that form a soft, spongy area of the young bone. The cells grow and add length to the bone, thereby determining the future length and shape of the mature skeleton. As a puppy grows and matures, the long bones of the legs grow from areas of immature bone located near the ends.

When a dog has finished growing, the growth plates close, meaning that they mineralize (become hard with calcium and other minerals) and no longer function as areas of growth. The growth plates of different bones close at different times, which can depend on the breed and size of the dog. Until they have closed, the growth plates are the weakest parts of the bones and are therefore more easily fractured. Great care must be taken with puppies and young dogs when playing, exercising, and training.

It is often difficult to diagnosis growth-plate injuries—even with the aid of X-rays—because displacement may be minimal or nonexistent. Symptoms depend on the area, to what extent the plate is injured or fractured, and the individual dog's temperament. Some dogs are more stoic than others, but symptoms generally include lameness, swelling, pain upon touching, or deformity. Growth-plate fractures are classified using the Salter-Harris classification method, which ranks fractures as type I through V, with the prognosis worsening as the grade increases.

Prognosis is unpredictable because the classification of the injury and the age of the dog at the time of the injury have a significant impact on treatment and recovery. A severe injury that closes the growth plate will be magnified in a young puppy, that must grow for an additional six to eight months following the injury. Injuries in dogs that are near skeletal maturity are less likely to result in deformity.

ride accompanied by a dog running off leash may be too much for a Poodle, but just right for a mature Australian Cattle Dog.

For young puppies, some experts suggest five minutes of exercise for every month of age. At eight weeks, they would get ten minutes of exercise several times a day; at three months, they would get several fifteen-minute sessions; at four months, twenty-minute sessions, and so on. You want to provide your puppy with plenty of exercise, but avoid exercising him to the point that he becomes frustrated or stressed. It's important to build up his tolerance to exercise gradually so that it is always fun for your puppy as he grows. Doubly important, until he is fully grown, his bones and ligaments are more susceptible to injury.

Mental Exercise

Mental exercise is as important as physical exercise, so it's your job to come up with fun games that can stimulate your puppy's brain. For example, in addition to obedience exercises, teach him to wave, walk backward, spin, twist, speak, jump through a hoop, or find a ball hidden in a box or bucket. Interactive exercises—you and your dog playing together—should include a lot of mentally stimulating games. However, for those times when you cannot play with him, chew toys will exercise your dog's teeth and gums, while food-dispensing and interactive toys will provide an hour or two of mental stimulation.

Walking

Most puppies are too young for strenuous exercise, but you can still give them the physical activity that they need. Daily walks at local parks or around the neighborhood are ideal. (Be sure that your puppy is fully vaccinated before exposing him to public venues, where the risk of infection is higher.) How far your puppy can walk will depend on his age and size and the type of terrain. Walking up and down hills or on sandy beaches will be more tiring to a young puppy than walking on flat sidewalks or grass.

Mix up his walks by taking him to new and different places. No doubt he will love experiencing new sights and smells. Group walks are fun and motivating, especially if your puppy likes other dogs, although a canine buddy may be too distracting for some puppies. Your puppy may be so excited that he goes into overstimulation mode, which can make on-leash walking difficult.

Ideally, you should use a buckle collar or harness as opposed to a choke or check chain, which can damage your puppy's throat and/or coat. The type of leash you use is really a personal preference, but you may find that a 4- or 6-foot soft leather or corded leash is gentlest on your hands.

Any fit dog—regardless of size or breed—can enjoy hiking and exploring the trails. Always keep your dog on leash when in an unfamiliar area brimming with enticing wildlife and other chaseable temptations.

Hiking

Hiking with your dog is great for two reasons: your dog gets to explore new, tantalizing scents, and he gets tuckered out in the process. An added bonus is that the two of you get to spend time together, which is ideal for strengthening the human-canine bond. Granted, your dog probably does not savor the scenery as much as you do, but some people say they hike simply because their dogs love it so much. However, you have a few things to consider before you head off the beaten path.

Most dogs can make excellent hiking companions, especially if they are physically fit. But some dogs, be they purebred or mixed, are better suited for hiking. That is not to say that a small dog, such as a Toy Fox Terrier or Bichon Frise, can't handle a good hiking path; however, small dogs have to take a lot more steps to cover the same amount of ground and may tire more quickly. They may need a boost over a downed log or some help scrambling up an embankment, whereas a larger dog probably will not. Plus, you may have second thoughts when you need to groom your Bichon's white coat after a day spent in the woods.

How far your dog can hike will depend on his age, his size, his physical condition, the terrain, and the weather. An extended hike over rough and rocky terrain may be a piece of cake for the conditioned dog but too taxing for some couch potatoes or young puppies. Remember, puppies and young dogs tire easily and may be more susceptible to sore muscles, fatigue, and injury than their older, more physically fit counterparts.

It's the rare Siberian Husky that can be exercised off leash. This obedient Husky is enjoying a jog with his owner on a cool day.

In addition to fitness, consider your dog's health. Some brachycephalic breeds have difficulty breathing, especially in hot weather. Any orthopedic conditions may preclude your dog from extended hikes, especially across steep or rocky terrain. When in doubt, always consult your veterinarian prior to hiking.

Jogging

If you are a jogger, a dog may be the perfect companion. After all, most dogs are almost always up for some fun, regardless of rain, hail, sleet, or snow. You will need to assess your dog's temperament and breed attributes before putting on your sneakers.

While a lot of dogs love to run, some breeds, such as the Alaskan Malamute and Siberian Husky, are bred for endurance. They can go the distance and are likely to tough out less than ideal conditions, but they are cold-climate dogs and can quickly overheat in warmer climates.

Canine Trail Etiquette

When hiking with your dog, you are responsible for his actions and safety. By following these simple tips, you will help keep your dog safe and make hiking enjoyable for everyone.

- Know and obey the rules specific to the trail you are visiting. Rules for dogs vary from one land agency to another. Some parks, be they national, state, or city, allow dogs; others do not. The same goes for public beaches and national forest hiking trails. Some areas allow dogs, but they must be leashed.
- Keep your dogs leashed in designated areas. Chasing wildlife is never a good idea. Your dog may become injured or lost dashing off after Chip 'n Dale or Bambi.
- Yield the right-of-way to other hikers or horses—making sure that your dog is under control, is calm, refrains from barking, and does not antagonize or startle other people or animals.
- No one wants to step in anything while hiking. Pick up and bury or, better yet, carry out your dog's droppings. (Leaving it under a bush or on the side of the path does not count!)
- Yours and your dog's safety is paramount. Always follow the rules, even when other hikers do not. It can mean the difference between a fun outing and a heartbreaking trip home.

Dalmatians, Airedale Terriers, and Parson Russell Terriers have boundless energy and can make faithful jogging companions. Most Whippets and Greyhounds love to run, but they are bred for sprinting, as opposed to endurance, and their short coats are better suited for more temperate climates.

Jogging can be a great exercise that you and your dog share together. However, as with any canine exercise program, safety is paramount. A puppy's growing bones and ligaments are prone to injury, and too much foot-pounding on hard or uneven surfaces can make his feet sore and may cause permanent injury. Equally important, a young dog's paws can be sensitive until they gradually toughen up. Therefore, you will want to start slowly to assess his energy and fitness levels.

Keep an eye out for signs of stress or fatigue, such as heavy panting, breathing problems, limping, flattened ears, or tail hanging down. If your dog can't keep up with you, lags behind, or stops and refuses to continue, you have probably gone too far too fast.

As with hiking, be sure to always carry appropriate supplies, including plenty of fluids for both you and your dog. Always consult your veterinarian before beginning a jogging program with your dog.

Safety Tips for Jogging and Biking

Hiking, biking, and jogging can be great fun for you and your canine companion, but these outings can be dangerous if you do not follow proper safety precautions. Before hitting the paths, consider these safety tips:

- Train your dog to jog on one side of you. Darting back and forth in front of or behind you while you are jogging or biking can cause you to trip and fall, resulting in injury to you and/or your dog.
- Dogs do not sweat like humans do. To avoid heatstroke, keep your workouts to early mornings or evenings when the temperatures are cooler.
- Hot pavement can seriously burn your dog's feet. If the pavement is too hot for your bare feet or hands, it is too hot for your dog's feet.
- Stay hydrated. Carry enough fluids for you and your dog.
- Allow your dog to cool down properly.
- After a workout, check your dog's feet for cuts, scrapes, or signs of injured pads. Check his coat for stickers, burrs, ticks, and other irritants.

Biking

If your dog has the energy and stamina to trot alongside you as you pedal, then biking may be an ideal way to strengthen the human-canine bond and get in some cardiovascular exercise at the same time. From the dog's point of view, biking is basically the same as jogging, but he will be working a lot harder than you are. You will want to follow the same safety precautions as with hiking and jogging, including assessing your dog's age, breed, temperament, physical fitness, and athletic ability.

Ideally, your dog should wear a properly fitted harness—rather than a collar—to avoid any damage to his throat caused by pulling too hard. Instead of holding the leash in your hands, purchase a Springer, which attaches to your bike frame and is designed specifically for biking with dogs. The dog's leash attaches to a specially designed coil spring on the Springer—leaving your hands free to steer and brake. The Springer also absorbs a good deal of the force of a dog's unexpected tugs and helps keep you and your dog balanced. The exceptionally adventurous owner with multiple dogs can attach a Springer to each side of the bike to cycle with two dogs at the same time.

If you decide not to purchase a Springer, holding the leash with your hands is an option, but never attach it to the handlebars. This is a disaster waiting to happen. If your dog zigs when you want to zag, it won't be pretty.

If you have never biked with your dog, start off by walking the dog alongside the bike to get him used to being attached to the bike. If possible, use paths that are soft, such as grass or dirt.

Once he is comfortable alongside the bike, you are ready to begin biking. Remember to start off slowly. Do not expect your young dog (or even an adult dog) to run for long distances in the beginning. This is not a race, so pedal at an average pace that allows your dog to trot, not sprint.

If your dog is small, such as a Chihuahua or Shih Tzu, there's no reason to leave him behind. Consider a specially designed handlebar basket for your dog to ride in.

Swimming

Swimming is an excellent nonweight-bearing exercise for cooling off, burning calories, and sharing quality time with your puppy. Of course, not all dogs enjoy swimming or being around water. The "doggy paddle" is not an inherited skill, and swimming does not necessarily come naturally to all dogs—even those bred for swimming like Labrador Retrievers. Generally speaking, dogs usually fall into one of three categories: dogs that naturally take to water, dogs that can be taught to swim and enjoy doing it, and dogs that do not have the body structure for swimming.

Dogs with "water" in their names and all retrievers are typically good swimmers that love the water. Many setters and Poodles tend to be good swimmers, too. Newfoundlands, of course, are renowned for their ability to save lives at sea, and many are right at home in the water. Each of these breeds has a strong history and tradition of swimming, and they have strong limbs that help propel them through the water.

Unlike their amphibious counterparts, some sturdy breeds are not genetically designed for swimming. Structurally, these dogs tend to be short-legged and top-heavy like Bulldogs and French Bulldogs. While they may try their best, breeds with large, heavy chests in relation to their hindquarters typically sink like rocks. Their short legs simply do not have the necessary thrust to keep them afloat. If you have a top-heavy dog, you'll need a life vest designed specifically for dogs anytime he is around water.

Pool owners must take safety precautions for their dogs. Don't let your dog drink from the pool. Provide clean water in a shaded area for your canine pool guests.

Brachycephalic breeds, such as the Pug and the aforementioned two Bulldogs, generally have trouble swimming because their restricted breathing causes them to tire easily. Small dogs, such as Chihuahuas and Miniature Pinschers, can be good swimmers, but they may have trouble because they can quickly become chilled. Many small dogs become frightened or fatigued in the water, which increases the risk of drowning.

Granted, exceptions to every rule exist, and many dogs bred for water or retrieving simply do not like the water. You should never assume your dog loves to swim simply because he comes from a long line of water dogs or retrievers. Some dogs have the physical capacity to swim but are terrified of water. These animals often panic in the water, which quickly leads to fatigue. On the flip side, some breeds that by design should never be able to swim manage to do so anyway. Bull Terriers and Rottweilers, for example, can be astoundingly good swimmers.

Your dog's individual temperament is an equally important factor in whether or not he can swim or likes to swim. If your dog likes the water but has trouble staying afloat, a flotation device or life jacket made for dogs will help keep your dog safe and happy in the pool, pond, or lake.

Most natural swimmers will not need coaxing, but dogs that are reluctant to get their feet wet will need to get used to the water gradually. For the hesitant dog, try to find a lake or shallow pond that has a gentle sloping bank. (Kiddie pools or wading pools are also excellent.) Encourage your dog to wade in the water with you and follow you as you swim around, but stay close to your dog. If he is comfortable and moves around well, he will probably learn to love swimming.

For dogs that like retrieving, toss a tennis ball or floatable toy, being careful in the beginning to toss it close to the bank or shallow end of the pond or pool. If you toss it too far, your dog will likely find the task of retrieving too daunting. If your dog swims out and retrieves the toy, encourage him to swim back to you, and praise enthusiastically. As your dog becomes comfortable at one depth, toss the toy into water that is progressively deeper. If your dog naturally loves the water, it won't be long before he is diving in on his own. And you may have trouble getting him out or keeping him out of the water!

Water sports are appealing to dogs of all sizes! You don't have to be a Labrador Retriever to hit the pool.

Swimming is a strenuous work—especially in deep water—and even physically fit dogs will get tired. Some high-energy dogs will play and swim until they exhaust themselves. Therefore, always watch for signs that your dog is getting tired, such as panting, slowing down, or slapping the water with his front feet. You need to put on your lifeguard visor and blow the whistle even if your dog wants to continue; a fatigued dog is at greater risk of drowning. Some dogs will not realize that they are in trouble until it is too late. Stay away from strong currents and areas where underwater debris, such as reeds, driftwood, kelp, and seaweed, can entangle or injure your dog.

Dog Parks

Wouldn't life be grand if all owners had plenty of space to allow their dogs to zoom around off-leash to their hearts' content, investigating new smells, wrestling with their canine buddies, and fetching toys? Some owners are fortunate to have large fenced areas for such activities. Others, including many city and urban dwellers, must rely on alternatives, which frequently include off-leash dog parks.

Dog parks have become increasingly popular across the United States and Canada, but they are a contentious topic, with opponents and proponents on both sides of the issue. Let's take a look.

Advantages:

- Dogs can run off leash.
- Dogs can get plenty of exercise, which can help reduce boredom, stress, and destructive behavior.
- Dogs can play with their canine buddies.
- Dog owners can brag about their dogs' awesomeness.

Some dogs are more boisterous than others. Safeguard your puppy from potentially overwhelming encounters at the dog park to make sure his experience is positive and fun.

- No cars, skateboarders, or bicyclists are allowed, so there's no chance your dog will get run over.

Disadvantages:

- Owners risk dog-to-dog aggression.
- Dog-to-people aggression is also a potential problem.
- Aggressive dogs can cause physical or psychological injuries to humans and dogs.
- Dogs can pick up unwanted behaviors, such as fear, aggression, and rough play.
- Problems can arise from owners who do not understand canine body language or who are generally ignorant about dogs.
- Dogs can become overstimulated and out of control.
- Dogs are exposed to a higher risk of parasites and bacteria.
- Your dog's getting into a fight can invite the potential for a lawsuit.

Theoretically, the concept of dog parks is well intended, and your dog certainly can have many positive experiences, running, romping, and playing with other dogs. You may decide that the benefits of dog parks outweigh the risks. If you go this route, consider the guidelines in the following paragraphs to help keep you and your puppy safe.

Socializing your puppy is important, but dog parks are not your best option because they can be a haven for parasites, such as fleas, ticks, and worms, as well as bacteria, viruses, and *Giardia*. Before they are fully vaccinated, puppies are vulnerable to potentially contagious diseases, such as parvovirus. Until your puppy is fully vaccinated, steer clear of dog parks and public dog areas, where exposure to dangerous pathogens is higher. Plenty of options other than dog parks exist for safe puppy socialization.

A backyard is the safer option for socializing young puppies. Dog parks can wait until the puppy is a bit older and fully vaccinated.

When your dog is off-leash at a dog park, it is your responsibility to focus on your dog 100 percent of the time. This point cannot be overstressed. Be aware of what your dog is doing and who he is interacting with at all times. It can mean the difference between a fun outing and a trip to the emergency clinic. Do not stand around, ignoring your dog, while you chat, text, or read a book. Small altercations may be happening behind your back that can lead to a serious larger altercation and a potential court case.

Not all dogs want to play—especially with other dogs. Just as you may not like all of your coworkers or neighbors, not all dogs like or want to play with each other. And just because a dog is playing with other dogs does not mean that he wants to play nice with your dog.

Not all dogs at dog parks are friendly, well mannered, or well trained. Even dogs that are well trained can become overstimulated when there are multiple dogs running, chasing, tussling, biting, and snapping. If you see signs that canine play is not going well, step in and break up the interaction before things get out of hand. It takes a nanosecond for fun to turn into an all-out canine brawl.

If an unruly dog shows up, leave the park. You may think that because you were there first, you have every right to be there. But you gain nothing by risking a dog fight, especially one that involves your young, impressionable dog. Young puppies are more susceptible to injury should they be rolled on, trampled, or attacked by a larger dog.

Monitoring your dog and his interactions with other dogs is extremely important, but do you know what dogs look like when they're friendly? How about when they are timid or shy or feeling bullied? Can you tell when your dog has had enough and wants to go home? Can you tell when canine buddies are not getting along? Knowing how to read canine body language will go a long way in helping you keep your dog safe while at dog parks.

Dog Park Decorum

To avoid any bad experiences for you and your dog, follow these simple and doable tips:

- Develop a reliable recall *before* going to a park. If your dog is not reliably trained, keep him on leash or on a long line when other dogs are around.
- Call your dog to you before he gets into trouble. Once trouble has started, it is highly unlikely he will respond to your frantic calls regardless of his training.
- Once your dog comes back to you, engage him in a fun interactive game.
- The dog-park entrance can get congested, thus it is a common area for dog fights to start. Do not allow your dog to mob other dogs that are entering or exiting the park. Give other dogs and owners plenty of leeway.
- Avoid letting your dog sprint up to other dogs he does not know.

PART IV

ADOLESCENCE
AND
BEYOND

CHAPTER 12

ADVANCED TRITION

N ow that you and your puppy have established a strong bond of trust and have mastered basic obedience skills, you can begin working on some advanced training, which can be as challenging as it is fun. Most advanced training exercises are a continuation of basic obedience exercises. In advanced training, you are simply asking more from your dog in distracting situations as he matures emotionally.

In the beginning, when your puppy was first learning, you asked him to learn behaviors in an environment that was mostly free of distractions, such as your living room or a quiet backyard. Most puppies and adult dogs are relatively easy to teach in distraction-free environments. To keep progressing, as your puppy matures into an adolescent and then an adult dog, you want to continue pushing the envelope by adding new distractions and new environments, as well as teaching the Stay command and building the duration of time that your puppy remains in the Stay position.

Stay

The Wait game is ideal for young puppies because most puppies are not physically or emotionally mature enough to handle a Stay command until they are about six, seven, or even twelve months old. It's fabulous that your four-month-old puppy can do a Stay while waiting for his food bowl in a quiet kitchen. However, it is unrealistic to think he can do a Sit/Stay or Down/Stay—or even just a Stay—while you are at the veterinarian's office or an outdoor café or when company arrives.

Staying in place, whether doing a Sit, Down, or Stand, takes a certain amount of emotional maturity. One trainer compared it to taking a child to Disneyland and expecting him to do algorithms. Never going to happen! The age at which a dog is emotionally mature enough to maintain a Stay no matter what else is going on around him depends on his breed, temperament, and personality. Some dogs can maintain a lengthy Stay at one year of age; others can still barely contain themselves at two years of age. By starting the Stay exercise too soon, rushing the process, or using rough physical or harsh verbal corrections, you run the risk of creating lifelong problems with the Stay command by putting too much emotional pressure and stress on a young dog.

To a large degree, a lot will depend on your training, too. Consider how often you train, how consistent you are with your commands, and how much you ask of your dog. For example, if you tell him to stay, yet he chooses to wander off and you ignore him, he will quickly learn that "Stay" means nothing. Equally important, if you ask him to stay in a very distracting situation—a situation that is beyond his emotional maturity—you set him up to fail, which is neither fair nor fun. Your job is to help him learn in a fair, humane, and fun manner.

Before starting, let's review some important points for success.

Every behavior you teach should be taught up close, within a few feet of your dog. Once your dog understands and can do the behavior with 100-percent compliance at a 3-foot distance, only then should you begin adding distance or distractions. If your dog cannot sit, lie down, or stay 100 percent of the time while 3 feet away from you, how can you expect him to sit, lie down, or come from 20 feet away amid high-level distractions (think squirrels, cats, or tennis balls)?

When releasing your dog from a Stay, be it a Sit/Stay, Down/Stay, or Stand/Stay, do so in a calm manner. If you go crazy and hoot and holler and do a crazy dance, your dog will think getting up is the best part of the exercise, which it is not.

Because Stay is a static exercise, many dogs—especially young puppies—find it stressful and can quickly become bored. Remember that training, be it obedience or trick training, is all about fun. It's not a test of authority over your dog. If you find yourself digging a hole—stop digging. Take a deep breath and play with your dog, toss his ball, have a quick game of tug, or do whatever you need to do to get yourself and your puppy happy and eager to train again.

If you have played the Wait game with your puppy, teaching a more advanced Stay command is relatively easy because you're simply building upon that game. It's worth noting that your dog will learn faster if you change only one criterion at a time. For example, if you are adding a new distraction, such as more toys or other dogs or a new location, do not also increase the duration at the same time. Likewise, if you are adding distance, do not add in a new distraction or increase the duration at the same time. If you are asking your dog to stay while a cat sits on a nearby fence or squirrels scurry around, keep the duration short.

The Wait exercise forms the basis of the Stay command.

Be proactive by reinforcing your dog's successes with yummy treats, his favorite toy, or any other reinforcement that he loves. Give your dog lots of reasons to want to continue learning and trying his hardest. Do not wait until he makes a mistake and then go back and attempt to correct the mistake. This can be very deflating to a dog's ego and can dampen his attitude and willingness to work. Always work within your dog's emotional threshold and ability, but don't baby him to the point that he never progresses.

Off-Leash, Long Lines, and Coming When Called

Have you ever been to a dog show or watched one on television and seen how the dogs only have eyes for their handlers? Dogs staring adoringly at their handlers, waiting to see what is going to happen next? Would you give your right arm (figuratively speaking) to get that type of focus and attention from your dog? It's 100-percent achievable for most dogs.

Granted, some breeds seem to naturally want to hang around their owners more than others do. Terriers, for example, were bred to work independently of their owners, so getting one to focus and stay close to you can take some doing. Also, some dogs may never be 100-percent reliable off leash. Think Siberian Husky, Shiba Inu, Whippet. The goal, however, is to work toward 100-percent reliability because one day calling your dog to come may save his life.

Being on or off leash should not be a condition of your puppy's working or wanting to be with you. When done correctly, puppies grow into adult dogs that continue to think that being off leash means something fabulous is going to happen. By instilling this behavior in your puppy while he is young and impressionable, transitioning to working off leash in new, strange, or distracting environments will be much easier.

This is where long lines come in handy. Trainers vary in their opinions when it comes to training dogs on long lines. A Recall in your backyard is not the same as a recall at a dog park or while hiking in the woods or walking on the beach. Where owners often go wrong is by allowing their dogs off leash too soon in distracting or unfamiliar environments. No doubt you have seen owners who have their dogs off leash at dog parks or beaches. However, unless you are 100-percent certain your dog will come amid chaotic distractions, he should *never* be off leash. The risk of him running off and becoming injured or lost is too high.

It takes thousands of successful Recalls before your dog can be given complete freedom to run in a public place.

Be realistic about your environment and the level of distractions. Having your dog drag a long line allows you to keep him safe and manage his environment so that he isn't allowed to develop bad habits, such as running away from you. If your dog is dragging a leash or long

Adding Distractions

Categorize distractions by various degrees. This varies from dog to dog, depending on temperament and personality. For example, a toy on the floor may be a minor distraction—say, a 2 on a scale of 1 to 10—for a Basset Hound, but a 9.5 for a Border Collie or another toy-crazy dog. Some dogs are super friendly and can't resist any friend who might appear, so that would probably be an 8 in terms of distractions for such dogs. A cat sitting on a fence might be a major distraction—a 10 on that same scale—for a sight-sensitive coursing, herding, or terrier breed, but not a big deal for a Newfoundland. Whether you are teaching fun Recalls, Sits, Downs, Stays, or tricks, as your dog becomes more proficient and reliable, begin increasing the distractions, but never progress to more difficult distractions until your dog is working reliably with low-level distractions. Manage your dog's environment so that you set him up to succeed, thereby always reinforcing him for doing the right thing.

line each and every time he goes outside with you, there will be no need for you to chase him down. A long line gives your puppy or adult dog the freedom to make choices about his behavior while enabling you to restrict his ability to run away from you.

If he starts to wander off, you simply step on the long line and say, "I've got you!" Then do something silly to make him come back to you. When he runs to you, praise and reward. If necessary, reel him with the long line and say, "There's my boy!"

Coming to you when called is the single most important command you can teach your dog, and you should start right away instilling the behavior as quickly and creatively as possible. The fun Recall games you've begun playing with your puppy will set the foundation for a first-class Recall as he grows and matures. By continuing with these fun games while gradually adding distractions along the way and reinforcing Come with treats or a favorite toy, your puppy will continue to think that running to you as fast as his legs will carry him is more fun than anything else in his world. And that's what you want.

Like the Stay command, you gradually begin adding distractions to the Recall command. For example, play chase Recall games in the backyard, where there are interesting smells or a few toys lying around. Maybe have a friend sitting in the yard or a few kids playing and chattering away. Set your dog up to succeed by using high-value reinforcements, such as steak, chicken, or that favorite toy. If he ignores a squirrel and comes darting over to you, you had better reward with 24-karat gold (e.g., cheddar cheese, boiled liver, heart, hot dog).

On the other hand, if your dog has a difficult time focusing, perhaps you increased the distractions too quickly. Try playing in a less distracting environment or trying harder to make yourself more exciting than the distractions. The long-term goal is for your dog to be able to focus on you despite enticing distractions.

CHAPTER 13

SOLVING BEHAVIORAL PROBLEMS

Are you beginning to wonder where that irresistible bundle of fur you brought home just five or six short months ago went? Has that cute puppy grown into an incorrigible adolescent that ignores basic commands, such as Sit, Stay, and Come? Does he dig, chew, or bark incessantly? Ransack the kitchen trash cans and overturn the outside garbage? Fence-fight with the neighbor's Poodles? Raid the cat's litterbox? Embarrass you in front of your friends and in-laws? Are you thinking that your ruffian is beyond hope? Think you should have bought a cat instead?

In the Real World

In a perfect world, your dog would never get into trouble. Unfortunately, that is utopia, not the real world, and in the world of dogdom, utopia exists only in your dreams. It is unrealistic to expect any dog to go through his life without getting into some sort of mischief or developing an annoying habit or two. Dogs and humans view the world differently. Dogs have different priorities. They live in the moment. They sniff rear ends, roll in stinky stuff, drink toilet water, and ravage your trash. They chase cars, cats, and kids on bicycles. They swipe food off counters and pee indiscriminately around the house. Again, perfectly normal behaviors from a dog's point of view.

Despite what many owners think, dogs don't lie around, conjuring up ways to make your life more difficult. When left to their own devices, they will do exactly what they feel like doing at that moment. Problems arise in the human-canine relationship because most if not all of these behaviors are objectionable to owners. A terrier's fanatical digging or an Australian Cattle Dog's persistent heel nipping is perfectly normal canine behavior.

You are not a bad owner for not wanting your dog to hike his leg on your couch, bolt out the door, or steal food off the table. The joy of interacting with a dog is the primary reason that most people have them as pets. However, when a dog's extracurricular activities cause him to wear out his welcome, interacting with him is not nearly as much fun. Don't despair. Most adolescent behaviors—even the most exasperating ones—are quite predictable and easily remedied.

Why Dogs Do What They Do

Canine genetics and behavior are complex topics well beyond the scope of this book. Without delving too deeply into the complexities of either, most dog behaviors fall into one of two categories: medical or behavioral.

Medical Issues

A number of seemingly naughty adolescent acts may actually be the result of an existing medical condition. If your dog is having house-training issues around the house, for instance, a urinary-tract infection, diabetes, or renal disease could be the cause; these are just a few of the painful medical conditions that can make getting outside to potty a problem for some dogs, making accidents in the house more common. Any number of health issues, from allergies and hormonal imbalances to serious diseases, could be to blame for house-training issues.

Think your dog has a temperament problem? Consider that pain, such as from a broken tooth, a torn ligament, or a pinched nerve, can cause an otherwise friendly dog to growl, bite, or snap. If your dog is showing signs of any behavior problems, first have him checked out by a veterinarian.

Behavioral Issues

Absent any medical issues, your dog's naughty behaviors may be caused by one or more factors—some of which you may inadvertently be causing. Before you throw up your hands and say, "I've tried, but my dog is too hard to train," consider that years ago, before dogs became our constant companions and treasured family members, most were bred for a specific working purpose, be it hunting, herding, guarding, or retrieving. The full-time jobs for which these dogs were originally bred required enormous amounts of energy, drive, stamina, courage, tenacity, and intelligence.

Boredom: All dogs, regardless of their size or breed, need daily physical and mental stimulation. Absent adequate physical and mental stimulation, most dogs become bored. Oftentimes, boredom can lead to obsessive-compulsive or self-destructive behaviors, such as tail chasing and excessive licking or chewing. You can prevent many of these unwanted behaviors by offering your dog more opportunities for physical and mental exercise.

Stress: Many behavioral problems in dogs can be attributed to stress. Like humans, dogs can experience stress, and for similar reasons. How a dog responds to negative stress is often dictated by a combination of genes and environment. Lack of socialization,

Trouble starts with "T," and that stands for "turkey bones in the garbage can."

Lack of Understanding or Training

Dogs are clever, but they cannot read our minds. They do not come preprogrammed, knowing how to understand our language or how to sit, come, or chew on their toys (as opposed to your expensive leather shoes). All of these behaviors must be trained, but too often owners expect their puppy or adult dog to do whatever is asked of him, regardless of whether or not he has been trained. Absent appropriate training and a consistent communication system, most dogs will inevitably get themselves into trouble.

unfamiliar surroundings, and the presence of other animals can trigger stress in some dogs. A sound-sensitive dog's stress level is likely to skyrocket when he is confined to a noisy kennel or a room filled with loud, boisterous kids. Unfamiliar people or the constant stimulation of being in a crowd of people can stress even the sweetest, most easygoing dog, provoking him to bolt, growl, or snap. Confining a high-energy dog to a small yard or apartment without adequate physical and mental stimulation also can trigger stress, possibly leading to neurotic or destructive behaviors. Understanding your dog's temperament and personality and reading his body language will go a long way in reducing his stress.

Solving Common Behavioral Problems

In moments of frustration and anger, it is easy to resort to punishment as a solution to your dog's "naughty behaviors." However, punishment rarely works. It might get you results in the short term, but at what cost? Yelling at, hitting, kicking, or berating your dog is not training—it is a crime in progress.

All training should be positive. Positive reinforcement is the method of choice for dog training, but equally important, if not more so, is the relationship you have with your dog. Every minute detail about the human-canine bond comes down to the relationship you have with your dog. How you look at him, talk to him, and pet him, and even the words you use to describe him, all reflect your relationship. So, too, do the methods you use to train him. Each dog's needs differ, and it is important to know what your dog needs so you can figure out how to provide it for him in a safe, humane, and positive manner.

Aggression

Aggression is a tricky and complicated topic because it refers to a wide variety of behaviors that happen under equally wide and varying circumstances. Entire books have been written on the subject, and so prevalent are some forms of canine aggression that trainers and behaviorists specialize in rehabbing dogs with particular aggression issues.

Aggression is classified in different ways based on the function or purpose of the aggression. Some of the most prevalent types include:

- defensive aggression
- dominance-related aggression
- fear aggression
- resource-guarding or possession aggression
- social aggression
- territorial aggression

Less common types of aggression include:

- frustration-elicited aggression
- redirected aggression
- pain-elicited aggression
- sex-related aggression
- predatory aggression

Further complicating the matter is the not-so-simple act of identifying the type of aggression that your dog is displaying. Aggression, with the possible exception of pain aggression, typically doesn't happen overnight. Some dogs are born with sour temperaments and skewed visions of the world. However, a dog is not hardwired to wake up one day and think, "I plan to bite my owner today." Generally speaking, owners inadvertently allow their dogs to develop improper behaviors and subsequently follow a path of aggression.

For most aggression, there are many warning signals that culminate in an attack. Warning signs are sometimes very obvious and include:

- barking or growling, sometimes explosive, which is intended to make the other dog (or person) move away so that a fight does not ensue
- lips drawn back to expose teeth
- tense body language, generally oriented in a forward motion and fully adrenalized
- eyes strong, staring, and making direct eye contact with the other animal or person

Is something new in your puppy's environment to cause him distress? Puppies can be sensitive to new people, other animals, noises, odors, and so forth.

- tail raised, usually held over the dog's back

Some warning signals can be subtle but equally important to recognize. These are signals that many owners tend to overlook:

- low, sometimes barely audible, growl
- guttural bark that sounds threatening
- curled lip
- ears drawn back
- quick nip that leaves no mark
- dog attempts to retreat to safety but is unable to or feels trapped

The more adept you are at recognizing potential problems, the sooner you can put a stop to them.

Always a serious problem, aggression is a complex behavior, and rooting out the underlying cause and rectifying it can be tricky. Most dog owners are not adequately skilled to handle aggression-related issues. If you suspect that your dog has an aggression issue, it is your responsibility as the dog's owner to decide how to treat the issue or to seek an alternative solution. After ruling out any medical issues that might be the underlying cause, you should seek professional help from a trainer or behaviorist who is specifically trained in dealing with canine aggression and can provide a modification program designed specifically for your dog's temperament and environment.

Barking

It's natural for dogs to bark, and it is highly unlikely that your dog is barking for no reason. Granted, some days it may seem as if your dog is barking just to hear himself bark. So what's the deal? Do dogs bark just to hear the sound of their own voices, or are they conveying specific messages?

Dogs that are usually 100-percent reliable can suddenly act aggressively due to a variety of factors, including pain, fear, and hormones.

Interestingly, little research has been done on the true meaning of barking. Sophia Lin, DVM, MS, whose research disputes earlier published works from the 1960s and 1970s, believes that our domestic dogs are so different from their wild ancestors that most barking is just a loud, obnoxious way for dogs to say, "Hey! Look at me!" as opposed to a specific form of communication. The more specific information, experts believe, comes from reading body language.

It's no surprise that more than a few owners and some accomplished researchers and behaviorists disagree. Much information about a dog's barking remains a mystery; however, as a dog owner, you know that dogs bark when they get excited, when they are playing with their canine buddies, and when the doorbell rings. They bark to alert their owners to intruders or protect their territory. They bark when they are fearful or anxious or when they are left alone. They bark when it's feeding time. Some dogs bark when you play with them. Some bark when you won't play with them. Some barkers might be spoiled or neurotic, or they lack adequate socialization or obedience training.

You can learn a lot from listening to the pitch of your dog's barking. Some barks are high pitched while others are low pitched, and some are more guttural. This may help you decode why your dog is barking. Most owners of chronic barkers, however, just want some peace and quiet.

For the most part, many dogs bark excessively because well-intended owners inadvertently allow their dogs to develop the habit of barking. It's one of those behaviors that might be cute for a four-month-old puppy but not so cute when he's three years old and barking at anything and everything. Some owners mistakenly think that dogs outgrow annoying behaviors, so they do nothing.

The best prevention against future barking is smart puppy management. It is much easier to prevent barking habits from developing in a puppy than it is to rehab a chronic offender. Properly socializing your puppy will help teach him not to bark incessantly. Also, never encourage your puppy or adolescent dog to bark.

Equally important, never allow your puppy to be in situations where he can develop bad habits. For example, leaving him in the backyard all day unsupervised. Barking at environmental stimuli is often self-rewarding for dogs. A dog barks at the mail carrier and, when the mail carrier leaves, the dog thinks, "Look how smart I am! My barking made that person leave!"

A lot of barking can be traced to a lack of physical or mental exercise. Absent appropriate exercise, most dogs release their excess energy through barking,

Years of scientific studies have yielded the astonishing discovery that most barking means, "Hey! Look at me!"

Bad Rap for Little Dogs

Interestingly, small dogs, such as Chihuahuas, Toy Poodles, Westies, and Norfolk Terriers, often get a bad rap for being yappy, yet there are no existing studies that indicate small dogs are more vocal than their large-breed counterparts. That said, it doesn't require scientific research to state the fact that some dogs are simply noisier than others.

Some dogs have a propensity to bark, and some are harder to keep quiet than others. "Woof! There's a raccoon up that tree! Woof! A leaf just fell from the tree! Woof! I'm a pretty pup! Woof! I'm here!" The good news is that dogs with serious barking problems can learn to be quiet. It takes time, commitment, and positive reinforcement, but it can be done.

chewing, or digging. In these situations, the solution might be as simple as some vigorous daily exercise, with the added benefit of strengthening the human-canine relationship.

Rather than wait until the problem gets out of control, teach your dog not to bark by calmly praising and rewarding him when he is quiet with "Good quiet" or "Good no bark." Think of all of the situations in which you can praise and reinforce him for being quiet, such as when he's patiently waiting for dinner, when you are putting on his leash, when you're riding in the car, when he is with the veterinarian or groomer, and when he stops barking at the door.

Finally, dogs learn not to bark or learn an appropriate alternative to barking when their owners are there to teach them. If your dog is left to his own devices most of the day, you can't expect him to learn on his own.

Begging

While begging is a natural behavior for dogs, it is also regularly reinforced either intentionally or inadvertently by well-meaning owners. It doesn't take long for this natural behavior to become an annoying ingrained behavior. It's adorable when a ten-week-old puppy sits up and whimpers for a potato chip, but it's not so cute when your 70-pound Golden Retriever drools, pesters you, and nudges you at the dining-room table.

Dogs do what is rewarding for them. If a dog begs and gets a tidbit of food, he will continue the behavior. Dogs are quick studies when it comes to begging, and it's a short leap from sad eyes to seasoned beggar. Preventing begging is easy: if your dog begs, ignore him. It's highly likely that he will discontinue the behavior. The hard part is getting cooperation from family members and visitors to your home. No one—this includes kids, in-laws, and neighbors—feeds the dog from the table or at any other time while he or she is eating.

If your puppy or adolescent dog is already begging, chances are good that someone is sneaking him tidbits of food. If you can't resist sharing your food, and some owners cannot, put scraps in the refrigerator and feed them at a later time as training treats. Use the treats to teach your puppy to sit up and beg properly—as a trick!

Chewing

Chewing is almost always lumped in with behavioral problems that need to be prevented rather than a natural canine behavior that should be managed by providing appropriate chew toys. However, if your puppy or adolescent dog has turned into a one-dog demolition team—chewing drywall, carpet, table legs, shoes, and everything else he can get his teeth on—you definitely have a problem. The good news is that it's a relatively simple behavior to curtail—even for an aggressive chewer that might be wreaking havoc in your household right now!

Understanding why dogs chew will go a long way in managing the behavior. Teething, which is the process of shedding baby teeth and growing permanent teeth, can cause an uncontrollable urge to chew as a means of relieving some of the discomfort and as a way to facilitate the removal of baby teeth. Dogs also chew when they are bored, frustrated, or anxious or when they are suffering from separation anxiety.

The key to minimizing destruction is managing your puppy's environment so he can't get himself into trouble. Ideally, this is best accomplished with baby gates so you can keep him in designated parts of the house, such as the kitchen or family room. Any puppy left unsupervised is trouble waiting to happen, and you should not be surprised when you come home to find a boatload of destruction. When you cannot closely supervise your puppy, keep him confined in

Puppies will chew anything they can get their paws (and teeth!) on. Direct your puppy's chewing to items that you provide for this purpose. Sticks in the yard, rocks in the grass, and mahogany legs in the dining room are off-limits!

the ex-pen, the crate, or a puppy-proofed area with a safe chew toy, such as a food-stuffed toy, bully stick, or marrow bone.

From day one, you must know where your puppy is and what he is doing at all times. Supervising your puppy not only allows you to monitor his whereabouts but also allows you to direct his chewing to appropriate items. If you catch your puppy chewing on something, such as your iPad or new leather boots, tell him "Trade you!" as you exchange the forbidden item for an acceptable chew toy. Make unacceptable items, such as table or chair legs or walls unpleasant to your puppy by spraying them with a no-chew spray that leaves a bitter taste.

As with most unwanted behaviors, the root cause of chewing is often a lack of physical or mental exercise. Therefore, be sure that your puppy has plenty of appropriate chews and mental-stimulation items.

Coprophagia

Statistics indicate that 24 percent of dogs have been caught eating poop, and 16 percent are serious poop eaters, meaning that they have been seen doing it at least five times. Further, 15 percent of dogs eat their own poop, while a whopping 85 percent eat the feces of other dogs. Somehow, those stats do not make the behavior any less distasteful! And if that isn't enough, more than 90 percent of dogs ate only stools that were one to two days old, and 75 percent ate stools only within the first twenty-four hours.

Why do dogs engage in *coprophagia* (the fancy term for this behavior)? No one really knows for certain, but it stands to reason that because dogs evolved thousands of years ago as scavengers, their discriminating palates are not too, well, discriminating.

Desperate but not starving, beggars at the table can only be cured cold turkey (not offering cold turkey, chicken, or anything else!).

What can you do about it? Not a lot. Research indicates that the behavior has nothing to do with a dog's diet. Yelling, chasing the dog away, electronic collars, or any other type of punishment does not work, either. None of the commercial anticoprophagia products has been proven to work. Better to invest your money in a pooper-scooper because promptly cleaning up after your dog seems to be the best solution. And count your blessings that it's only poop and not rocks, wood chips, socks, or other inedible items that can cause life-threatening intestinal blockages.

Counter Surfing

Counter surfing might seem like a funny habit, but it should be discouraged as soon as your puppy can reach the counter. When your older and bolder (and taller) puppy checks out the table and countertops, he isn't being naughty in his mind. After all, your puppy is observant, and he knows that you keep the good "people food" and that jar of dog treats on the kitchen counters.

There are several ways to curb counter-surfing behavior. One is to keep your counters free of food and treats; that way, if your dog does take a peek around, there won't be anything to swipe. This is not always realistic or practical, though. After all, who does not occasionally have a package of hot dogs thawing on the counter? And who has not had to run to the bathroom or stop to answer the door while cooking breakfast or dinner? That small window of opportunity is all it takes for an enterprising young dog to snatch a donut or turkey leg or pot roast.

An alternative is to have baby gates strategically placed to corral your dog and keep him out of the kitchen and away from countertops. Another option is to have him drag his leash around the house. When you see his front feet headed in the direction of the countertop, grab his leash and guide his feet back to the floor while telling him "Off!" Do so swiftly and immediately so that it's clear to your puppy that putting his feet on the counter (or table) is unacceptable. Then be sure to reward him with plenty of praise and treats for sitting on the floor. At some point, the light bulb will turn on, and he will realize that counter surfing doesn't work to get food, but sitting nicely does.

Finally, another suggestion is to purchase a "scat mat," which is a touch-sensitive mat that emits low-power electronic pulses similar to static electricity. Place the battery-operated mat on the counter (it works on furniture, too), and when the dog's feet touch it, he gets a mild zap, which is usually enough to keep the dog from returning to the scene of the potential crime.

If you can't stop your digger from excavating your garden, you might consider providing a special area of the yard for the dog to enjoy digging.

Digging

You may loathe your dog's digging—especially when he uproots your newly planted African violets or vegetable starters, but dogs love to dig. It's another natural canine behavior that owners usually tag as naughty or unwanted. Dogs dig for a couple of reasons. For some dogs, digging is in their DNA. Terriers, for example, were originally bred to "go to ground," which means that their job is to root out vermin from underground dens. Many dogs dig to bury their favorite toys or bones. Others dig to find cool spots to escape the heat. Most dogs, especially high-drive or high-energy dogs, dig out of frustration or boredom.

The best solution for digging is prevention. If your dog is bored, you will need to find an appropriate job for him to exercise his mind and body. It can be anything that you and he enjoy, such as swimming, jogging, obedience training, or fetching a Frisbee or ball. Also, try to come up with fun interactive games that stimulate his mind, such as trick training or food-dispensing puzzles.

If your puppy is digging to escape the heat, the potholes in your yard may be the least of your problems. Most dogs, especially heavily coated breeds, black dogs, and brachycephalic (flat-faced, short-muzzled) breeds, do not tolerate hot weather. You need to get your dog out of the heat and provide him with a cool spot.

If digging is in his blood, set your dog up with his own piece of heaven. Find an out-of-the-way area of your yard, dig a pit, fill it with sand or clean soil, and teach your puppy to dig in his pit. Also, do not allow your dog free access to the garden or yard areas where he can dig and wreak havoc. If you notice him digging somewhere other than his pit, run to his pit and encourage him to dig in it. Praise and reward.

In a flash, this door darter willl be showing you his tailless rump in motion.

Door Darting

For most dogs, whatever is outside is more exciting and rewarding than what is indoors. Puppies, and more than a few adult dogs, love darting through open doors. Puppies must be taught early on not to barge through doors or gateways. Too many dogs have been lost, seriously injured, or even killed because they darted out open doors onto busy streets.

The goal is to have your puppy sit and wait—or at the very least wait—while you open the door and go through first. Only when you release him with his release cue may he follow you. When you stop at the door, your puppy should stop, too. Think of it as a doggy version of asking "Please, may I go outside?"

For better control while teaching this exercise, it is

helpful if your puppy is on leash. Some owners want their puppy to sit when they approach a door. Others don't mind if the dog stands, as long as he isn't diving at the door. You will need to decide your criteria and stick to it.

- Approach a closed door with your puppy on leash.
- Verbally praise (or click) and reward any tendencies not to lunge or bolt at the door. Be generous with the treats so your puppy understands that you pay well for desired behaviors.
- If you're going to require him to sit for this exercise, hold the food slightly over his head but close to his nose so that he is encouraged to drop his rear into a Sit.
- Release him, back away from the door with the puppy, and then practice the door approach several times.
- As he becomes more proficient at waiting (and sitting, if that's a requirement), practice reaching for the doorknob and praising (or clicking) and rewarding for his not lunging or bolting at the door.
- Progress to opening the door, then stepping through the door while the puppy remains sitting or standing in place, and then calling the puppy through the door.
- To cement the behavior, put your release word to it, such as "Fido, OK," so he understands that he must be released to go through the door, which will prevent him from bolting out the door as soon as you are through it.

Teach your puppy that being released to come through the door does not mean that he gets to tear off down the driveway or across the yard. Practicing these exercises on leash will teach him that he must pass through the door and stay close to you. Plenty of tasty rewards will help reinforce staying with you.

The same process can easily be adapted to car doors; however, teaching your puppy to ride in a crate is the best preventive measure. You will need to teach your puppy not to bolt out his crate door, or you can have problems with him escaping your grasp or running off into traffic.

Eating Inappropriate Things (Pica)

Pica is the medical term for eating stuff that is simply not meant to be eaten. Experts do not know why dogs eat

Do down feathers taste like goose? It's hard to know what makes a dog want to chow down on inappropriate stuff.

Curing Phobias

Plenty of options exist when it comes to helping dogs with fears and phobias. If your dog needs help, don't hesitate to contact a veterinarian, behaviorist, or trainer. A professional may recommend nutritional programs, homeopathic supplements, flower essences, pharmacological treatment (e.g., benzodiazepines or selective serotonin reuptake inhibitors, such as fluoxetine and sertraline), exercise, obedience training, or trick training.

inappropriate things. Some theorize that dogs that engage in pica may lack proper nutrients, suffer from a biological imbalance, or have a behavioral disorder. But, again, no scientific data exists to explain this oddity in dogs.

Your veterinarian can help you rule out possible causes. Treatment consists of stopping the behavior or, at the very least, monitoring it. Some items, such as rocks and wood chips, can cause serious intestinal blockages, which may require emergency surgery to unbind the intestines. Some dogs have been known to eat paper (cardboard, wrapping paper, telephone books) with seemingly no problem passing it in their stools. When in doubt, always seek veterinary attention, as many situations can be life-threatening.

Fear and Phobias

Dogs that suffer from fear- or anxiety-related behaviors can pose real challenges for owners and trainers. Some dogs have a genetic predisposition to fear, which can result from poor breeding and compounded with a lack of socialization. Fear can also be a learned behavior. For example, dragging an eight- or ten-week-old puppy by his leash while excited children surround him and reach out to pet him is not socialization. While it may not bother some dogs, the puppy that is trembling and shaking is undoubtedly overwhelmed and is learning to be afraid.

A puppy that is bullied or attacked by a bossy or aggressive dog can develop a fear of other dogs. Some dogs can be fearful of all dogs or just one particular dog or even one breed or one color of dog. A puppy that is smacked with a rolled-up newspaper can learn to be afraid of newspapers—and his owner! A dog that has a painful experience during a veterinary visit might start panting, drooling, and shaking the next time the car pulls into the clinic's driveway.

Most, but certainly not all, dog-aggressive dogs have fear-based aggression. While it is easy to write them off as bad or untrainable, it's important to know how these dogs became fearful in order to help them.

How frightened a dog remains throughout his life depends a lot on genetics, what countermeasures are taken during his development, and how traumatic and psychologically damaging the fearful event was for the puppy. A lot also depends on the owner's emotional state at the time. If an owner goes into hysterical overload when his precious pooch is slightly nipped by another dog, the puppy will sense the owner's panic and may possibly overreact himself.

Jumping Up

Have you ever seen dogs when they greet and play with their canine buddies? They mouth and jump on each other. It's what dogs do. It's great fun and perfectly acceptable doggy manners. Unfortunately, dogs don't understand that many humans take offense to this behavior. Of course, you may not have a problem with your dog jumping on you—many owners do not. If, however, your puppy is a canine pogo stick, he may be cute now, but his antics will be far from amusing when he reaches his 80-pound adult weight.

If you do not want your puppy to grow into an adult dog that jumps up on you, you need to discourage the behavior while he is young and impressionable and hasn't yet developed any bad habits. It is unfair to allow him to jump up when he's a cute, irresistible puppy but then scold him for the same behavior as an adult dog. It's equally unfair to allow him to jump on you when you're in your gardening duds but not when you are dressed for work.

Try these tips to prevent jumping up:

- Teach him to sit for a treat. Dogs are smart, but even the smartest dog hasn't figured out how to sit and jump at the same time!
- To prevent your puppy from jumping on visitors, put his leash on before you open the door to greet them. This will allow you to control the behavior without grabbing at his fur or collar. When he sits nicely without pawing or mauling your guests, reward him with a treat and calm verbal praise: "Good sit" or "That's my good boy." Calm praise will help keep your puppy calm. High-pitched or excited praise will rev him up, which is not what you want.

It's helpful if you can deliberately set up situations to teach your puppy not to jump up on people. Perhaps you can enlist a friend to help you by passing by you and your puppy when you're out walking. This allows you to practice teaching your puppy to sit in a controlled environment.

Some people don't mind dogs jumping on them. However, if your goal is no jumping up, you should tell your friends ahead of time that no jumping is allowed. Not even a little bit of jumping. Remember, dogs learn through repetition and consistency, and your puppy will quickly learn the rules when they are implemented.

How cute is a puppy jumping up to say hello? Not at all. Turn your back and ignore him. Dogs must greet you on all fours.

Loud Noises

Some dogs are terrified of loud noises, such as an automobile backfiring, thunder, or firecrackers. While humans may recognize the noises as harmless, the anxiety that noise-phobic dogs experience worsens the situation a thousand times over. Many owners are frustrated by their moderately or very noise-sensitive dogs and opt to seek the help of experienced trainers or behaviorists to desensitize the dogs.

Marking

Marking, like chewing, is not a behavioral problem. It's a highly complex and frequently misunderstood method of canine communication. Primarily, dogs that mark are "branding" or "staking their claim" to what they believe is their territory. Whether a dog hikes his leg on a tree, a fence post, or your couch, he is saying, "This is mine." Then other dogs come along and check the message, and they may leave messages of their own by marking over or adjacent to the original spot.

Guarding breeds like the Belgian Tervuren develop strong territorial instincts, which can be manifested in marking behaviors.

Dogs that urine-mark may do so in a variety of situations, such as while on walks in the neighborhood or at dog parks. Some dogs, although not all, mark both in their own homes and outdoors. Some male dogs mark only when in the presence of female dogs—especially if they are in heat—as a way of impressing the females; other males mark only when interacting with other male dogs—usually rival males. Some females mark as a form of competition. Many dogs never mark in their own homes but will mark while in unfamiliar places, such as the veterinary clinic or a friend's home.

Dogs don't mark out of spite. Dogs urine-mark indoors and/or outdoors for two primary reasons: first, for territorial purposes, to define and redefine their turf; and second, due to anxiety issues, which can include:

- separation anxiety
- a new pet in the household
- conflicts with other pets or people in the household

- a new baby, boyfriend, girlfriend, spouse, relative, or other person living in the house
- the departure of a family member from the house
- an unfamiliar dog urinating in the yard
- new objects, such as luggage or furniture, in the house that have unfamiliar smells or another animal's scent

If your dog's marking has become an issue—especially indoors—you may need the expertise of a knowledgeable dog trainer or behaviorist to determine what circumstances are eliciting the behavior and possibly to implement counterconditioning strategies, such as spaying or neutering.

It is important that you not correct or scold your dog, even when he is caught in the act. Allow your dog some leeway to mark while outside in the yard or during walks. By preventing him from marking altogether, you may frustrate him and actually exacerbate the situation.

To discourage indoor marking, consider a proactive approach with the following strategies:

- Spay or neuter your dog. This will decrease or eliminate sexual motivation for marking but may not completely remedy any learned marking behaviors.
- Clean up all signs of marking so your dog is not further stimulated to leave "pee-mail." Use products designed to eliminate urine odor. Do not use ammonia, as this can attract him back to the same spot to mark again.
- Supervise your dog like a hawk when he is indoors. Constant supervision is critical; otherwise, the problem is likely to continue.
- Address the dog's underlying anxiety or territorial insecurity that is causing him to mark repeatedly. His reasons can be complicated; consider the services of a certified animal behaviorist.
- Consider using a synthetic hormone (pheromone) diffuser, which can, in some cases, have a calming effect on dogs.
- For repeat offenders, consider discussing medications, such as antidepressants and selective serotonin reuptake inhibitors, with your veterinarian. Medication alone will not be effective, however, especially if the underlying causes have not been addressed.

Male dogs tend to mark their territory by raising their legs on vertical objects. While on a walk, your dog may mark trees and poles to let other dogs know he's been there.

Urine Marking Is Not House-Soiling

House-soiling and submissive/excitement urination are completely different behaviors from urine marking. If your dog is having potty accidents in the house, there are a few reasons why this might be happening.

- He is not house-trained (despite your best intentions).
- He has a medical issue that is causing incontinence.
- He is taking a medication that may be causing more frequent urination.
- If you are not sure what is going on, consider these facts:
- House-soiling generally results in a good deal of urine.
- House-soiling may occur in corners or other areas that you are less likely to notice.
- Submissive or excitement urination generally occurs during greetings, physical contact, or scolding.
- Urine marking generally involves small amounts of urine.
- Urine marking usually happens on vertical surfaces, such as walls or furniture.
- Marking normally occurs in prominent locations.

In many cases, it may take a combination of strategies to diminish marking. A veterinary checkup may be necessary because some medical conditions, such as cystitis, kidney dysfunction, endocrine abnormalities, and incontinence, or the onset of old age can inadvertently be mistaken for marking.

Resource Guarding

Resource guarding, or food guarding, is a form of aggression. While food is a common object of guarding, dogs can guard a treasured toy, a tasty bone, or your favorite chair. Some dogs even guard their owners. Signals can include the dog's casually turning his head, crouching over the item, growling, lunging, or biting.

To prevent a young puppy from developing a guarding habit, teach him early on in a humane and positive way that you can take away any possession at any time and that no protesting or backtalking is acceptable. Obviously, you should not abuse the practice. After all, you don't want to make your puppy neurotic.

Sit on the floor and hand-feed your puppy a piece of kibble or two at a time. Talk to him and praise him for taking the food nicely. Now place his food bowl on the floor and, while he's eating from it, reach down, touch the bowl, and drop a tidbit of food in it. Praise him for being good. He should understand that you can touch his food, bowl, toys, and the like at any time. Again, don't abuse the right, but let him know that your touching his stuff is perfectly acceptable.

While playing with him, take away his toy, praise him for giving it up, give him a kiss, and then give the toy back. You should also utilize the Leave It and Drop It cues. These commands apply not only to his food but also to anything he might pick up that could be potentially harmful, such as a dead bird, a paper clip, a medicine bottle, and so forth.

If you accustom your puppy to having his food and possessions handled by you on a regular basis, he should remain relaxed and unthreatened by your presence around his food or toys.

Running Off or Not Coming When Called

Dogs are curious creatures. When left to their own devices, they can develop the annoying and dangerous habit of running away or refusing to come when called. Some breeds, such as Siberian Huskies, Whippets, and Shiba Inus— even really, really well-trained ones—can never be completely trusted off leash. Their inherent desire to run makes controlling or confining them at all times a necessity. Other breeds can be equally frustrating, but, honestly, any dog can develop the behavior of running off.

It should come as no surprise that prevention is the key to success. By managing your puppy's environment, he never has the opportunity to learn the unacceptable behaviors of running off and not coming when called. But it's a fine line between managing your puppy's environment and stifling him. You need to set him up to for success by teaching a strong Come command and then, when he is older, giving him little bits of freedom so he can show you what he has learned.

Remember, your young puppy has an inherent follow response and will follow you just about anywhere. Unfortunately, many owners of puppies and adolescent dogs expect their new dogs to automatically follow them everywhere, but this is not always the case. Often, they lack adequate training and cannot be called back once they run off. Obviously, this causes a good deal of grief for dogs and owners.

It's perfectly OK to let your puppy or adolescent dog run around and explore his surroundings in a fenced area, but he should be dragging his leash or long line and be supervised at all times. If your puppy starts to wander off, simply step on the leash or line and reel him back in.

Enclosed environments provide excellent opportunities to practice all of the recommended puppy skills, such as chase Recalls, hide and seek, Follow Me, and Find Me. These skills help instill the

Don't allow your puppy to become possessive of his bowl or toys. Teach your puppy that what's yours is yours and what's his is yours, too.

behaviors that make you fun and interesting and prevent your puppy from running off. When you establish a solid relationship with your maturing puppy, he will look to your for leadership, fun, and excitement when he is an adult. A dog that is bonded to his master is less likely to wander away to find his own fun.

Separation Anxiety

Separation anxiety (a fear of being alone) is a common fear in many dogs. It is a real problem for many owners because dogs can become extremely anxious and destructive when left alone. Before you say, "Ah ha! That's why my puppy shreds everything in sight!" it's important to recognize that true separation anxiety doesn't occur simply when a puppy is left alone and becomes a little bored.

Dogs with true separation anxiety come unhinged when their owners leave them alone—even for short periods of time. Many dogs chew furniture, drywall, carpeting, rugs, and linoleum. Some dogs urinate and defecate, and they frequently whine, pace, drool, howl, or bark and oftentimes work themselves into uncontrollable frenzies. For a severely affected dog, the mere anticipation of an owner leaving is enough to trigger a sense of anxiety, nervousness, hyperactivity, or pacing. It's a sad situation for both dogs and owners, and owners should never think that dogs with separation anxiety are being intentionally naughty or destructive.

You can do a lot to prevent separation anxiety by conditioning your young puppy to being left alone for short periods of time—starting with one minute or less and gradually increasing to three to four minutes, and then ten to fifteen minutes, and so on. You can start doing this when he is a very young puppy and chewing on a marrow bone in his exercise pen. You simply walk out of the room and come back again. No fuss. No drama. No histrionics.

No matter how irrational you deem your puppy's phobias, they're very real to him. Always be calm and reassuring (without rewarding the fear).

Maybe you're cooking in the kitchen, and you go to the laundry room to put clothes in the dryer. Gradually, in small increments, you increase the time that your puppy is left alone. If he's chewing on a tasty marrow bone, he is less likely to care that you have disappeared for a minute or two. The key is to link good feelings with your departure.

Despite your best efforts to raise a well-behaved dog, things can occasionally go wrong, and you may need to call in an expert. Some behavioral issues, such as aggression and separation anxiety, are difficult and challenging to decode and generally require expert guidance. Many behavioral issues are complex and have underlying causes, such as lack of socialization, sexual maturity (or lack thereof), lack of training, or having been corrected inappropriately.

If you find yourself frustrated and angry, which, from time to time, happens to even the best of owners and trainers, there is no shame in calling in an expert. As mentioned previously, training goes beyond teaching your puppy the basic commands and dealing with naughty behaviors. Every aspect of your dog's behavior, be it good or bad, desirable or undesirable, is reflected in the relationship you have with him. If that relationship begins to deteriorate, you owe it to your dog to repair what has gone awry. As a responsible owner, seeking professional help can put the human-canine relationship back on a positive track.

If your puppy already has a serious case of separation anxiety, you will need to work much harder and be more patient. In these instances, contacting an experienced trainer or behaviorist is your best bet. Well-intended owners may exacerbate the problem if they overreact or underreact to the situation. Severe cases may require a combination of behavior modification and pharmacological therapy. Antianxiety medications, which are similar to what humans take, can make a big difference in a dog's quality of life. These medications are not intended for long-term or permanent use, but rather to be used in conjunction with training to facilitate rehabilitation/counterconditioning by helping improve trainability.

Submissive Urination

Submissive urination is another frequently misunderstood behavior that stems from canine anxiety. Perhaps your puppy exhibits this behavior by urinating when he greets you. Most common in young or shy dogs, it is a reflexive sign that a dog accepts his owner's authority. In the wild, this behavior is normal and functions to dissuade dominant pack members from aggression.

Owners often mistakenly read submissive urination as a house-training accident or, worse, a willful act of disobedience. They mistakenly believe that the dog can control himself and is simply urinating on purpose. If an owner immediately shifts into freak-out mode and scolds the dog, the problem becomes more pronounced because the dog must urinate even more in order to block his owner's aggression. In the dog's mind, he has acknowledged his owner's authority by urinating. When scolded for doing so, he becomes even more submissive in an effort to appease his owner.

CHAPTER 14

ACTIVE COMPANIONS

Your companion dog lives to be by your side—at home, in the backyard, at the beach or park, or at an organized event like a dog show, a flyball competition, or an agility trial. Traveling with your dog can be fun and rewarding for you, your dog, and your family, whether you're just going to take a hike in a nearby town or take a weeklong adventure in the mountains.

Traveling with Your Dog

Who doesn't love traveling with his or her dog? Wide-open spaces, endless blue skies, swimming, hiking, and hotels! AAA reports that nearly 90 percent of US pet owners say that they travel with their pets. Obviously, some dogs might not like traveling, and not all dogs are suited for all travel, but when conditioned at an early age—when they are young and more receptive to new adventures—most puppies grow into adult dogs that make wonderful traveling companions, be it across town or across the country.

By Car

For many dogs, riding in the family car is part of everyday life, as natural as eating, sleeping, and playing. These dogs usually associate car rides with fun activities such as hiking, swimming, or playing with their canine buddies at the dog park. One of the best ways to accustom your new puppy to traveling is to put him in his crate and take him places with you (weather providing, of course). Take him for rides around town or to visit your dog-friendly friends and family. Make the experience fun by giving him treats and telling him he is perfect!

Some puppies that have never been in cars or that have developed phobias are often anxious about car rides. If, for instance, a puppy's first few car rides are associated with fear or apprehension, such as his dislike of the car's movement or his inability to control his surroundings, he may begin to equate car rides with drooling, a general sense of queasiness, or vomiting. He also may associate car rides with unpleasant experiences at the journey's end, such as a stressful visit to the vet's office or a noisy obedience class. For some shelter and rescue dogs, a ride in the car ended in being abandoned by their owners. A few bad experiences can ruin a puppy's enthusiasm for car rides.

Motion sickness, on the other hand, is normally associated with an inner-ear problem. While all breeds appear equally susceptible, it appears more common in puppies and young dogs than

Tips for Helping Control Car-Related Anxiety

If your puppy is experiencing motion sickness while riding in the car, consider these tips to help squelch the nausea.

- Always travel with your puppy in his crate, which provides a sense of familiarity and security for him. If you are using a specially designed canine seatbelt/harness and buckling him in the front seat, be sure he is as far back as possible from the dashboard and air bags, which can be hazardous to dogs. The crate is the better option, though, because doggie seatbelts are unreliable.
- Visibility out the side windows can cause a queasy sensation, which can cause or compound motion sickness. Consider a fiberglass crate with solid sides to limit his view, or cover the sides of his crate with a lightweight towel or sheet.
- Lower the car windows a few inches to equalize inside and outside air pressures.
- Keep the vehicle cool.
- Limit your puppy's food and water intake before travel.
- Give your puppy a small treat or two every time he gets in the car.
- If he has had a negative response to your vehicle, try using a different vehicle, if possible.
- Take short rides to fun places, such as the park, the lake, or a hiking trail.

Unfortunately, some dogs never do get over their car-related anxiety or motion sickness. However, with perseverance, the chances are good that you will have a successful outcome with your puppy. If the problem persists, consult a veterinarian or behaviorist who can help determine whether the cause is truly motion sickness or another issue.

in older dogs, with experts presuming it is because the ear structures that help balance are not fully developed in puppies.

Most dogs—especially well-trained dogs—can be remarkable traveling companions, and there is no limit to the fun you can have exploring together. So it is well worth the training to help your dog overcome his fear of riding in a car.

Here are some travel tips that every owner needs to know:

- Never allow your puppy to travel in the open bed of a pickup truck or with his head hanging out an open window. Dust, debris, and bugs are ever-present dangers that can damage his eyes and nostrils. A sudden, unexpected stop could throw him from the truck or car, causing serious injury or death.
- Be careful that your puppy does not overheat. Use a window shield to keep the sun from beating through the window on him, and never, *ever* leave him in the car unattended during warm weather. Even on a pleasant day, temperatures inside a car can soar to

well over 100°F or 37.8°C in the time it takes you to run inside the store and grab a few supplies.

- Never leave your puppy in the car unattended. Puppies left unattended in parked cars can be stolen.
- Walk your puppy in areas designated for pets. Pick up after your dog and deposit his waste in the nearest trash bin.

By Air

Like anything pertaining to dogs, airline travel has opponents and proponents regarding its safety. While there are horror stories about pets being lost or injured, there certainly are more success stories about owners who have flown with their dogs. Before you book your reservation, be sure to understand the risks and take all necessary precautions.

Dogs traveling by air are protected by the Animal Welfare Act (AWA), which is enforced by the US Department of Agriculture's (USDA's) Animal and Plant Health Inspection Service (APHIS). That in itself does not guarantee that your puppy will be safe flying the friendly skies. However, there are safety regulations and precautions to help minimize potential dangers, including the following:

- Dogs must be at least eight weeks old and be weaned at least five days prior to traveling.
- A licensed veterinarian must examine your dog and issue a health certificate within ten days of traveling.
- Brachycephalic breeds, such as Pugs, Boston Terriers, Bulldogs, and Pekingese, are particularly susceptible to respiratory problems that may come with stress and exposure to increased altitude pressure.

Small dogs can fly in the cabin, like this Chihuahua in his jet-setting owner's carry-on.

- If your puppy fits under the seat in a carrier, he may be able to fly in the passenger cabin with you. Otherwise, he will travel in the cargo hold.
- Dogs must travel in airline-approved crates that meet stringent USDA regulations for size, strength, sanitation, and ventilation. Your puppy may be refused a boarding pass if his kennel does not meet the government's requirements.
- Dogs flying outside the continental United States may be subjected to quarantine regulations.
- Sedation should never be administered without your veterinarian's approval.

Regulations vary from airline to airline, so it is important to always plan ahead. Not all airlines accept dogs, many limit the number of dogs accepted on each flight, and many impose flight embargos during summer travel or when temperatures exceed a designated temperature anywhere on the route.

Call the airlines well in advance of your travel plans to schedule flights. Ideally, when booking a flight, try to:

- book flights during the middle of the week, avoiding holiday or weekend travel
- be sure that you and your puppy are traveling on the same plane
- avoid layovers and plane changes, if possible
- choose flights early in the morning or late in the evening in warm months
- choose midday flights in cooler months

Ask about "counter-to-counter" shipping in which your puppy is loaded immediately before departure and unloaded immediately after arrival. (Additional fees may apply for this service.)

Specific regulations for national and international air travel are available on the APHIS website: http://www.aphis.usda.gov.

By Train or Bus

If you and your puppy to plan to travel by train or bus, you are out of luck. Neither Amtrak trains nor Greyhound bus lines allow pets other than service dogs to travel. (Local rail and bus lines may allow pets, but always double-check.) For decades, pets were allowed to ride the rails until Amtrak did away with the policy in 1976. However, H.R. 2066, The Pets on Trains Act of 2013, requires Amtrak to propose a policy that would allow passengers to transport dogs and cats on specified Amtrak trains. This new law would lift the Amtrak pet-travel ban and enable owners to include certain pets in their travel plans. The legislation will include certain caveats, including a fee for each pet, a 750-mile travel limit for pets, and designated "pet-friendly" cars in which pets must travel.

When You Can't Take Your Puppy with You

Family emergencies, unexpected business trips, and inclement weather conditions may exclude your best friend from your travel plans. Whatever the reason, occasions may arise when you need to leave your puppy for a few days or a few weeks. Yes, it's heartbreaking, but there are a few options that may give you some peace of mind.

Microchipping is the most reliable way to permanently identify your dog.

Boarding facilities have come a long way in the last ten or fifteen years. Many are now designed with the discriminating pet owner in mind, and they provide a variety of services in addition to boarding, including training, daily exercise, and grooming. Some facilities provide live video feeds that allow you to view your puppy via the facility's website.

Your puppy's physical safety and emotional well-being are paramount. Here are some tips on choosing the best facility and reducing your and your dog's stress.

- Visit and tour the entire facility. A clean and inviting reception area does not guarantee clean kennel runs. If the proprietors do not want you touring the facility, hightail it to the nearest exit.
- Check the cleanliness of the kennels, runs, and exercise areas. Make sure they are free of debris and excrement and that they are cleaned and disinfected between boarders. Check the security of the facility. It should be completely fenced, the kennels and exercise yards should have secure latches, and the fences should be sturdy and at least 6 feet high.
- Find out if your puppy will be boarded indoors or out (or a combination of the two). The indoor facilities should be heated, and the outdoor facilities should offer protection from the weather.
- Look at what your puppy will be sleeping on. Do you need to bring his bed or favorite blanket?
- If you have more than one dog, ask if you can kennel them together and what, if any, additional costs this might incur.
- Find out how frequently and for how long your puppy will be walked or exercised each day. A good boarding kennel will have someone interact or play with him and not just leave him unattended in an exercise yard.
- It can be dangerous and stressful to have your puppy housed with other dogs, so ask whether he will be alone or with other dogs.

If it's not possible to bring your dog, consider using the services of a reputable boarding kennel in your area.

- Ask about the facility's veterinarian and if there is a twenty-four-hour emergency clinic nearby.
- Ask about their admission policies, drop-off and pickup hours, and what happens if your return is delayed.
- Get a list of required vaccinations.
- Once you have decided on a facility, remember to book early. Many facilities are booked months in advance,

especially during the holidays. Always leave special care instructions, your itinerary, and phone numbers to contact you or a trusted friend or relative in the event of an emergency.

Therapy Work

We've all heard reports that petting a dog can lower a person's blood pressure, anxiety, and stress levels. Research shows that people's levels of oxytocin (the "feel good" neurohormone) double while they are petting a dog. So it should come as no surprise that dogs, dogs, and more dogs are just what the doctor ordered!

Get Involved in Therapy

Therapy work is hard work, but it can be extremely rewarding, and most people who work with therapy dogs and who are visited by therapy dogs say that it is the highlight of their day or week. Most hospitals, nursing homes, and schools require therapy dogs to be certified. For information on therapy-dog certification, contact an organization such as Pet Partners (www.petpartners.org), Therapy Dogs International (www.tdi-dog.org), or Love on a Leash (www.loveonaleash.org).

A basic foundation of obedience training, including Sit, Down, and Wait, is necessary, and it helps if your dog has his AKC Canine Good Citizen (CGC) certificate.

Everyday therapy dogs help people—the mentally ill, the sick, the disabled, the elderly, the lonely, and even the forgotten. Countless stories have been told about therapy dogs' providing physical, psychological, and social benefits to people, such as patients undergoing chemotherapy, children of deployed military families, and people with advanced Alzheimer's disease. They visit people in hospitals, rehabilitation centers, and nursing homes, providing love and comfort and nonjudgmental companionship. Most importantly, they help people walk, talk, smile, laugh, and reminisce about their own animals, and who doesn't want that?

Many dogs are naturally gifted and have an uncanny instinct for knowing who needs them. But just because you love your puppy doesn't mean that he is a good candidate for therapy work. Not all dogs have the physical and mental fortitude to cope with strange noises and smells, distractions, and, often, erratic behavior. A good therapy dog must be physically and mentally calm and well trained. He needs the right temperament and personality because the work can be tiring and stressful. A therapy dog can't jump up on elderly people or knock down toddlers. He can't bolt at the sight of a wheelchair or panic when someone screams or grabs his ear, when a child hugs him a little too hard, or when a food tray crashes to the ground behind him. Therapy dogs need to behave in a way most dogs do not, which can be too much pressure for many dogs.

Equally important, you need to be your dog's advocate while he is working. You need to be sharply in tune to his body language and be an expert at reading him. You need to know when he is tired or overwhelmed, when he has had enough, and when it is time to call it a day. You need to interpret his visual signals every minute of every interaction and watch for signs of stress or discomfort. You cannot dismiss the signs that your dog gives you.

Sports and Competition

While your puppy is too young for most competitive events, it never hurts to plan ahead if you are interested in the myriad dog sports available. Some puppies grow into adult dogs that do extremely well in multiple sports or in a particular activity because of their breed, while others excel because of their individual personalities and intelligence. Many herding and sporting breeds, for example, excel in agility and dock diving. Plenty of pit bulls and American Staffordshire Terriers dominate canine weight-pulling competitions. While many sheepdog trials are open to any breed, Border Collies tend to dominate, though many other dogs—from German Shepherds to Schipperkes—perform well.

That's not to say you must limit your choices based on your dog's breed. Plenty of activities are available, and the following list is a small sampling of the most popular ones. The key is finding the perfect match. You may have to try a few different activities, but chances are there is a canine sport—or two!—with your dog's name written all over it.

Remember, your puppy is young and still growing. His bones are soft and susceptible to injury until his growth plates close, which can be anywhere from six to eighteen months. While it is best to hold off on any serious training until he is about one year old, plenty of groundwork exercises, such as basic obedience commands and retrieving, let you get started on the foundation skills. Always check with your veterinarian before starting any training or strenuous exercises with your puppy.

Dog Shows

Dog shows have been around for a long time, but the date of the first show is a matter of debate.

This young Great Dane is being stacked for the judge's initial evaluation.

Some say that the first hound shows took place in 1776. However, the first "official" show is generally accepted as being held in Newcastle-upon-Tyne in England in 1859, with the competition being restricted to pointers and setters. Dog shows became a part of American life in the 1870s, but, again, there are mixed opinions about the date and location of the first US show. Today, the country's most prestigious show, the Westminster Kennel Club dog show, is held every February at Madison Square Garden in New York City.

Conformation shows are, as the name implies, all about a dog's *conformation*—how he is structurally put together, how he moves, and how closely he adheres to the breed's standard. Conformation shows are considered by many as the signature event of the competitive dog world. The breed ring provides a forum for breeders and handlers to showcase the best in their breeding stock.

So what is the gauge for a great show dog? More than just good looks, show dogs are athletes in competition. In addition to representing outstanding specimens of their breeds, top dogs must be physically conditioned and have an outstanding temperament to handle the stress of the noisy, crowded show-ring environment. The dogs need showmanship, and they must look like winners. This "presence" in the ring often separates the great dogs that win from all the rest.

Agility Trials

Agility is one of the fastest growing dog sports and one of the most exciting, fast-paced canine sports for spectators. It was developed and officially introduced in 1978 at Crufts, England's largest dog show, as an entertaining diversion for spectators. The sport made its way across the pond and was promoted by the United States Dog Agility Association in the mid-1980s and then officially recognized by the AKC ten years later.

In an agility trial, dogs demonstrate their athleticism and versatility by maneuvering through a timed obstacle course that includes jumps, tunnels, and weave poles as well as an A-frame, teeter-totter, and table (or pause box).

This Sheltie is deftly maneuvering his way through the weave poles at an agility trial.

Agility is addicting because it can never quite be mastered. Each course brings new challenges and tests your handling skills as well as your dog's skills and training. Handlers race against the clock as they try to regulate their dogs' speed and precision while simultaneously stay the heck out of the dogs' way and trying to remember the correct order of seventeen to twenty obstacles!

Agility training helps dogs build confidence and develop body awareness. They learn how to jump correctly (yes, some dogs need to be taught), climb, change direction, speed up, slow down, and read your body cues. Training also helps a dog build confidence in you—his handler.

You must develop a communication system with your dog so that you can teach him in a fun and humane

AKC Rally® is a combination of agility and obedience, sort of. The emphasis is less on speed and precision and more on how well dogs and handlers perform together as a team. Created by the AKC with the average dog owner in mind, the goal is to help promote a positive human-canine relationship with an emphasis on fun. It's much less pressure than competing in a formal obedience environment while still allowing owners to showcase their dogs' obedience skills.

Dog and handler move at their own pace through a preset course of ten to twenty stations, depending on the level. Each station has a sign that provides instruction regarding the skill to be performed, such as Halt and Sit; Sit, Down, Right Turn; About Right Turn; or While Heeling Perform a 270-Degree Left Turn.

Unlike in traditional obedience, handlers are permitted to talk to their dogs, use praise, clap their hands, pat their legs, or use any verbal means of communication and body language throughout the performance. Handlers may not touch their dogs or make physical corrections. Any purebred or mixed-breed dog that is eligible for AKC registration or Canine Partners enrollment can enter Rally.

manner all of the things he needs to know to compete successfully. You need to build a mutually strong bond and working relationship so that he is comfortable working off leash and focusing on you and his job while in a busy, chaotic environment.

Canine Good Citizen®

The American Kennel Club's Canine Good Citizen® (CGC) program, implemented in 1989, is a public education and certification program designed to promote good dogs and good owners. By rewarding responsible dog ownership and good pet manners, the program encourages owners to get involved with and obedience-train their dogs, thereby helping foster and develop a positive, mutually loving, and respectful human-canine relationships.

The CGC program is a noncompetitive, ten-part test that evaluates a dog's behavior in practical situations at home, in public, and in the presence of unfamiliar people and other dogs. The pass-or-fail test is designed to test a dog's reactions to distractions, friendly strangers, and supervised isolation. Additionally, a dog must sit politely while being petted, walk on a loose leash, walk through a crowd, and respond to basic obedience commands including Sit, Down, Stay, and Come. The evaluator also inspects the dog to determine whether he is clean and well groomed. Any dog that successfully completes the test receives a certificate stating that he is a Canine Good Citizen, and he is entitled to use the initials CGC after his name.

Obedience

America's introduction to obedience began in Mount Kisco, New York, in 1933. Organizer and promoter of the sport, Helen Whitehouse Walker, felt that her Standard Poodles were every bit as smart and competent as any sporting or working dog. She set out to prove it by organizing her own obedience test. And that's how the sport of obedience began.

Many decades later, obedience competition has been modified and refined, but the purpose of obedience training remains the same. That purpose, according to the AKC, is to "demonstrate the usefulness of purebred dogs as the ultimate companion of man and helpmate to man, and as a means of recognizing that dogs have been trained to behave in the home, in public places, and in the presence of other dogs." Despite the fact that the AKC now allows mixed-breed dogs to strut their stuff in the obedience ring, the purpose of the sport remains unchanged.

Obedience trials test your dog's ability to perform a particular set of exercises. There are three levels of competition: Novice, Open, and Utility, with each class increasing in difficulty. A perfect score in each class is 200, and handler-dog teams are faulted for being out of position, bumping into each other, executing slow or crooked sits, retrieving the wrong article, and so forth. A score of 176 is needed to pass.

Dock Diving

From the smallest jumpers to the highest flyers, what could be more fun for water-loving dogs than running full speed ahead and hurling themselves into a giant pool of water? Owners and spectators alike have taken to this high-flying canine sport, and for good reason. It's all about speed and how far or how high a dog can jump, and both experienced and amateur dogs can make a big splash.

Few dog sports are as exciting as dock diving!

Safety is, of course, paramount, and rules and regulations are in place to help prevent injuries. However, compared to many canine events, the rules are pretty simple. Several organizations, including DockDogs and Ultimate Air Dogs, sponsor regional and national events. While the rules vary slightly between organizations, the premise remains basically the same. For long-jump competitions, the dogs run down a dock, get airborne, and land in a specially constructed pool of water. Owners can use a "chase" object as long as it is throwable, buoyant, and retrievable, such as a bumper, ball, dead fowl trainer, or Frisbee. The official jump distance is measured from the end of the dock to the point at which the base of the dog's tail breaks the water's surface. An added twist, for those brave enough to try, requires dogs to catch the thrown object in order for the jump to count.

Practices and competitions are open to all breeds and mixed breeds. Dogs must be at least six months old and know how to swim. Not all dogs are natural swimmers, so you will want to be sure that your dock-diving dog loves swimming.

Flying Disc

Part of the flying-disc sport's popularity is that it requires not much more than an open, flat field; a Frisbee; and a dog that loves to run, jump, and catch. Of course, your dog will need basic obedience and socialization skills, and even though he knows how to catch, he may not immediately understand the concept of the game. You may need to refine his training to show him how to turn and chase a disc that is thrown over his head.

Competition is regulated by the International Disc Dog Handlers Association (IDDHA) and the Flying Disc Dog Organization (FDDO). Events are held all over the country and are divided into beginner and intermediate classes. Formats include short distance, long distance, and freestyle, with some dogs using their owners as launching pads.

While any dog can excel, most flying-disc dogs tend to be medium-sized, lean, and agile. While your puppy is young, you can begin instilling a drive and enthusiasm for flying discs. However, this is an athletic sport, so you will want to be sure that your puppy is fully grown and his growth plates are closed before you start any jumping maneuvers or strenuous training.

Frisbee can be either a casual game in your backyard or a canine Olympic sport!

Flyball

Flyball has been around for more than thirty years and is another fast-paced sport that you can do with your dog regardless of his size or pedigree. It is the perfect game for all tennis-ball-loving dogs because this high-octane relay race showcases your dog's speed and agility.

The course consists of four hurdles (small jumps) spaced approximately 10 feet apart. Fifteen feet beyond the last hurdle is a spring-loaded box that contains a tennis ball. The goal is for each dog to take a turn running the relay by leaping each of the four hurdles and then hitting a pedal or lever with his paw to trigger the box, which shoots a tennis ball up in the air. Once the dog catches the ball in his mouth, he races back over the four hurdles to the finish line, where the next dog is anxiously awaiting his turn. The first team to have all four dogs run without errors wins the heat. If a dog misses a hurdle or fails to retrieve the ball, he must repeat his turn. Jump height is determined by the smallest dog on the team.

Weight-Pull Competitions

If speed sports aren't your thing, canine weight-pull competitions might be more to your (and your dog's) liking. Don't worry—your dog does all of the pulling in this muscle sport. Similar to tractor-pull competitions, dogs compete within their individual weight classes to see which dog can pull the most weight over a distance of 16 feet within one minute. A dog can pull a weighted sled on snow or a wheeled cart on a natural surface, and the weight is gradually increased until one dog remains.

Dogs wear specially designed harnesses that disperse tension and reduce the possibility of injury. It's important to mention that you can't force a dog to pull any more than you can force him to catch a Frisbee, run an obstacle course, or herd sheep! Dogs excel at this sport because they love to work—not because they are forced to perform— and because they have been properly trained and conditioned.

Dogs must be two years old to compete in weight pulls sanctioned by the International Weight Pulling Association (IWPA), but you can begin teaching lots of puppy socialization and obedience skills during his formative puppy months. As with all canine activities, your dog needs basic obedience training, handling, and socialization. Always start slowly and progress at a rate suitable for the mental and physical capabilities of your dog. When in doubt, consult your veterinarian.

Earthdog Tests

Looking for a competitive outlet for your terrier's abundance of energy? Earthdog tests are a lot of fun. The terrier breeds are feisty, energetic dogs whose ancestors were bred to hunt and kill vermin by tracking game above and below ground, barking at their quarry in the den, and then bolting or drawing it for the hunter. Many of today's terriers are pets, and few are regularly hunted to ground in natural hunts. However, noncompetitive AKC earthdog tests offer these game little dogs an outlet for their energy and instincts, while providing

It's a dirty job, but someone's got to do it! Dachshunds and most of the terrier breeds actively participate in earthdog events.

owners a standardized gauge to measure their dogs' natural aptitudes and trained hunting and working behaviors. The American Working Terrier Association also holds field trials and issues certificates of gameness (CG), hunting certificates (HC), and working certificates (WC).

Herding

Looking for a competitive outlet for your herding dog's seemingly endless energy and drive? While many herding dogs, which have been selectively bred for hundreds of years for their superb ability to maneuver livestock, are still utilized in a working environment, many are treasured family pets and companions living in cities and suburbs, far removed from the sights, smells, and activities of sheep, goats, and cattle. The good news is that you and your herding dog—even if he is a city slicker—can still get involved and compete in recreational or competitive herding.

Sheepdog trials in the United States are fashioned after the British trials and are considered to be the true test of sheepdogs. They are designed to parallel the everyday work of a sheepdog in a farm environment, and while each trial is a bit different, they normally consist of an outrun, lift, fetch, drive, pen, and shed.

Many owners of herding dogs dabble in AKC-sponsored herding events designed to test a dog's herding instinct. These events differ from sheepdog trials in that they are simulations of working ranch or farm conditions and not always reflective of true farm work. However, they do provide a standardized test by which owners can measure their dog's inherent herding abilities and training—and have a lot of fun in the process!

The king of herding trials (and quite a few other events), Border Collies excel in herding and sheepdog trials.

Other organizations, such as the Australian Shepherd Club of America (ASCA), require dogs to be at least six months old on the day of competition. The ASCA, in addition to its stockdog program that certifies a number of non-Australian Shepherd breeds, offers a Ranch Dog program that is open to multiple herding breeds and crossbreeds.

To get started, look for obedience trainers who instill basic commands in a fun and humane manner, and stockdog trainers who are knowledgeable about herding as well as about your breed's herding style. Look for stockdog trainers who use their dogs in working or competitive environments.

Lure Coursing

Lure coursing in the United States traces back to the 1960s, but it was developed as a performance event in the early 1970s. This competitive environment recreates the physical requirements of open-field coursing, allows owners to continue testing the functional abilities of their sighthounds, and permits dogs to simulate the pursuit of prey in an open field.

Dogs chase a lure (usually nothing more than a plastic bag) around a field in a pattern meant to resemble the route that prey might take when pursued by hounds. Courses are usually between 500 and 1000 yards in length but can be longer. Dogs are scored on speed, enthusiasm, agility, endurance, and coursing abilities.

While most sighthounds love to run for the fun of the chase, they can also earn titles under various organizations. Several organizations, including the American Sighthound Field Association (ASFA) and the AKC, sponsor events. These swift coursing breeds find their prey by sight, not scent. While a few organizations allow all breeds to compete, sighthounds excel.

Tracking

Tracking is a popular sport that tests a dog's ability to recognize and track a human scent over varying terrains and with climatic changes. It is designed to showcase a dog's intelligence and extremely high level of scent capability, which should be pretty easy for most hound, herding, and retrieving breeds.

The primary goal is for the dog to follow a scented track and locate an article left at the end of the trail by a tracklayer. The tracks are aged longer and the courses become increasingly more difficult as the dogs move up in the classes.

Unlike obedience and agility titles, which require a dog and handler to qualify three times, a dog only needs to complete one track successfully to earn each title. If you and your dog love the great outdoors, tracking might be the sport for you. The best way to get involved in tracking is to contact a local dog obedience club or your national kennel club.

You'll soon find that the possibilities are nearly endlessness for you and your active, overachieving pooch. For as long as humans can dream up new pursuits for their willing canine companions, there will always be new sports to conquer. Just a few short generations ago, no one would have imagined we'd see dogs running on obstacle courses, Dachshunds racing, retrievers diving from docks, or dogs competing in carting or barn hunts!

Sporting dogs were originally bred for hunting and tracking, and retriever field trials test dogs' ability to excel in the field.

PART V

CANINE
HEALTH
CARE

CHAPTER 15

KEEPING YOUR PUPPY HEALTHY

A healthy puppy is a happy companion, and keeping him happy and healthy requires daily feeding, regular grooming, and quality veterinary care. Your puppy is counting on you to take care of him—especially when he is sick—which means you must pay close attention to him every day and be wary of any hint of illness. A number of serious illnesses can hamper your puppy's well-being, and some breeds are more prone to certain illnesses and conditions than others, though nearly all purebred dogs have some predisposition to disease.

Do you know what a healthy puppy's eyes, ears, and nose should look like? What about his stools—are they normal looking? The more time you spend interacting with your puppy, the more likely you will recognize what is normal. Most owners can recognize the obvious signs of sickness, including vomiting, diarrhea, coughing, nasal discharge, and runny eyes. These are excellent visual indicators that something is wrong. Familiarizing yourself with the more subtle symptoms is equally important. By recognizing these symptoms early on, you help ensure that your puppy grows into a healthy, happy adult dog.

Obviously, dogs can't talk, so veterinarians use the term *clinical signs* as opposed to *symptoms* because it indicates that what is being reported is based on observation, usually by the owner. For the sake of clarity and simplicity, *clinical signs* and *symptoms* are used interchangeably here.

Signs of Wellness
Ears, Eyes, Nose, and Mouth

Your puppy's eyes should be clear and bright, with no watery or mucous discharge. A healthy dog will occasionally have a small amount of discharge that gathers in the corners of the eyes, which requires periodic cleaning with a clean cloth and warm water. Always question any redness, swelling, squinting, excessive blinking, or closing of the eyelids, which could indicate an injury, a foreign body, viral or bacterial infections, allergies, hereditary conditions, or tumors.

The same goes for your puppy's ears. A healthy ear should have a clean, healthy smell. Honey-colored wax in the ear is normal, but a crusty, dark substance may indicate ear mites or another problem. Other red flags include ears that have discharge, smell bad, or are red, inflamed, or dark in color. If the puppy is showing signs of discomfort, such as depression or irritability, scratching or rubbing his ears or head, or shaking or tilting his head to one side, it also indicates a problem.

A puppy's nose should be neither hot nor cold to the touch. Nasal discharge that is any color other than clear could indicate problems caused by allergies, fungal infection, or even cancer.

Puppies should have firm, pink gums and healthy, white (and sharp!) baby teeth. Gums and teeth should be free of bleeding with no visible inflammation or decay. Pale or blue gums are symptomatic of serious health issues, which can include anemia, shock, or lack of oxygen. Bad breath (halitosis) also usually indicates a problem.

Coat and Skin

Your puppy's coat and skin should look, smell, and feel healthy to the touch. His coat should be free of dandruff and neither dry nor broken. His skin should be healthy and pink with no rashes, hot spots, lice, or fleas. Persistent scratching or licking almost always indicates a problem.

Alertness and Movement

Puppies differ in their activity levels. A healthy puppy should be able to move freely and unencumbered. Normal canine gait (movement) requires that the bones, joints, muscles, and ligaments work together harmoniously. Lameness may indicate something minor, such as a sticker stuck in a paw or a broken toenail; or possibly something more serious, including a structural issue or injury.

Signs of Illnesses and Emergencies

If you suspect that your puppy is feeling a bit under the weather, it's always best to err on the side of caution. Many illnesses, such as gastrointestinal disease and cancer, have multiple symptoms that can vary from mild to life-threatening. Always consult your veterinarian if you are concerned about your puppy.

A clean, shiny coat is an excellent indicator of the dog's overall health.

Bleeding

Bleeding from your puppy's nose or mouth and blood in the urine, stool, or vomit suggest a serious health issue. A puppy exhibiting any of these signs should be taken to the veterinarian immediately. Prolonged bleeding from a cut or puncture wound may be indicative of a damaged artery or vein. Bandaging can be dangerous if not done correctly. Seek immediate veterinary attention.

Breathing Problems

Anything that indicates abnormal breathing, including shallow, rapid, noisy, or breathy breathing; open-mouth breathing while resting; gagging; or pale or bluish-colored gums or tongue, should be checked by your veterinarian. Any number of medical issues can cause difficulty breathing; these include obstructions, ruptures, swelling, pneumonia, bleeding, or heartworms, to name a few. Many brachycephalic breeds have noisy or impaired breathing, which may be reasonably normal, considering their compromised airways.

Changes in Appetite

Be observant of your puppy's eating habits. An increase or decrease in his appetite may be worth consulting your veterinarian. If your puppy is not feeling well, it stands to reason that he may not feel like eating much. If your normally ravenous puppy goes off his food temporarily, it may be something minor. If his lack of appetite persists or is out of character for your puppy, it may indicate a broken tooth or something more serious. If accompanied by lethargy, vomiting, diarrhea, weight loss, or other signs of illness, consult your veterinarian immediately.

An increase in appetite may be a normal response to an increased need for nutrients. Exercise, cold temperatures, and pregnancy are examples of normal situations that require increased food and nutrition. Some medications—especially corticosteroids—can increase a puppy's appetite or thirst. Unless you monitor your puppy's food intake daily with scheduled feedings, as opposed to free feedings, you may not notice an increase or decrease in appetite.

A lack of enthusiasm at the breakfast buffet is a sure sign that your puppy isn't feeling well.

Changes in Water Consumption

Like food intake, water consumption varies with environmental temperature, exercise, and diet. Hot weather and vigorous exercise increase a puppy's water requirements. If you notice that your puppy is drinking more or less water than normal and/or urinating more or less than usual, it could be voluntary or involuntary. Voluntary decreases in water are often associated with other signs of disease, such as lethargy, vomiting, diarrhea, and fever, and may be indicative of diabetes or kidney issues. Involuntary decreases in water usually stem from cold weather that freezes a water bowl, making fresh water inaccessible; or from the owner's failure to replenish the dog's water bowl. Dogs that don't drink enough water run the risk of dehydration, which is a serious problem.

Changes in Urination

Urination is a complex process, with urine carrying waste products out of a dog's body and keeping his internal environment balanced. Male and female urination patterns differ, with a lot of factors working together to form urination habits. Puppies urinate more frequently than adult dogs because they lack bladder control until about six to eight months of age. Like water consumption, changes in urination can be voluntary or involuntary. If your puppy is urinating more frequently or passing more urine when he does his business, if he appears to be experiencing pain or straining, or if you notice a change of color or blood in his urine, you should have him checked by a veterinarian right away. Any number of medical issues, including infections, obstructions, urinary stones, ingestion of toxins, and cancer, can cause changes in urination.

Choking

Puppies that are choking can be extremely anxious and may even attempt to bite. If your puppy is choking on food or a foreign object, you can try to remove it by performing a mini-Heimlich maneuver—similar to the human procedure. Press quickly around the chest to force an object out of the upper throat area. If his gums and tongue are pale or blue, he is not getting enough air and requires immediate veterinary attention. Don't delay.

Constipation

If your puppy is straining to defecate, or if he has not passed feces for several days, contact your veterinarian. It could simply be constipation, which is often confused with more serious issues, such as inflammatory bowel disease (IBD), also known as chronic colitis. Gastroenteritis or impacted or infected anal sacs could also be culprits. Constipation can result from a number of reasons, including overly long confinement while traveling or a diet lacking in fiber and water.

Don't let Jaws Jr. chew on everything he finds in the yard. Choking on a foreign object can occur in a matter of seconds.

Tumors or trauma can also be a contributing factor. Intestinal blockage caused by bones, corncobs, rocks, fruit stones, food wrappers, wood chips, bottle caps, or countless other foreign objects is a common cause of constipation.

An intestinal blockage can be life-threatening. If you suspect that your puppy has swallowed a foreign object, seek veterinary attention right away. Diagnosis is usually made with an X-ray of the gastrointestinal (GI) tract. Absent GI blockage, and if no other symptoms are present, medication may be all your puppy needs to start feeling better. Always consult your veterinarian before giving over-the-counter medications to your puppy.

Coughing

Have you ever heard your puppy cough? Coughing can sound either harsh and dry or moist and wet. Depending on the quality of the cough, it can be indicative of infection, obstruction, allergies, structural abnormalities, parasites, pneumonia, trauma, blood-clotting disorder, heart or lung issues, or various other medical issues.

Diarrhea

Diarrhea can indicate a disease or illness, such as infection, defective transport of nutrients, or internal parasites—especially if it persists longer than twenty-four hours. It could be a result of overeating, eating spoiled or rotten food, a change of diet, stress, or too much excitement. If your puppy has additional symptoms—vomiting, lethargy, loss of appetite, weight loss, or blood in the stool—it warrants an immediate trip to the veterinarian. If possible, take a stool sample with you.

Dizziness or Lack of Balance

Puppies stumble and fall all the time while playing, as if their uncoordinated bodies can't keep up with their brains. Dizziness or lack of balance is a separate issue and should not be ignored because it can indicate multiple health issues, including infection, dehydration, or toxin ingestion, to name a few.

Lethargy

If your happy, active puppy isn't his normal self and is acting unusually drowsy or dull, it is worth taking a closer look. Lethargy or restlessness is an important sign that your puppy is not well and could indicate any number of diseases or illnesses, including parvovirus or bloat. Always err on the side of caution and consult your veterinarian.

Limping or Stiffness

A normal gait requires a puppy's muscles, ligaments, bones, and joints to move together harmoniously for maximum efficiency. Limping, stiffness, or general problems with a puppy's gait could indicate a bone or joint problem. It, of course, could be something very insignificant, such as a splinter in a pad or untrimmed nails. Symptoms vary from subtle pain or tenderness to an inability to place any weight on a limb. Be sure to let your veterinarian know.

Pawing at the Mouth

Pawing at the mouth may mean that something is stuck or embedded in the puppy's mouth, in the gums, or in or under the tongue, or that he is choking. Check inside your puppy's mouth immediately; he could have a stick wedged behind his jaws or have something clumped inside his cheek. Your puppy may rub his face on the floor, drool, gag, lick his mouth repeatedly, or hold his mouth open. A condition left untreated can result in an abscess, with the principal signs being lethargy, bad breath, and refusal to eat.

Scratching or Itching

Excessive scratching or itching, hot spots, rashes, or patches of missing fur indicate an underlying skin issue. Among the wide range of possibilities are flea allergy dermatitis, parasites, fungal infections, allergies, and poor diet. Hormonal issues such as hypothyroidism and Cushing's disease can also contribute to skin problems. A puppy suffering from skin issues is no doubt miserable, so take him to your veterinarian right away.

This sluggish little slugger is not his usual wild "Jack" self.

Titer Instead of Vaccination?

A titer test is a simple blood test that measures the amount of antibodies that develop after a puppy (or adult dog) is vaccinated or after exposure to an infectious disease. It indicates whether a puppy has enough protection—or effective immunity—against a disease, such as parvovirus, distemper, or hepatitis. (A blood titer for rabies is available, but currently no state will accept a titer in lieu of a rabies vaccination.) Blood titer results allow a veterinarian to determine if a booster vaccination is necessary. Many owners go this route to avoid the side effects that can be associated with vaccinating or overvaccinating their dogs. While there appears to be no downside, not all veterinarians support titering in lieu of booster vaccinations, believing it is not a valid method of determining a dog's immunity to infectious diseases. And, of course, there is the cost of a titer test, which is considerably more expensive than that of a vaccine. As with all things pertaining to your dog, consult your veterinarian and do your due diligence.

Shaking or Trembling

Puppies shake and tremble when they are excited—such as when they see their owners! Otherwise, shaking and trembling can indicate shock and/or the puppy's fight or flight instinct. It also may indicate any number of issues, including injury, pain, nausea, poisoning, or kidney disease. Seek veterinary attention right away.

Swelling

Swelling of the muzzle area often results from an insect bite or bee sting. Veterinary attention depends on the severity of swelling and whether or not there are accompanying symptoms, such as vomiting, diarrhea, drooling, or collapsing. When in doubt, always seek veterinary attention.

Temperature

The normal rectal temperature of a dog is 101°F to 102.5°F or 38.3° and 39°C. An increase in temperature can be caused by excessive exercise or excitement as well as a rise in the environmental temperature (e.g., a heat wave, the dog's being confined to an enclosed car, or the dog's being left outside in the yard with no shade). An elevated temperature can be indicative of a problem, which includes infection, abscess, internal parasites, or other health issues.

Vomiting

Dogs vomit for all sorts of reasons and, unlike humans, they occasionally do so with little discomfort. Dogs vomit when they get excited, drink too much water too fast (especially after exercise), gulp their food, go for car rides, or eat grass.

If your puppy appears to be healthy, a single vomiting episode should not send you running to the vet. It may be nothing more than a mild stomach irritation. Persistent vomiting can mean a severe problem, especially when it is seen in combination with other symptoms, such as lethargy, pain, fever, diarrhea, stomach bloating, listlessness, labored breathing, or blood or bile in the vomit. Causes can include an intestinal blockage, ingestion of toxic substances, or an infection, to name a few. Persistent vomiting indicates that something is wrong and also can lead to loss of water and important electrolytes. Contact your veterinarian right away and bring a sample of the vomit with you.

Vaccinations

Most experts agree that vaccinations are an important part of preventive care and essential when it comes to keeping your puppy healthy. The majority of veterinarians supports puppy vaccinations and the need to vaccinate all dogs against rabies. However, the rules for vaccinating dogs have changed in recent years, and many experts feel that puppies are vaccinated too early and too often, and with too many vaccines at once. What does this mean to you and your puppy?

While many veterinarians still recommend annual boosters to protect against the most common canine diseases, an estimated 40 to 50 percent of US veterinarians now recommend a three-year booster schedule, recognizing that overvaccination may jeopardize a dog's health. The judicious use of vaccines, they say, is paramount. Others advocate rotating yearly vaccines using a single-component vaccine for each disease—a vaccine, for example, that contains only parvovirus rather than a combination vaccine for parvovirus, distemper, and hepatitis.

Vaccinations were once a straightforward topic, but not so much today.

There is no question that some vaccinations are an absolute necessity. Veterinarians are slowly coming to terms with the risks and side effects associated with vaccines, but the controversy surrounding them is not likely to fade anytime soon. The long-term health risks associated with vaccinations have yet to be clearly defined, and many question the necessity of vaccinating for Lyme disease, *Giardia*, or even rattlesnake bites. Proper vaccination protocol includes vaccinating only healthy dogs, vaccinating at the appropriate ages, and following an appropriate vaccination schedule. Your puppy's lifestyle, where you live, and how much traveling you plan to do will factor into your puppy's vaccination plan. Therefore, it is important to discuss with your veterinarian a program to help your puppy grow into a happy, healthy adult dog.

How Vaccines Work

Vaccines are designed to trigger a protective immune response and prepare a dog to fight future infections from highly contagious and deadly disease-causing agents. Think of your puppy's immune system as a border patrol that guards his body against foreign invaders. When your puppy is vaccinated or exposed to something foreign, or *nonself*, such as bacteria or viruses, his immune system reacts by producing antibodies or sensitized lymphocytes (a type of white blood cell) that seek out and destroy the intruders. This is called *active* immunity. These fighting cells not only destroy the organism but also remember what it looked like so they can fend it off in the future, preventing or minimizing illness if a puppy is exposed to the same organism again. In other words, this *immunological memory* enables vaccines to protect a puppy against future disease long after the original infection.

When puppies nurse, they receive immunity from their mother through colostrum (first milk), which is rich in antibodies and provides *passive* immunity. These maternally derived antibodies (MDAs) provide adequate protection for six to sixteen weeks. The exact age at which these MDAs disappear will vary greatly from one puppy to another. The same MDAs that help protect your puppy also can interfere or block the ability of vaccines to do their job because

Most vets agree that all dogs must be initially vaccinated against the four core diseases.

MDAs do not distinguish between the real virus and the vaccine virus. In other words, the vaccine is inactivated or neutralized by the presence of MDAs.

To overcome this problem, vaccines are generally administered as a series of inoculations. The AAHA (2011) guidelines recommend that puppies receive their vaccinations every three to four weeks between the ages of six and sixteen weeks, depending on the vaccine that is being used and the disease being vaccinated against. Because experts assume that most puppies nurse from previously immunized females, and therefore consume significant quantities of MDAs within the first three days of life, many strongly recommend that all puppies receive the last dose in the initial series of core vaccines at fourteen to sixteen weeks of age, more specifically between fifteen and sixteen weeks of age, as many puppies maintain interfering levels of antibodies until fourteen weeks of age.

By giving a series of vaccinations, the period during which puppies are most susceptible to natural infection is minimized. The goal is to minimize the puppy's susceptibility to disease by immunizing as close as possible to the time that MDA levels are low enough to not interfere with the vaccine. For example, if a puppy loses his MDA protection at eight weeks of age and is not vaccinated until sixteen weeks of age, he will be unprotected for eight weeks. If, on the other hand, a puppy loses his MDA protection at seven weeks of age and receives his first vaccination at eight weeks of age, the period of relative susceptibility is much shorter.

Core Vaccines

Due to the multitude of vaccines available and the recognition that not all dogs need all vaccines, the AAHA vaccination guidelines center on core and noncore vaccines. Core vaccines are considered essential for every dog because they help to prevent against high-risk, highly contagious, and potentially fatal diseases. Veterinarians differ in their vaccination protocol, but most inoculate against the four most common diseases: distemper, hepatitis, parvovirus, and rabies.

Dogs that are boarded or attend doggy daycare will need to be vaccinated for kennel cough in addition to receiving the core vaccines.

Parvovirus is a highly contagious and often lethal gastrointestinal disease. To keep your puppy safe, experts recommend the following:

- Vaccinate your puppy. Puppies have immunity from their mother early in life but should receive their first vaccination between six and eight weeks of age and then two boosters at three-week intervals. Many experts recommend administering the final vaccination at sixteen weeks of age to avoid maternal antibody interference.
- Avoid taking your puppy to high-risk areas, such as dog parks, pet stores, doggy-daycare centers, boarding kennels, and other areas frequented by dogs until the puppy has received his complete set of vaccinations.

If you suspect your dog has been exposed to parvovirus or if he shows symptoms (vomiting or diarrhea), seek veterinary attention immediately. Time is of the essence.

Distemper: Highly contagious and potentially fatal, distemper is similar to the human measles virus. Puppies less than six months of age are most susceptible. Spread through the air or direct contact with an infected animal's urine, feces, or saliva, distemper affects many organs, including the skin, the respiratory system, and the nervous system. Symptoms usually include nasal and eye discharge, coughing, diarrhea, and vomiting.

Hepatitis: Canine hepatitis typically affects the liver, tonsils, and larynx but can also attack other organs. Spread primarily through infected fluids, including saliva, nasal discharge, and urine, symptoms include a sore throat, coughing, and occasionally pneumonia. It spreads rapidly to other organs and develops quickly; dogs can die within hours of exhibiting symptoms. Unvaccinated dogs of all ages are at risk, but it is most prevalent in puppies less than one year old.

Parvovirus: A highly contagious and life-threatening gastrointestinal disease, canine parvovirus (CPV) has been documented since the late 1960s, and particles are literally everywhere, in every environment. Sterile environments can be quickly reinfected because the virus is shed in large amounts in the stools of infected dogs for several weeks following infection and can be carried on a dog's feet and hair, as well as on shoes, clothing, tires, pet crates, and other animals. CPV is extremely hardy, and viral particles are capable of surviving for months in the environment—even through winter.

CPV normally affects puppies, but unvaccinated dogs of all ages are susceptible. The typical incubation period is three to seven days between initial infection and onset of symptoms, which include diarrhea (oftentimes bloody or odorous), vomiting, and dehydration. Lethargy, depression, and loss or lack of appetite, followed by a sudden onset of high fever, may also occur.

Diagnosis is confirmed with an enzyme-linked immunosorbent assay (ELISA) with results normally available within fifteen minutes. The gold standard for treatment consists of intensive veterinary management, including intravenous fluids to control dehydration and antibiotics for infection, which almost always require a costly hospital stay. Oftentimes, the cost is prohibitive for many owners who do not have veterinary insurance.

Rabies: A highly infectious viral disease that affects the brain, rabies is almost invariably fatal once symptoms begin to appear. All warm-blooded animals—including humans—are at risk, with rabies still being prevalent in many parts of the world. Transmission of the virus is almost always from a bite from a rabid animal, such as a bat, raccoon, or skunk. The virus is relatively slow moving, with the average incubation time from exposure to brain involvement (in dogs) being between two weeks to six months. Behavior changes are frequently the first symptom, and infected dogs have trouble swallowing and will drool or salivate. Advanced symptoms include paralysis and convulsions. Although the disease is incurable, properly vaccinated animals are at a relatively low risk of contracting the disease. Vaccination protocol varies from state to state. Always err on the side of caution and seek veterinary assistance immediately if you suspect a wild animal or an infected dog has bitten your puppy.

Noncore Vaccines

Noncore vaccines are sometimes referred to as "lifestyle" vaccines and are recommended based on geographical location, likelihood of infection, and a dog's individual risk factor. For example, does your puppy go to doggy daycare or dog shows? Does the geographic area where you live or travel with your dog have increasing outbreaks or incidences of a particular infectious disease?

Kennel Cough: Also known as canine infectious tracheobronchitis, kennel cough is highly contagious and normally characterized by a harsh, dry coughing or hacking, which may be followed by retching and gagging. Caused by the bacterium *Bordetella bronchiseptica,* the disease is airborne and can spread rapidly among dogs that live together. Four to six days is the normal incubation period. Dogs at shows, boarding kennels, grooming shops, veterinary clinics, and dog parks are at an increased risk to exposure. The disease is rarely dangerous to healthy dogs, and most puppies will recover in a week or two, while others may develop secondary bacterial infections, bronchopneumonia, or chronic bronchitis, with symptoms lasting for many weeks. Diagnosis is made based on a case history

Only permit your pup to play with dogs whose vaccination history you know.

(e.g., recent kenneling or exposure to infected dogs) and the unmistakable honking or harsh cough. Treatment often is limited to letting the cough run its course. Some veterinarians may prescribe antibiotics for secondary bacterial infections, cough suppressants, or fluid therapy to maintain normal hydration if necessary.

Leptospirosis: Transmitted primarily through the urine of infected animals, spiral-shaped bacteria known as leptospires can get into water or soil and survive for weeks to months. Warm, stagnant, or slow-moving water is a haven for leptospires.

Contaminated urine can infect dogs and humans as well as vegetation, food, soil, water, and even bedding. Most infections occur when a dog or human goes swimming in or drinks water harboring these bacteria. The leptospires enter the body through mucous membranes or abraded skin, where they enter the bloodstream and multiply rapidly. After reproducing in the bloodstream, the bacteria invade their target organs, including the kidney and liver.

Symptoms vary from dog to dog and can include fever, joint or muscle pain, vomiting, abdominal pain, diarrhea, loss of appetite, nasal or eye discharge, jaundice, weakness, and lethargy. Some dogs are asymptomatic but can be severely ill and die spontaneously. Diagnosis is based on clinical observations as well as on laboratory testing of blood and urine. Treatment generally consists of antibiotics to control the bacterial infection.

Lyme Disease: Depending on where you live, your veterinarian may choose to vaccinate against Lyme disease—a bacterial infection caused by corkscrew-shaped bacterium identified as *Borrelia burgdorferi*. Lyme disease is transmitted to humans and dogs through the bite of

Follow your vet's advice on noncore vaccines.

an infected deer tick. Illness may not show up for months after initial exposure to an infected tick, and the severity of the disease may vary depending on the dog's age and immune status.

Fever, shifting-leg lameness, swelling in the joints, and lethargy are the most common symptoms. Lameness occurs an average of two to five months after tick exposure. Symptoms are often reoccurring, which makes the disease difficult to cure. Occasionally, Lyme disease develops into a chronic state, becoming a "waxing and waning" illness in which the symptoms come and go.

Diagnosis includes history of exposure to ticks in an endemic area, typical clinical signs (lameness with or without fever), a positive antibody test, and a prompt response to antibiotic therapy. The enzyme-linked immunosorbent assay (ELISA) is useful for diagnosis if the dog has not yet been vaccinated against Lyme disease. Prognosis is good, with most dogs responding well to antibiotic treatment and complete recovery expected in the majority of cases.

Parainfluenza: This virus is one of several viruses attributed to kennel cough in dogs. It is easily spread when a dog coughs, which is one of the primary symptoms. A highly contagious respiratory infection that emerged in the United States in 2003, parainfluenza is closely related to the virus that causes equine influenza, which is thought to have mutated to produce the canine virus. Easily spread by airborne respiratory secretions (e.g., a dog coughing or sneezing), the virus is commonly mistaken for kennel cough because the symptoms are similar. Any situation that brings dogs together increases the risk of infection; however, high dog populations at places such as doggy daycares, boarding kennels, and pet stores are most problematic.

Symptoms include dry or hacking cough, fever, difficulty breathing, runny nose, sneezing, runny eyes, eye inflammation or conjunctivitis, loss of appetite, and lethargy. Symptoms may persist for ten to thirty days or even longer, despite antibiotics and cough suppressants. Some dogs progress to a more severe form of the illness that is complicated by pneumonia. Approximately 20 to 25 percent of infected dogs are asymptomatic but can still shed the virus. Treatment generally consists of antibiotics, cough suppressants, and supportive treatment, including hydration.

Additional Options

The AAHA classifies some vaccines as "not recommended," but your veterinarian may choose to vaccinate your puppy based on specific circumstances.

Coronavirus: Spread through the stool of infected dogs, coronavirus is a highly contagious intestinal infection. Symptoms include vomiting, loss of appetite, and acute diarrhea, which may lead to dehydration, further endangering puppies. Puppies less than twelve weeks of age are at the greatest risk. Laboratory tests are necessary to differentiate coronavirus from the deadly canine parvovirus.

Crotalus Atrox (Rattlesnake) Venom: The efficacy and experimental challenge data in dogs for this vaccine is not yet available. However, for owners living in high-risk areas, where rattlesnakes are common, this vaccine may buy

The tall tales of puppyhood: "That snake was 90 feet long, and, yes, I killed it to keep you two cool cats safe."

your dog the time he needs until emergency veterinary help is reached. It is intended to protect dogs against the venom associated with the bite of the western diamondback rattlesnake but may have some cross-protection against other rattlesnakes.

The vaccine works by stimulating a dog's immune system to develop neutralizing antibody titers, and it helps lessen the dog's potential reaction to a snake bite. For the vaccine to be effective, a dog must be inoculated at least thirty days prior to a bite. The vaccine does not prevent all reactions and does not negate the need for emergency veterinary treatment should a dog be bitten.

External Parasites

Parasites are not exactly dinner-table conversation—except among a few diehard dog enthusiasts—but it is a conversation you need to have with your veterinarian. Keeping your pet healthy is much easier if you understand and recognize the most common parasites before they lead to major health issues.

Parasites are divided into two broad categories: internal parasites and external parasites. Internal parasites, such as worms, live inside the host (i.e., your puppy), primarily in the gastrointestinal tract, liver, and lungs. External parasites, such as fleas and ticks, are found on or within the host's skin.

Fleas: Few things spoil summer fun like fleas. These tiny, nearly invisible creatures have been pestering animals and humans since the beginning of time, or pretty close to it. One bite from these wingless bloodsuckers can cause itching for days, and there is never just *one* flea. If you spot one, it's a safe bet that you will find plenty more living in your carpet, furniture, and bedding in addition to on your four-legged pal. Worse yet, some dogs are sensitive to fleas and can have an allergic reaction known as flea-allergy dermatitis (FAD), one of the most common skin diseases seen in small-animal practices. One flea bite can make a dog's life miserable, plunging him into a vicious cycle of biting, scratching, and licking.

Fleas can spread diseases to both dogs and humans. The most common risk is tapeworm infestation, which can be

A scourge of mosquitoes can collect in stagnant puddles. Sweep them away before your puppy decides to take a dip.

transmitted when a dog swallows a flea, which often happens inadvertently during grooming. Extreme flea infestations can cause anemia, especially in puppies.

In North America, the aggressive and tenacious *Ctenocephalides felis*, also known as the domestic cat flea, is the most common. Fleas are active year-round in many regions of the United States. Optimal temperatures for fleas to thrive range from 65°F to 85°F (18°C to 29°C) with 75- to 85-percent humidity being ideal. The cat flea is susceptible to cold, which means it can't survive for more than a few days when exposed to temperatures below 37°F (3°C). So instead of cursing at freezing temperatures, think of all the fleas that are dying!

Fleas feeding on your dog inject their saliva, which contains different antigens and histaminelike substances, resulting in irritation that causes the dog mild to downright nasty itching. Dogs with flea allergies usually itch over their entire bodies, experience generalized hair loss, and develop red, inflamed skin and hot spots.

Today, flea-control products—ranging from once-a-month topical treatments to chewable tablets—are readily available with varying safety and efficacy, making eradicating fleas a lot easier than it was a decade or two ago. Additionally, a number of shampoos, sprays, dips, and powders are available. Many of these products may be toxic and irritate your puppy's skin or cause health problems. Be sure to consult your veterinarian before using flea-control products.

Flea products alone won't do the job because 95 percent of flea control involves rigorous treatment of the dog's living environment. That means a regular and consistent flea-control regimen both indoors and outdoors. Flea-control and treatment recommendations vary with individual situations and can be multifaceted. The route you take will depend on the severity of the infestation, number of dogs in the environment, and your compliance with the regimen, and your finances. A good starting point includes the following:

- Treat all pets in the household that can serve as hosts, including dogs, cats, and ferrets.
- Clean anything and everything that your puppy has come in contact with. Wash his dog beds and blankets weekly— and your own bed linens if he sleeps with you. (Some say that adding apple cider vinegar to the rinse cycle discourages new fleas.)

Wild birds, including swans, ducks, and geese, can be vectors of disease. Keep your puppy away from wildlife in the park for his own safety.

- Mop floors and vacuum all carpets, rugs, and furniture. Don't forget to vacuum your car, too. Immediately dispose of vacuum bags because eggs can hatch in them.

Any effective flea-control program includes treating your pets and their environment. Remove dense vegetation near your home, yard, or kennel area because these spaces offer damp microenvironments that are favorable to flea development.

For immediate short-term relief, but not always a long-term solution, consider these tips:

- Bathe your dog with hypoallergenic or colloidal oatmeal shampoos to help remove allergens. Shampoos containing neem, peppermint, spearmint, clove, cedar, or eucalyptus oil may help combat fleas.
- Topical anti-itch creams, shampoos, or oils containing lavender may help to soothe your pet's skin.
- Fatty acid supplements such as omega-3 and omega-6, which are found in fish oil, for example, are helpful in reducing the amount and effects of histamine.
- Organic coconut oil given orally with a dog's food can help with hot spots and skin irritations.
- Tea tree oil applied to the skin is excellent for irritations, such as rashes and hot spots.
- Despite your best efforts, in some cases, your veterinarian may need to prescribe corticosteroids to reduce itching.

Ticks: Classified as arachnids (not insects), ticks burrow their heads into their hosts' skin and engorge themselves with blood, expanding to many times their size. They can secrete a paralysis-causing toxin and can spread serious diseases, including Lyme disease, Rocky Mountain spotted fever, Texas fever, and canine ehrlichiosis. Ticks can also be infected with and transmit more than one disease. In severe infestations, severe blood loss, anemia (low red-blood-cell count), and even death may occur.

Longhaired dogs, such as this plushly coated Pomeranian, can be a challenge to keep flea-free.

Approximately 850 species of ticks exist, with the brown dog tick (*Rhipicephalus sanguineus*) and the American dog tick (*Dermacentor variabilis*) commonly feeding on dogs. Dogs pick up ticks often while walking or playing in wooded or grassy areas, in overgrown fields, and near low, overhanging branches or shrubs. Ticks commonly embed themselves between the toes and around the head, neck, or ears, but they can be also found elsewhere on the dog's body.

Preventing a tick infestation is more effective than eliminating one. The protocol is very similar to controlling fleas: it includes treating your house, your yard, your dog's blankets and beds, and your dog with products designed specifically to repel ticks. A number of over-the-counter products are available, such as sprays, foggers, powders, dips, shampoos, and collars. Again, these products may be toxic. Read all labels and follow directions carefully. When in doubt, always consult your veterinarian before purchasing and using tick-control products.

Unlike fleas, ticks are not susceptible to cold weather. Different species have evolved to survive under different conditions of humidity and temperature. You may need to treat your yard year-round. However, most tick infestations are seen in the spring and summer, when ticks are most abundant.

Ticks, especially the engorged ones, are pretty distinctive looking. Once you see one, you are not likely to forget what it looks like. If you find a tick on your puppy, remove it right away. Removing a tick is not terribly difficult—once you get past any queasiness about doing it! Use tweezers or a specially designed tick-removing tool to grab the tick as close as possible to where it enters your puppy's skin. Pull slowly, firmly, and steadily in an outward direction. Clean the bite wound with a disinfectant and apply an antibiotic ointment. Dispose of the tick by immersing it in rubbing alcohol. If you simply cannot bring yourself to remove the tick, take your puppy to the veterinarian. Ticks must be removed as soon as possible.

Internal Parasites

Internal parasites, or endoparasites, live inside your puppy's body (*endo* means "within"). Heartworms, hookworms, roundworms, tapeworms, and whipworms are the most common, and all are capable of wreaking havoc on your puppy's health and well-being. Most internal parasites live primarily in the gastrointestinal tract, causing GI-type symptoms. If a puppy's immune system is compromised by malnutrition, stress, or immunosuppressive drugs (e.g., corticosteroids), the potential for disease may be enhanced.

While deworming medications are available at pet stores and retail outlets, they differ drastically in their safety and efficacy in expelling worms from a dog's body. Always have your veterinarian diagnose the specific type of internal parasite and prescribe the proper deworming medication.

Heartworm: Transmitted by mosquitoes, heartworms are dangerous and deadly internal parasites. The larvae grow inside your healthy dog, migrating through his tissues into the bloodstream and eventually into the pulmonary arteries and the heart, where the adult worms do lethal harm. An infected dog can suffer from pulmonary hypertension (elevated blood pressure), an enlarged pulmonary artery, enlargement of the right side of the heart, and congestion in the liver. Pulmonary embolism (sudden blockage of a vessel) may also result.

Some dogs are asymptomatic, and oftentimes symptoms may not appear until the damage is extensive and the disease is well advanced. Clinical symptoms vary with the severity of the infection (number of heartworms present). When present, first symptoms generally include coughing, a decrease in appetite, weight loss, and listlessness, as well as fatigue after light exercise. Unlike fleas and ticks, you can't look at a dog and say that he has heartworms. A veterinarian must make a diagnosis through a heartworm antigen test. X-rays and ultrasounds of your dog's heart and lungs may be recommended to determine the severity of the infection and to develop a prognosis.

The best approach to heartworm is prevention. Preventive medications are readily available and recommended by most vets. You are also well advised to eliminate stagnant or slow-moving water from your property, including kiddie pools, bird baths, water barrels, puddles, and even standing water in rain gutters, all of which can be a haven for mosquitoes.

Hookworms: With their teethlike hooks, hookworms (*Ancylostoma*) attach to the lining of your puppy's small intestine, feeding on his oxygen-rich blood. Like other internal parasites, hookworms pass eggs in the dog's feces, where they hatch into larvae. Depending on the species, hookworms can enter the dog's body by oral ingestion or through skin penetration. Ingesting contaminated food or water, licking their contaminated feet, or ingesting an infected host are the primary ways that dogs become infected. Puppies often become infected through their mother.

Good sanitary practices will help prevent the spread of hookworms, which is why it is important to pick up dog droppings right away. When walking in public places, do not allow your dog to come in contact with other dogs' feces. Diarrhea, vomiting, and life-threatening anemia are a few of the serious health problems associated with this roughly half-inch-long parasite. Symptoms may also include pale gums, weakness, and black, tarry stools. Some puppies take on an unkempt or disheveled appearance. Some hookworms and/or eggs may be, but are not always, detected in the stool; their presence in the stool enables the veterinarian to make a primary diagnosis. Treatment involves deworming medication, with multiple treatments often being necessary. Some year-round heartworm/intestinal-parasite-prevention combination products kill hookworms and help prevent future infections.

Roundworms: The most common roundworms, *Toxocara canis,* live and feed in a dog's small intestine—feeding off partially digested intestinal contents—causing serious problems for dogs and huge headaches for owners. Roundworms absorb nutrients, interfere with digestion, and can damage the lining of your puppy's intestine. In severe infestations, dogs may be thin, have a pot-bellied appearance, and cry out from intestinal discomfort. A dry, dull, and rough-looking coat is also symptomatic of roundworm infestation.

Puppies can be born with roundworms when a pregnant mama dog passes them to her puppies via transplacental transmission (from mother to fetus across the placenta) or through transmammary transmission (in first milk while nursing). In any case, all puppies require deworming at an early age. Puppies or adult dogs also can become infected when they eat infected animals, such as rodents; ingest contaminated soil; come in contacted with infected feces; or snack from the cat's litterbox.

A definitive diagnosis is confirmed via a stool sample, which means that you will need to take a stool sample to the veterinarian's office. Treatment involves a dewormer. Roundworms are resistant to environmental conditions and most common disinfectants. They can adhere to your puppy's skin, hair, and paws, so good hygiene and strict sanitation practices are essential to minimize further contamination. Roundworms can live for months or even years in soil. Some year-round heartworm-preventive products also kill roundworms and help prevent future infestations.

Minimizing the risk of infection is key; it includes the prompt disposal of dog feces, especially in yards, gardens, and public parks. Don't allow your dog to do his business in areas frequented by children, such as sandboxes and playgrounds. And don't forget to wash your hands!

Tapeworms: *Dipylidium canium*—the most common tapeworm infecting dogs in the United States—is not normally life-threatening. However, tapeworms are a problem because they attach to the wall of a puppy's intestine and absorb nutrients, though not in the same volume as hookworms do. Tapeworms grow by creating new segments, which makes getting rid of them especially difficult—unless the head is successfully eliminated, a tapeworm can grow a new body.

Your job as your dog's owner is to keep him worm-free.

Mature tapeworm segments contain egg capsules that are ingested by the intermediate host (flea larvae or lice), which is then eaten by the dog. If the flea has consumed tapeworm eggs, the eggs will be released into your puppy's digestive system during the digestive process. Without an aggressive flea-control program, controlling tapeworms is nearly impossible because reinfection can occur within as little as three weeks after treatment.

While tapeworms generally do not cause any symptoms, they are often visible on a puppy's rear end, in his stool, or on his bedding. Severe infestations may cause diarrhea, vomiting, abdominal discomfort, and weight loss if left untreated. Diagnosis can be confirmed with a stool sample examined under a microscope in search of characteristic eggs. Treatment involves an appropriate dewormer and an aggressive indoor/outdoor flea-control program.

Whipworms: Named after the whiplike shape of the adult worm, whipworms (*Trichuriasis vulpis)*live primarily in the large intestine (colon), where they feed on blood and tissue fluids as they slash, puncture, and tunnel their way into the intestinal wall, using their mouthparts to lacerate blood vessels. Females lay eggs that can pass in the feces. An infected dog can easily contaminate the soil in his kennel run or fenced yard, where the worms remain in the ground for up to five years. Uninfected dogs that bury their bones, dig, or eat grass in infested areas can pick up eggs.

Mild infestations may not produce any obvious symptoms, but heavy infestations can produce acute or chronic inflammation of the intestinal wall, diarrhea, mucus and blood in the stools, and weight loss. Anemia is possible if hemorrhaging occurs. Diagnosis is confirmed via a stool sample and detection of characteristic eggs. However, diagnosis can be difficult because eggs are often shed only in small numbers at irregular intervals.

Because the eggs are resistant to the environment and can live in moist soil for long periods, whipworms can be difficult to treat and control. Reinfestation is common. Treatment is straightforward with deworming medications. Some heartworm-preventive medications also control whipworms. To help reduce or prevent contamination, owners must pick up fecal matter daily and clean kennel areas or dog runs thoroughly.

DENTAL PROBLEMS
Periodontal Disease

Bad breath, tartar accumulation, and red, swollen gums are classic symptoms of periodontal disease, which is the progressive loss or destruction of the tissues that hold the teeth in the jaws. It starts the same way in dogs as it does in humans: when the bacteria come in contact

Provide appropriately sized safe chew toys for your puppy.

with the gums, or gingiva, they provoke an inflammatory reaction known as gingivitis. Yellowish brown crust on a dog's teeth and red gums are signs that you need to visit a veterinarian. In the earliest stages, when only plaque and minimal tartar are present, gingivitis is reversible.

Treatment at this stage includes a thorough oral examination and professional dental cleaning, which means that your dog will need to be anesthetized. While he is asleep, the veterinarian can remove all of the tartar from the teeth, below the gum line, and between the

Growth Plates

Every bone in your puppy's body—from the top of his skull to the tip of his caudal appendage (tail)—have growth plates. These growth plates, or epiphyseal plates, are rich in immature, noncalcified cells that form a soft, spongy area of the young bone. These cells grow and add length to the bone, thereby determining the future length and shape of the mature skeleton. As a puppy grows, the long bones of the legs grow from areas of immature bone located near the ends.

When a dog has finished growing, the growth plates "close," meaning that they mineralize (become hard with calcium and other minerals) and no longer function as areas of growth, indicating the end of significant bone growth. The growth plates of different bones close at different times, which can depend on the breed and size of the dog. Until they have closed, the growth plates are the weakest parts of the bones and are therefore more easily fractured.

teeth. Left untreated, the bacteria can spread under the gum line, causing deep pockets between the teeth and gums. These pockets encourage more bacteria growth, causing infection in the deeper periodontal tissues—a condition known as periodontitis. In this stage of the disease, the tissues and bones that support the teeth erode, resulting in pain and eventual tooth loss. In advanced stages, bacteria can enter the bloodstream, causing secondary infections that can damage your dog's heart, liver, and kidneys.

Periodontitis is irreversible, but in some cases, treatment can slow the progression of the disease, prevent infection, and ease pain. Treatment for periodontitis generally includes a professional dental cleaning and, depending on the severity of the disease, may include tooth extraction or periodontal surgery to clean the root surfaces or remove excessive gum tissue.

Fractured Teeth

Like humans, dogs with fractured teeth can suffer a great deal of pain, especially if the broken tooth exposes the pulp, the soft inner portion of the tooth that contains blood vessels and nerve tissues. If a broken tooth goes untreated, it can create a superhighway for bacteria to lodge in the damaged tissue, causing inflammation and abscesses.

Eventually, the tooth dies and becomes a bacterial haven. As with periodontal disease, the blood vessels in the area pick up the bacteria, spreading it to and infecting other areas of the body, specifically the liver and kidneys. Dogs usually break their teeth chewing on hard bones, rocks, ice cubes, and, yes, chain-link fencing. Fighting or fence fighting are common causes of broken teeth (especially canines).

Treatment depends on the dog's age and the time that elapses between the fracture and treatment, as well as which parts of the tooth are broken and the break's severity. If only the

Exercise Guidelines

- To prevent possible lifelong injuries, avoid running or jogging with your puppy until his bones and joints are fully developed and his growth plates have closed.
- Avoid hot surfaces, including sidewalks and roadways. Your puppy's feet can be easily burned. If it's too hot for your bare feet, it's too hot for your puppy.
- Never wake your puppy up to play. You wouldn't do this to a toddler, so why do it to your puppy?
- Supervise play and exercise between your puppy and young children. Roughhousing is not productive exercise, and it teaches your puppy bad habits.
- Break up your puppy's exercise into multiple daily sessions. It's better to take the shorter route five times a day than the longer route once a day.

enamel is broken, treatment may be minor, such as smoothing the sharp edges to prevent irritation to the lips or tongue. More serious breaks may require removal, a root canal, or a crown—not unlike the dental procedures performed on people.

Obesity

Did you know that keeping your puppy at a proper and ideal weight throughout his life can increase his life span by two years? It's true! It is one of the easiest ways to keep your puppy healthy and cut down on expensive veterinary bills. Unfortunately, studies indicate that as humans become more obese, so too do our dogs. The Association for Pet Obesity Prevention estimates that nearly 53 percent of US dogs are overweight or obese—that means roughly 37 million dogs are at increased risk for obesity-related diseases, such as diabetes, increased blood pressure, and congestive heart failure.

Health Issues and Obesity

Fat works as an insulator, which is great if you're a hibernating bear. Otherwise, consider that overweight dogs:

- have difficulty breathing because extra fat restricts the expansion of their lungs
- are less capable of regulating their body temperatures and therefore are more susceptible to heatstroke
- have less stamina and endurance
- have increased surgical risks, decreased immune functions, and greater susceptibility to osteoarthritis as well as injuries to joints, bones, and ligaments
- are more susceptible to hypertension, digestive disorders, and certain cancers
- have mild but significant elevations in cholesterol, triglycerides, and phospholipids

Some medical conditions, such as hypothyroidism and Cushing's disease, can contribute to weight gain. So too can certain medications, such as prednisone and phenobarbital, which can affect a dog's metabolism and appetite. Yet those cases represent a very small portion of overweight dogs, perhaps less than 5 percent, according to experts.

The primary cause of canine obesity is a disparity in the "energy balance equation." Simply put, if your dog consumes more calories than he burns, he's going to pack on the pounds.

Is Your Dog Too Fat?

Dogs are considered overweight when their weight is 15 percent above ideal and are obese when their weight is 30 percent above ideal. For instance, a small dog whose ideal weight is 12 pounds would need to gain only 2 pounds to be considered overweight and 3.5 pounds to be in the obese category. Like humans, some dogs require very few surplus calories to result in extra weight.

Some owners think that if they can feel their dog's ribs, he is too thin. Not so! You want your dog to be fit and lean—not too skinny, but not too fat. To assess your dog's weight, run your fingers up and down along his rib cage. You should be able to feel his ribs without pressing in. Run your hand over his croup (rump). You should be able to feel his two pelvic bones with little effort.

Ideally, when looking at your dog from the side, his abdominal tuck—the underline of his body where his belly is drawn up toward his hind end—should be evident. When standing over your dog and viewing him from above, his waist—the section behind his ribs—should be well proportioned. If your dog is more sausagelike than fit and trim, he probably needs to shed a few pounds. (Yes, even Dachshunds—"wiener dogs"—have waists!) It is impossible to arbitrarily set a correct weight for a dog, which is why it is important to put your hands on your puppy and feel his neck, ribs, and hips. If you are uncertain about your dog's ideal weight, your veterinarian can help you determine it and develop a long-term plan to condition him so that he'll enjoy a longer, healthier, and more active life.

Whether a toy dog, a guard dog, or a working dog, every puppy is an individual. Don't push your puppy past his comfort zone.

CHAPTER 16

NATURAL DOG CARE

Natural health for dogs is perhaps one of the most fascinating—and most frequently misunderstood—subjects for dog owners. A wide variety of health-care techniques, ranging from acupuncture to chiropractic therapy to herbal medicine, is steadily gaining popularity as treatment for many canine ailments and behavior problems. As interest in alternative medicine for humans grows, many owners are looking outside the traditional approaches of veterinary care and exploring alternative treatments for their pets.

Before jumping in headfirst, it's important to first define *natural health care*. *Natural* doesn't necessarily mean "organic" or "healthy." As someone once said, "Snake venom is 'natural,' but that doesn't mean it's good for you." *Alternative medicine* and *natural health care* are broad terms used to describe anything other than conventional medical treatments and practices. The terms are a bit misleading because they suggest performing one treatment in lieu of another option, which is not the case. To counter any confusion, the more popular terms *complementary therapy* or *complementary and alternative veterinary medicine* (CAVM) are frequently used. *Integrative medicine* is a term used by practitioners who incorporate both conventional Western-style medicine with holistic practices.

While the topic of alternative and complementary medicine is too complex to cover thoroughly here, the following brief descriptions are intended to familiarize you with some of the more popular treatments.

Traditional veterinary medicine is rooted in physics, chemistry, and biology, and its practices are backed by scientific data. While alternative medicine has been around for thousands of years, the evidence for it comes mainly from anecdotes, personal observations, and testimonials of veterinarians and dog owners rather than from clinical trials. Therefore, it's not surprising that alternative medicine is controversial. As with anything pertaining to dogs, different opinions abound.

Opponents cite the lack of controlled scientific evidence and uncertain diagnostic and therapeutic standards as the primary opposition, while others dismiss the practice as quackery or hocus-pocus medicine. Are holistic veterinarians treading in scientifically unsound waters? Can superfine surgical needles inserted into body parts or remedies diluted to incredibly miniscule amounts really cure disease? Let's learn a little about acupuncture and homeopathy... and more.

Homeopathic Care

The terms *holistic* and *homeopathic* are often used interchangeably; however, they are quite different. A veterinarian who practices holistic medicine employs an array of therapies to treat the whole animal, both body and spirit. Homeopathy is one of those therapies.

Dr. Samuel Hahnemann (1755–1843), a German physician, is credited with formally conceiving the principles of homeopathy. However, the roots of this practice go back to ancient civilizations. Holistic medicine focuses on caring for the "whole animal" as opposed to treating the disease or symptoms alone. The underlying principle of holistic medicine is that symptoms are the result of the body's energy field's attempting to heal the underlying imbalances. Homeopathy addresses the whole body and helps the body to heal itself. One key belief of homeopathy is the "similars principle" or "like cures like," meaning that a substance that could produce symptoms in a healthy dog (or human) could cure an ill patient with the same symptoms. Hence, the prefix *homeo-* (similar) and the suffix *-pathy* (suffering), thus *homeopathic*.

Theoretically, the homeopathic principle is similar to that of inoculations. A vaccine, which purposefully contains live, weakened, or dead pathogens, stimulates a dog's immune system to produce disease-fighting antibodies against infectious disease. Homeopathic remedies, which are tiny amounts of substances, are theorized to stimulate recovery in a similar manner. They nudge the immune system toward *homeostasis*, an internal balance or equilibrium.

Consider, for instance, a dog with a health problem that produces a symptom of itching. Rather than simply continuing to treat the itching with pills (such as steroids), homeopathy's principle of similars states that the patient's itching can be cured by a remedy that, in its original form or in larger amounts, also produces itching.

Think of it this way: if you have ever encountered poison ivy, you know that it can cause nonstop itching as well as rashes and sores. Based on the principle of similars, the homeopathic remedy Rhus tox (aka *Rhus toxicodendron*), derived from poison ivy, could be used to control itching. Similarly, sulfur, in a large dose, can cause a rash, yet it has been used in remedies to treat seborrheic dermatitis and alopecia.

While the list of homeopathic ingredients is unbelievably long, a dozen or so of the most common are have many uses. For

Holistic medicine aims to treat the whole animal instead of focusing on specific symptoms or diseases.

example, *Arnica montana*, from the plant leopard's bane, is frequently used as an arthritis remedy but also soothes inflammations, cuts, and other symptoms associated with trauma or physical injury. *Thuja occidentalis* has long been recommended to counteract the undesirable effects of vaccines.

These remedies are severely diluted—down to miniscule concentrations—and therefore no longer cause the symptoms. Yet, despite the repeated dilutions, these microdoses of natural substances—herbs, plants, barks, seeds, berries, flowers, bacteria, minerals, and animal matter—retain their biological activity, or "vibrational energy," which promotes healing and rebalances the dog's body. The healing power of homeopathy doesn't come from the remedies themselves; instead, they stimulate the body to heal itself.

Flower Essences

One of the more popular homeopathic remedies available without a prescription is Bach Original Flower Essences®. They work in the same manner as homeopathic remedies do for physical ailments, but flower remedies are also for the emotions. They were first prepared in the 1930s by a British physician named Dr. Edward Bach. He isolated thirty-eight flower essences with apparent healing effects, which he believed would remedy negative states of mind. Like other homeopathic practitioners, Bach believed in mind-body medicine and that mental and emotional states of mind play an enormous role in illness and recovery from illness.

While it's easy to confuse flower essences with other herbal remedies, there are significant differences. Flower essences and herbal remedies share a history of being nature's purest ingredients. They also work with, rather than suppress, the healing process. But flower essences differ from other herbal remedies. Herbal products are made from many parts of a plant,

Certain flowers possess healing properties that can be used to relieve both physical and behavioral issues.

including the root, stem, leaves, fruit, seeds, and blossoms, and are made using a number of methods, including infusion, decoction, and tincture. Flower essences, however, begin with an infusion in water and use only the freshest blossoms of the plant. After a specific amount of infusion time, these flower essences become diluted and suitable for use as remedies.

Essential Oils

While the use of essential oils for canines may not be as commonplace as some of the other natural techniques, they have been used for the health and well-being of people for centuries. In fact, essential oils have been found in Egyptian tombs. As people become more aware of the healing benefits of essential oils for the body and mind, it's no wonder that owners and veterinarians are interested in using them for dogs' emotional, cognitive, and physical well-being, too.

Essential oils are found in the roots, stems, leaves, flowers, and seeds of plants. These naturally occurring oils are extracted by distillation. Unlike herbal and homeopathic remedies, which are used internally and externally, essential oils are usually used topically or in a diffuser. The quality of essential oils used is, well, *essential* to success. The oils are highly concentrated, and it takes a lot of plants to fill a 1-ounce bottle. Therefore, a five-dollar bottle from the corner market probably doesn't contain a high-quality grade of essential oil. Most problems arise from the use of poor-quality or synthetic-grade oils, or sometimes owner misuse. Always consult your veterinarian or work with an experienced holistic veterinarian for the best results.

Aromatherapy

Aromatherapy for dogs? It's true! Dogs are extremely scent driven, and everyone knows that their olfactory skills are far superior to ours. And aromatherapy is all about scent. While it's the practice of using essential oils distilled from various plants for their fragrances, who's to know if aromatherapy works the same for dogs as it does for people. Does lavender smell the same to dogs as it does to us? How do we know it's not offensive? It seems that dogs perceive scents differently than humans do. After all, they like rotting garbage and stinky horse manure. Do scents heal, calm, or invigorate dogs as they do some people? Anecdotal evidence suggests they do, but no scientific data exists (yet!).

Some theorize that aromatherapy, such as lavender, has a calming effect on owners, which, in turn, may indirectly calm their dogs. Even though the evidence is completely anecdotal and empirical, if controlling your aromatic environment makes you feel better, it's bound to improve the human-canine relationship.

Some veterinary clinics now use electric aromatic diffusers in their waiting and exam rooms to help provide calming and relaxing effects on their human and canine clients.

Consider that your puppy's nose is thousands of times as effective as your own. Now imagine what lavender smells like to a dog!

Herbal Remedies

Many owners have personal experience with herbal remedies, which is what started them thinking that herbal medicine could work for their dogs. As mentioned, herbal remedies differ from flower essences, but they remain an important part of alternative medicine. Herbal medicine focuses on using plants and other natural ingredients to enhance well-being. They emphasize therapies that are designed to optimize systems' functions and correct immune, digestive, and metabolic deficiencies. Traditional herbal remedies are based on standard formulas created thousands of years ago, which reportedly have antibiotic, antifungal, and even anticancer properties. Proponents believe that prescribing whole plants provides both synergistic and safety advantages.

Literally hundreds of plants are available for use in herbal remedies, and many, such as chamomile and echinacea, can be combined. How you use them—fresh, dried, in teas or tinctures—depends on the plant and your dog. You can grow herbs and plants in your garden or buy commercial products. Herbal remedies provide a wonderful opportunity for owners looking for alternatives to synthetic medications. They may even help you save a few dollars on veterinary visits.

Acupuncture

Acupuncture is part of the holistic system known as Traditional Chinese Medicine (TCM). The original technique, which is still practiced today, involves the insertion of very fine needles into acupuncture points that are just under the skin or in muscles that have a good nerve supply. Acupuncture points are found on meridians, or energetic pathways, which correspond with circulatory and nervous pathways. These meridians carry the body's vital life force or energy, referred to as *qi* or *chi*. Stimulating these acupuncture points corrects the flow of qi so that the body can rebalance and heal itself and maintain its internal stability (homeostasis).

The strategic placement of needles is believed to stimulate the release of pain-relieving chemicals in the brain and spinal cord, which produces more generalized analgesia. According to the ancient Chinese, pain is a blockage of qi energy, and the strategic insertion of needles corrects and rebalances this flow.

Acupuncture is used to treat dogs with skeletal disorders, such as arthritis and hip dysplasia, as well as allergies; gastrointestinal, respiratory, urinary, and musculoskeletal disorders; and chronic or severe pain. The length and frequency of treatment depend on the specific medical issue and condition of the dog.

Chiropractic Therapy

A holistic approach to the treatment of many health and locomotion problems of dogs, chiropractic manipulation involves the movement of the joints to correct alignment and to

Common Herbal Remedies

A few of the more common—and not so common—herbal remedies include:

- **Aloe vera,** which is used primarily to reduce inflammation and heal wounds. Who hasn't rubbed the natural gel from an aloe vera leaf on a burn or scrape?
- **Calendula,** whose petals applied as a paste help heal wounds, reduce inflammation, and promote the growth of healthy new tissue. As a tea, it can be used as a wound flush. Mixed with comfrey to form a balm, it can help soothe dry, sore, scaly skin.
- **Capsaicin,** the compound found in hot peppers and is responsible for their pungency. When applied as a balm, it may help reduce the inflammation and pain associated with osteoarthritis.
- **Chamomile,** one of the most common herbal remedies. It's wonderful for the digestive system and has a calming effect on irritable or whiny dogs. You've probably had chamomile tea to calm your own nerves.
- **Dandelion,** which stimulates digestion and is good for reducing inflammation.
- **Echinacea,** known for its ability to stimulate the immune system, which helps attack foreign invaders and fight infection. Plenty of people drink it as a tea to ward off colds and flu. In a tea, tincture, or capsule, it can be applied to a dog's wounds, such as a bite.
- **Milk thistle,** which helps to protect against liver damage. It is an important extract if your dog has been on medications or has ingested toxins that may affect the liver.
- **Peppermint,** which is soothing to the digestive tract and helps control nausea and vomiting.
- **Slippery elm,** which helps calm gastrointestinal issues, including colitis and diarrhea.

return the body to homeostasis. Chiropractic treatment is based on the principle that the body can heal itself when the skeletal system is correctly aligned. When the spine is even slightly displaced, nerves become irritated. Chiropractors feel for irregularities (subluxations) and adjust them, which restores correct vertebral alignment.

Some chiropractors adhere strictly to the established practice, believing that problems with the spine are a leading cause of disease. On the flip side, many chiropractors eagerly incorporate other therapies, including conventional medicine, nutritional supplements, herbal remedies, and so forth. If you are interested in exploring chiropractic with your dog, your veterinarian may be able to help you choose a chiropractor best suited to your dog's needs.

Massage and Tellington TTouch® Therapy

Touch is an essential component of the human-canine relationship. It helps establish a deeper rapport between you and your dog, and, as a bonus, it teaches him to accept being handled. You can massage your puppy at home by stroking him while you're watching television or reading.

Be sure to use calm, gentle strokes—you're not attempting a deep-tissue massage. Vigorous rubbing will only serve to stimulate and invigorate your puppy rather than relax him.

TTouch® is a popular touch therapy developed by Linda Tellington-Jones. Based on circular movements of the fingers and hands all over the body, the Tellington method's intent is to "activate the function of the cells and awaken cellular intelligence—a little like 'turning on the electrical lights of the body,'" according to www.ttouch.com. While it sounds complicated, it's relatively easy to learn, and it has been used to help with excessive chewing and barking as well as with jumping up and carsickness. It has been shown to reduce stress, fear, shyness, excitability, and nervousness and to help relax animals so they can learn more efficiently.

Certified practitioners can show you how to use TTouch therapy to help your puppy as well as to build a strong human-canine relationship. If you're looking for a more precise form of touch, consider visiting a canine massage therapist, who uses a hands-on approach to working directly with muscles—encouraging the cells of the muscles to move in specific directions. A knowledgeable and experienced massage therapist works to realign cells within a muscle, such as by removing a knot or charley horse, and lengthen cells to help with muscle memory.

A canine massage therapist pays close attention to how the muscles connect to the bone,

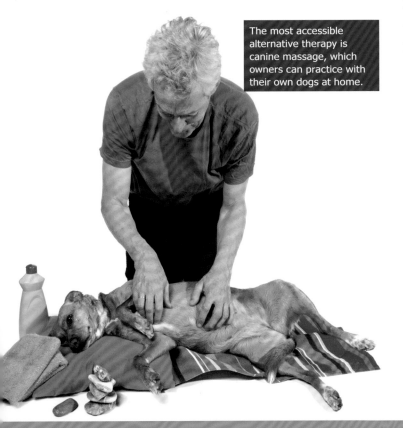

The most accessible alternative therapy is canine massage, which owners can practice with their own dogs at home.

how the ligaments and tendons connect, and how all of these parts work together to move efficiently. Muscle cells sometimes get confused, and something goes wrong. So after making a connection with your puppy, a massage therapist typically warms a muscle and its cells, shows the muscle where it belongs and how it should work, and encourages it to stay in position.

Certification for canine massage therapists varies from state to state, with some states requiring no training or testing. Before selecting a practitioner, ensure that he or she has received training specifically

Online Resources for Alternative Medicine

For additional information on alternative and complementary approaches to veterinary health care, visit these websites:

- American Veterinary Chiropractic Association (AVCA), www.animalchiropractic.org
- Academy of Veterinary Homeopathy (AVH), www.theavh.org
- American Academy of Veterinary Acupuncture (AAVA), www.aava.org
- American Holistic Veterinary Medical Association (AHVMA), www.ahvma.org
- International Association of Reiki Professionals (IARP), www.iarp.com.
- National College of Natural Medicine (NCNM), www.ncnm.edu

for working with dogs, as well as anatomy and physiology courses and hands-on training. Be certain that your dog is comfortable with the person and that the person knows how to handle him. As always, trust your dog's instincts.

Energy Therapy

Reiki (pronounced *ray-key*) is a "healing art" and one of the more recognized energy therapies becoming increasingly popular for dogs and other animals. As with most other energy therapies, the underlying principle is that all living things contain a life force that encompasses the physical and spiritual being. A reiki practitioner uses his or her life force—through either a light touch directly on the patient's body or by placing his or her hands above the patient's body—to direct and manipulate the patient's energy. In other words, the healer, or practitioner, serves as a universal energy conduit to stabilize or balance the patient's energy field. Reiki proponents believe that this activates the patient's own natural healing abilities.

Reiki is used for a variety of canine health issues, to enhance overall well-being, strengthen the immune system, accelerate healing after surgery, reduce stress and anxiety, and strengthen the human-canine bond.

Alternative and Complementary Care

Alternative medicine does not replace traditional veterinary medicine or surgery but can provide a valuable alternative or complementary method of care. The AVMA has established guidelines for veterinary acupuncture, chiropractic, homeopathic, and holistic medicine. However, the Food and Drug Administration (FDA) does not regulate herbs and natural supplements, which can cause side effects or result in adverse reactions if combined with other supplements or medications. Quality control is also a major concern. Consumerlab.com, an independent testing facility, provides analysis of many popular products. To prevent problems, always consult with your veterinarian

CHAPTER 17

ALLERGIES AND OTHER ISSUES

All dogs itch sometimes. It's normal. But when a dog's itching turns into a full-time job of scratching, biting, digging, and chewing at his skin, it becomes a real pain—literally and figuratively!

Allergies Affecting the Skin

Allergies are one of the most confounding conditions for pets and owners—and no doubt for veterinarians, too—because they are widespread and can be difficult to pinpoint. All sorts of things can cause itching in dogs, but the four most common categories are food allergies, inhalant allergies, contact allergies, and flea-allergy dermatitis. The classic symptoms include excessive scratching, licking, chewing, and biting, often resulting in hair loss, recurrent ear problems, or changes in the skin, including redness, sores, or hot spots. Left untreated, these conditions can make your dog not only miserable but also quite ill.

Atopic Dermatitis (AD)

Atopic dermatitis (also called atopy and previously called allergic inhalant dermatitis) is an allergic skin condition caused by a genetic predisposition and hypersensitivity to environmental substances, called allergens, such as house dust, dust mites, mold spores, grass, and weed pollen. Many of these allergens, which are often the same allergens responsible for human allergies such as hay fever and asthma, occur during the summer and fall, when pollen activity is high. Dogs are exposed to these allergens either through the skin or by inhaling them. These allergens trigger a dog's immune system, causing itchiness and inflammation, which in turn causes a dog to scratch, dig, and chew at his skin. As the disease progresses, clinical signs may go from seasonal to year-round. Secondary infections of the skin and ears can complicate and aggravate the itching, creating a vicious cycle.

Second only to flea-allergy dermatitis in frequency, AD affects about 10 to 15 percent of dogs. Why some dogs have issues and others do not is perplexing, but progress is being made on understanding the mechanisms and the complex interaction between a dog's genetic makeup and environmental factors. Symptoms generally appear between one and three years of age, with some dogs showing symptoms as early as four to six months of age.

No tests exist to confirm a definitive diagnosis. Therefore, diagnosing AD is a bit of an art and a science. Veterinarians resort to a process of elimination—first looking at the dog's history (age, breed, sex, affected areas of the body, response to previous treatments), then considering clinical symptoms (scratching, biting, chewing, inflamed skin, hair loss), and then ruling out other conditions (food allergies, flea infestation, parasites, and mange), all of which have overlapping symptoms similar to those of AD.

No cure exists for AD, but it can, in many cases, be controlled. Successful treatments are multifaceted and typically are comprised of the following:

- avoidance (removing or reducing exposure to the triggering allergens)
- immunotherapy (using specific allergens in a vaccine-mediated hyposensitization protocol)
- immunosuppressive or drug therapy
- Atopica® and Apoquel®, currently the only FDA-approved nonsteroidal drugs for the management of atopic dermatitis

Changing the diet of AD-affected dogs may be useful when combined with conventional therapies. Utilizing household air filters; hypoallergenic, colloidal-oatmeal, or corticosteroid-containing shampoos; topical anti-itch creams; antihistamines; and fatty-acid (omega-3 and omega-6) supplements may be helpful.

Flea-Allergy Dermatitis (FAD)

If a dog is sensitive to fleas, one bite from this tiny pest can make his life (and yours!) miserable. Flea-allergy dermatitis, also known as bite hypersensitivity, is the most common allergy dermatitis in dogs. Some dermatologists believe that where fleas are common, FAD comprises between 50 and 80 percent of allergic skin disease.

Dogs suffering from FAD will commonly scratch everywhere, not just the site of the bites. They commonly lose hair and experience nasty red, inflamed skin patches. Scratching, licking, and chewing at themselves become the full-time occupation of these very unhappy pooches.

Any breed is susceptible, and symptoms are more common in dogs six months of age or older.

Specially formulated shampoos can offer temporary relief for dogs suffering from FAD.

Although no tests exist, you can rule FAD out if you see no signs of improvement after several months of strict and aggressive flea control. Remember, it takes only one flea bite to wreak havoc on your dog, so you must treat all of the animals in your house. Veterinarians frequently recommend hypoallergenic or colloidal-oatmeal shampoos and topical anti-itch creams to soothe the skin, but they are rarely a long-term solution. Fatty-acid supplements, such as omega-3 and omega-6, found in flaxseed and fish oils, prove helpful in reducing the amount and effects of histamine. In many cases, veterinarians prescribe corticosteroids to reduce the interminable itching.

Food Allergies and Food Intolerance

What owners call "food allergies" are often "food sensitivities," though they are definitely different and have different immunological responses. W. Jean Dodds, DVM, a foremost expert in pet health care, explains it this way: "A classic example of a food allergy is anaphylactic shock caused by peanuts. As soon as the person or animal comes in contact with the allergen—the peanuts—his or her airway closes and he or she cannot breathe."

Boom! The response is instantaneous. The allergen triggers an immediate, and sometimes life-threatening, immunological and physiological reaction. This is known as a Type I hypersensitivity reaction.

Food sensitivity (or intolerance), according to Dr. Dodds, is "typically a chronic condition and often does not involve an immunological response." Generally, it builds up over time, perhaps months or even years of exposure to the offending food. Food sensitivity is caused by Types II and III hypersensitivity reactions. Therefore, animal-based proteins—meats, eggs, and dairy—are most often the culprits, but sometimes a carbohydrate source is implicated, too.

What makes food allergies frustrating is that clinical symptoms (scratching, chewing, etc.) often mimic those of other skin issues. Affected dogs often have recurrent ear infections, while others experience gastrointestinal upset. A dog's paws, flank, groin, neck, and ears are commonly affected.

Determining the source of a food allergy is a time-consuming and often frustrating process.

Unlike FAD or AD, food allergies are not seasonal. Most generally, adult dogs are affected, as opposed to puppies, because to develop true food intolerances/sensitivities, the dog must be exposed to the allergen for a period of time.

Diagnosis usually involves a strict elimination diet with only one protein source (e.g., fish) and one carbohydrate source (e.g., potato). If, for instance, you are feeding a food that has multiple protein sources, such as turkey, chicken, and salmon, and your dog is having problems. you will need to find a food that does not contain any of those proteins. The same goes for carbohydrates.

Some companies make foods designed specifically for dogs with allergies or sensitivities. In many instances, a home-cooked or raw diet may be necessary. This is a daunting task for many owners because the process of uncovering the allergen(s) is time-consuming, as is locating good-quality ingredients. (If you go this route, be sure to work with a holistic veterinarian or certified nutritionist.)

Finding a Qualified Dermatologist

Food allergies, parasites, and flea infestations can have overlapping symptoms similar to atopic dermatitis and demodectic mange, so it is important to consult a veterinarian as soon as possible. To locate a canine dermatologist, ask your regular veterinarian for a referral or visit the American College of Veterinary Dermatology (ACVD) website at www.acvd.org.

The goal is to provide a protein (such as bison, rabbit, venison, or duck) and carbohydrate source (such as potato) that the dog has never been exposed to. Years ago, neither lamb nor rice was used in dog foods, so it could be used for an allergic pet. Today, lamb and rice are common ingredients, so they are not suitable. Many of the "exotic" proteins are also becoming more popular and have been fed by some owners. Short of feeding ostrich, kangaroo, or alligator, finding a novel protein source can be taxing and expensive! For this reason, some veterinarians recommend a hydrolyzed protein, which involves turning intact proteins into a mixture of amino acids and smaller proteins, thereby turning the protein into a type that is novel again.

Once the offending ingredient(s) have been isolated and eliminated, reduction in itching may be seen in a few weeks, but in most cases it can take a lot longer, with some veterinarians estimating six to twelve weeks or longer. Owner compliance is paramount, so you can give absolutely no table scraps, treats, chews, or flavored medications while the dog is on the elimination/trial diet. Once the offending allergen(s) is identified, it can never be fed for the rest of the dog's life.

Other Skin Problems
Hot Spots

Pyotraumatic dermatitis and *acute moist dermatitis* are fancy scientific names for hot spots, those painful red, itchy, oozing skin infections that can drive a dog to self-mutilation. Most generally, they begin as an irritation to the dog's skin, such as a flea bite or a moist area where bacteria gathers. Allergies, both food and environmental, can also cause hot spots.

Typically, hot spots are created when a dog's natural bacteria overpopulates parts of the skin. Less common causes, although certainly worth consideration, are mental or emotional issues, such an obsessive-compulsive behavior, separation anxiety, or boredom, all of which may

Long-Term Commitment

Getting significant skin problems under control can take months to years, depending on the issue. With either a veterinary dermatologist or holistic veterinarian, you must be committed to long-term treatment. Many owners are unable or unwilling to go down this road because it can be expensive and time-consuming. Controlling the symptoms with medications such as prednisone and antihistamines works relatively fast and provides relief for suffering pets. Holistic treatment can work, but it is not usually quick.

trigger licking and chewing, resulting in hot spots. Identifying the underlying cause of hot spots is important to avoid future occurrences; otherwise, your dog will be forced to suffer through a painful, vicious cycle of chewing, digging, and scratching.

Most likely, you will see a hot spot emerging on a dog's hip area, on the head, and/or along the side of the chest. For dogs with a lot of coat, a telltale sign is usually a gooey, matted mess. Hot spots can come on very quickly and spread rapidly. In some instances, hot spots can result in fever and serious underlying skin problems, so you will want to see your veterinarian as soon as possible.

Treatment consists of drying out the area, which means getting air to the area, and that necessitates shaving or trimming the hair around the hot spot. You may be able to do this at home, depending on your dog's cooperation. Hot spots can be very painful, so you may need a second set of hands or even veterinary assistance. If not shaved, the dog's hair can mat over the hot spot, causing additional problems, and you will have a much harder time healing the wound.

Once the area is shaved, you can disinfect the area with organic iodine, available at most pharmacies and health-food stores. The goal is to disinfect and then manage the hot spot so that it stays clean and dry at all times. Some veterinarians recommend a topical solution, such as colloidal silver, raw aloe, or raw manuka honey. Your veterinarian may recommend a wound-healing spray or a topical hydrocortisone cream. Be careful not to use anything on your dog's skin that he may lick off and ingest. If your dog wants to lick or dig at the sores, you may need to consider using an Elizabethan collar (one of the lampshade-shaped collars) to keep him from getting to the hot spots. In some cases, antibiotics and/or antihistamines may also be recommended.

Acral Lick Granuloma

Another maddening skin problem in dogs is known as acral lick granuloma (or lick granuloma, acral lick dermatitis, or canine neurodermatitis). Dogs with this condition repetitively lick their skin, sometimes for hours every day, resulting in a hairless, infected, ulcerated plaque that will not heal. Once a dog creates the wound, it becomes a vicious cycle of licking, which creates more irritation, which stimulates more licking. These self-inflicted wounds vary in size, with some lesions covering an entire limb. The normal sites affected are the front and sides of the lower leg (*acral*, meaning on the extremities). In rare cases, acral lick granulomas can occur on the flank or at the base of the tail.

What makes lick granuloma so frustrating is that it is multifactorial, meaning that many factors may contribute to its development, including a potentially hereditary and obsessive-compulsive component that manifests itself as self-mutilation. Other factors include allergies, atopic dermatitis, boredom, obsessive-compulsive disorder (OCD), pain (less common, but a potential factor), and stress.

Dogs that lick repetitively generally have other behavior problems, including separation anxiety, phobias, or OCD behaviors such as tail chasing, circling, or fly biting. Dogs over the age of three are most often affected, and male dogs may be more commonly affected than females.

Diagnosis is based on the dog's history (breed, temperament, daily activities, other skin conditions), clinical signs, process of elimination, and, in some instances, a biopsy. A treatment plan includes identifying and addressing the underlying cause, which can be a frustrating and complicated process.

Behavior-modification protocols, including pharmaceuticals intended to decrease anxiety and obsessive-compulsive behaviors, may be recommended. Antibiotics to treat secondary infections, topical therapies, bandages, an Elizabethan collar, and/or surgical removal of the lesion may also be recommended. Because allergies (atopic and/or food sensitivity) are often a primary factor, allergy medications and/or corticosteroids may be prescribed.

Deafness

Like humans, dogs can suffer hearing loss ranging from mild to complete deafness. This can present unique and challenging problems, not to mention frustration and heartache, for both owners and breeders. Deafness can be either acquired or congenital. Acquired deafness can result from an infection, drug toxicities, old age, or trauma. Present at birth, congenital deafness in dogs is predominantly associated with the merle or piebald gene, which are pigmentation genes responsible for the white or light skin and fur coloration in some breeds. For example, the piebald gene is what gives Dalmatians their brilliant white coats. The merle gene, which gives various breeds their unique coat colors and eye colors, is associated with deafness and, in some cases, blindness. A number of popular breeds carries the merle gene.

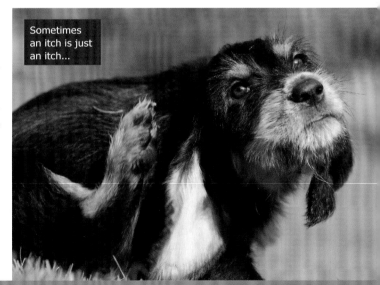

Sometimes an itch is just an itch...

Melanocytes (pigment-producing cells) play an important role in helping to translate air vibrations caused by sound into electrical impulses that travel to the brain. If pigment-producing cells fail to reach the inner ear, deafness usually results about three weeks after birth, while the ear canal is still closed. In some breeds, the lack of melanocytes is related to excessive white markings on the head. Researchers believe that susceptible breeds develop deafness because of the suppression of pigment-producing cells that are necessary to the health of the cochlea.

In the simplest of terms, the inner ear contains a tiny organ called the *cochlea* that contains a fluid and is lined with tiny hairlike nerve cells. Vibrations travel through the ear canal and vibrate the fluid within the cochlea, which wiggles the hairlike cells that connect the nerve endings to the brain. If the pigment-producing cells in the blood supply are absent, the nerve cells of the cochlea die. Without the hairlike cells, sound can't be transmitted, and the result is deafness. While the mechanics of the vascular degeneration are not known, veterinary researchers believe it is associated with the absence of melanocytes in the blood vessels.

Dogs can be deaf in one ear (unilateral) or both ears (bilateral). Many times, owners do not recognize a problem until they begin to train their puppy when he is several months old. Diagnosing unilaterally deaf dogs can be challenging. The most conclusive diagnosis comes from performing a BAER (Brainstem Auditory Evoked Response) test. Similar to the way a television detects its signals, a BAER test recognizes electrical activity in the cochlea and auditory pathways in the brain. If your veterinarian does not offer BAER testing, you may need to travel to a small-animal clinic that offers the service.

The piebald gene (responsible for those amazing spots) is linked to deafness in Dalmatians.

Ear Mites

Several mites can cause problems in a dog's ear, but *Otodectes cynotis* is the most common ear mite found in dogs and cats. Ten percent of all ear problems in dogs are thought to be caused by the *Otodectes cynotis* mite. Ear mites are highly contagious and can be spread from the dam to her puppies or between different species. Interestingly, the *Felis catus,* also known as your domestic cat, is a major culprit in spreading these eight-legged mites to dogs. (For some reason, ear mites don't bother cats to the same degree as they irritate dogs.) Common in young dogs, mites can affect dogs of any age.

While the mites' life cycle is only three weeks, they feed on wax and oils in a dog's ear canal and frequently cause intense irritation and inflammation. Dogs that scratch or dig at their ears may damage their ear canals or ear drums. Dogs that have an immune hypersensitivity may have complications resulting from intense irritation of the external ear.

Typical symptoms include:

- shaking of the head and ears
- scratching or pawing at one or both ears
- a foul odor from the ears
- a yellowish, brown, or black discharge
- inflammation or redness of the earflap or opening to the canal
- pain around or on the ear
- head tilted to one side
- lethargy, depression, loss of hearing
- loss of balance, stumbling, or circling to one side

Using an otoscope (a mechanical instrument equipped with a light), a veterinarian can look into the ear canals, where mites will be visible. Treatment consists of thoroughly cleaning the ears and administering mite-killing medications. Because mites are highly contagious, treating all animals in the house is recommended.

If you notice any of the signs, consult your veterinarian right away. Ear infections are painful and, left untreated, can cause permanent damage to your dog's hearing. The best ways to prevent ear infections are to establish a regular ear-care program, be aware of possible ear problems, and seek immediate veterinary attention if you suspect a problem.

If your puppy is frantically scratching at his ears, a visit to the vet is in order. Ear mites are readily eradicated with prescribed ear drops.

CHAPTER 18

FURTHER HEALTH
CONSIDERATIONS

One of the most important aspects of dog ownership is recognizing when there might be a problem. Many health problems can occur in any dog or breed, and other problems are more breed-specific. Although there are no guarantees, it is completely possible that your dog will never experience any health issues during his long and happy lifetime. Smart owners are prepared and knowledgeable, so familiarity with the more common health issues in dogs is well advised. If you have questions or concerns, always seek veterinary assistance.

Anemia

Anemia refers to a reduced red-blood-cell count. It is not a disease, but rather a result of some other disease or condition. It's an indicator that something is going on in a dog's body. If you remember high-school biology, red blood cells, also known as erythrocytes, are rich in an iron-containing protein called hemoglobin. Hemoglobin delivers the oxygen required for all normal body function. When a dog's red-blood-cell count drops, anemia occurs.

Any number of medical issues can cause anemia, including chronic blood loss from an injury or internal bleeding from ulcers or tumors. Chronic kidney disease or cancer involving the bone marrow can cause anemia. An autoimmune disease like autoimmune hemolytic anemia, in which the body attacks its own red blood cells, can cause severe anemia. Very poor nutrition or nutritional imbalances, and even a severe infestation of hookworms, fleas, or ticks, can result in a reduced red-blood-cell count.

Symptoms generally include pale to white gums, and inside the dog's ears may be pale, too, rather than pink. Weakness, lack of energy, and listlessness are overriding symptoms, as is loss of appetite. A complete blood-cell count (CBC) will quickly confirm a diagnosis of anemia. Other tests, such as a blood smear, bone-marrow biopsy or aspirate, biochemical profile, urinalysis, and fecal parasite exam can give your veterinarian a clearer picture of the underlying cause of the anemia. Treatment varies depending on the cause but may include corticosteroids, deworming medications, or surgery.

Cancer

Few diseases cause dog owners as much alarm as cancer. And rightly so—the statistics are sobering. Two of the more common cancers in dogs are hemangiosarcoma and lymphoma.

Hemangiosarcoma

Hemangiosarcoma (HSA) can affect all breeds, but the incidence rate is higher in certain breeds. A common cancer of middle-aged or older dogs, HSA targets the spleen in 50 percent of affected dogs. Visceral hemangiosarcomas (tumors that form on the internal organs) are aggressive and can metastasize quickly, while tumors that occur in or under the skin typically show less aggressive behavior. This type of cancer is nearly impossible to detect until it reaches the advanced stages, which makes it unbelievably frustrating and devastating. Once symptoms appear, an ultrasound can provide a definitive diagnosis. Symptoms usually result when a tumor ruptures, accompanied by subsequent internal bleeding, and include anemia, weakness, collapse, difficulty breathing, or even sudden death. No curative treatment exists.

Lymphoma

Lymphoma, also known as lymphosarcoma or LSA, is one of the five most common types of tumors in dogs. Lymphoma is caused by a cancerous proliferation of lymphocytes, which are a type of white blood cell that circulates in the blood and functions as part of the immune system. While the cause of LSA is not known, it can affect dogs of any breed and age, although it mainly tends to strike young to middle-aged dogs. LSA is a systemic disease and is not considered a cancer that spreads to other organs. Symptoms typically include enlarged lymph nodes, lethargy, poor appetite, fever, vomiting, and an overall sense of illness. Lymph-node aspirates can provide a definitive diagnosis and help determine the stage of the disease.

It's best to become an informed owner who knows what to look for and when to seek professional assistance.

Overall, the tumors are not considered curable in dogs. However, in most instances (an estimated 75 percent), dogs experience a period of remission when a course of chemotherapy, which is the mainstay of treatment, is followed. Chemotherapy does not appear to affect dogs with the same nauseous side effects as it does humans. In some instances, surgery or radiation therapy also may be recommended.

Degenerative Myelopathy

Canine degenerative myelopathy (DM) is a devastating adult-onset neurological disease with many similarities to the human form of amyotrophic lateral sclerosis (ALS), or Lou Gehrig's disease. DM affects nerve fibers called axons and damages the myelin, which serves as insulation. The onset of clinical signs starts around eight years of age and usually begins with early signs of knuckling of the hind paws or dragging of the toenails, which is what owners notice first. Over the next year, dogs begin to show decreasing muscle control and weakness in their rear limbs that can lead to frequent falls and difficulty getting up. Nerve transmission is progressively reduced, resulting in hind-limb clumsiness and partial paralysis with an increasing loss of mobility in the hindquarters. Eventually, the nervous system is unable to transmit sensory information or movement commands between the brain and hind limbs, resulting in complete loss of muscle function. Affected dogs are usually paralyzed within eleven months, and euthanasia is not uncommon at this point.

The time you invest in locating an excellent veterinary clinic will pay off tenfold when you encounter a serious problem with your dog.

Epilepsy

Epilepsy is a term used to describe a disorder of recurring seizures, characterized as either primary or secondary epilepsy. Secondary epilepsy, also known as acquired or symptomatic epilepsy, refers to seizures for which a cause can be determined. As the name suggests, it is secondary to some kind of identifiable brain damage, such as a stroke, a tumor, trauma, metabolic disease, a congenital defect, or infection. In these instances, treating the underlying cause, such as removing a tumor, is the primary goal.

More often than not, unfortunately, veterinarians can't find a reason for epilepsy. Idiopathic, or primary, epilepsy refers to recurrent seizures that are of unknown cause. As the mouse Remy says in the movie *Ratatouille*, "The only thing predictable about life is its unpredictability," and the same thing can be said about idiopathic epilepsy.

Epilepsy is considered one of the most common neurologic diseases in dogs. Studies estimate that up to 4 percent of all dogs are affected, but those numbers may be higher because many breeds are predisposed to developing epilepsy. The mode of inheritance is believed to vary considerably among breeds. While a hereditary component has been identified in several breeds, in others it is simply a strong suspicion.

What triggers a seizure is also anyone's guess. A biochemical defect in the brain cells or the brain environment is thought to cause idiopathic epilepsy. An estimated 66 percent of dogs with idiopathic epilepsy experience their first seizures between one and three years of age. Some dogs appear to have seizures regularly, while seizures in other dogs appear to be triggered by events such as stress or changes in weather. However, for many dogs, no pattern of seizure activity exists.

Seizures are divided into two types: generalized and focal (or partial). Generalized seizures are further divided into subtypes: major motor seizures (grand mal), which is the classic seizure; and absence seizures (petit mal), which don't appear to occur in pets. Symptoms associated with the classic seizure, also called a tonic-clonic seizure, usually include rigidity or jerking of the body or limbs, anxiety, hysteria, unconsciousness, vocalizing, salivation, drooling, urination, and defecation. While the seizure seems to last a lifetime,

Be sure to discuss treatment options with your vet before embarking on a care regimen.

it normally last less than 30 seconds and gives way to rhythmic movements (the tonic part). Normally lasting less than two minutes, tonic symptoms consist of chomping of the jaws and jerking or running movements of the limbs.

Focal or partial seizures begin in an isolated area of the brain. Depending on the location of the seizure, symptoms may include twitching or blinking on one side of the face. Limbs may be affected if the seizure spreads. The dog usually remains alert and awake, though he may seem confused and search out his owner. The electrical activity may stay localized, but if it spreads to the whole cerebral cortex or the entire brain at once, a generalized seizure may occur.

Canine idiopathic epilepsy is a chronic disease with no cure. Treatment usually involves antiepileptic drugs with the goal of reducing the frequency and severity of seizures to a level that does not compromise a dog's quality of life without severe side effects associated with medications. With proper medications, most epileptic dogs can lead a normal life.

Eye Problems

A number of eye disorders can cause serious problems for your puppy. Some breeds are known to have eye issues that are genetically inherited, such as progressive retinal atrophy (PRA), Collie eye anomaly, and cataracts. Research has discovered the mode of inheritance in some breeds, which helps breeders avoid mating dogs that carry the genes responsible for a particular disease. Some eye issues are a result of trauma from working or from debris that gets into a dog's eyes. Many of these diseases have no treatment, which is why it is important to ask about breeders for proof of eye exams and clearances for breeding stock and puppies.

Your vet may recommend an Elizabethan collar to prevent your dog from scratching his eyes after an operation.

Cataracts

Dogs get cataracts the same as people do. Cataracts are the leading cause of blindness in dogs (and humans), affecting an estimated one hundred breeds, with most cataracts being inherited—especially in purebreds. Despite the large number of breeds affected, little is known about the genetics of cataracts. Some cataracts are known to be hereditary, while others are considered to hereditary but lack scientific data.

Cataracts can be congenital (present at birth) or developmental (developing early in life). Some occur as secondary complications to eye disorders such as PRA, glaucoma, and inflammatory uveitis, while others are secondary to health conditions such as trauma or metabolic disorders like diabetes. Cataracts can develop rapidly over weeks or slowly over years and can assume a variety of appearances depending on the severity of the situation. They may appear in one eye or both, be of any size or shape, and affect the entire lens. Hereditary cataracts have breed-specific characteristics relating to appearance, age of onset, and rate of progression.

The degree of vision impairment is determined by the size and location of the cataract, and vision loss ranges from partial to complete. Loss of vision is caused by the cloudy opacity that develops in a normally clear lens. The opacity inhibits the lens from focusing light on the retina. As the condition worsens, the amount of light reaching the retina is reduced until a dog eventually becomes blind.

Cataracts are classified by several factors, including the age of onset, the cause, the location, and the degree of opacity. Your veterinarian may be able to confirm the presence of mature or complete cataracts, but a veterinary ophthalmologist is better able to detect small cataracts—especially in young puppies. No medication is available to prevent, reverse, or shrink cataracts. For eligible candidates, surgery to insert a new prosthetic lens is the only known treatment. New, improved microsurgical techniques have increased the success rates of restoring vision to dogs to an estimated 90 percent.

Older dogs may develop nuclear sclerosis, which is characterized by a slight graying of the lens and is a normal change that occurs in the structure of the lens. Frequently mistaken for cataracts, nuclear sclerosis usually occurs in both eyes at the same time and mostly in dogs over six years of age. The condition normally doesn't significantly interfere with vision.

Intense at-home eye-drop therapy is required after cataract surgery.

Collie Eye Anomaly

Collie eye anomaly (CEA) disrupts the normal development of the back of a puppy's eye. CEA is not just a problem for Collies, as it affects a number of breeds. A recessively inherited eye disorder, CEA (technically known as choroidal hypoplasia) causes abnormal development of the choroid—an important layer of tissue under the retina of the eye. Because the choroid does not develop normally, it can be diagnosed by a canine ophthalmologist in puppies as young as five to eight weeks of age. The disease is congenital, meaning that it is present at birth and the abnormalities develop along with the eye, but it does not progressively worsen with age.

The severity of CEA varies among affected dogs, between parent and offspring, and even within a litter. Disorders can range from mild to severe, with severe disease leading to vision loss, although this disorder only rarely results in total blindness.

Ectropion and Entropion

Ectropion is a conformational defect in which the eyelids sag or roll out (eversion). Abnormal exposure of the eye is a common clinical sign, which often leads to tear pooling, bacterial or allergic conjunctivitis, and frequent irritation and infection. Affected dogs may develop

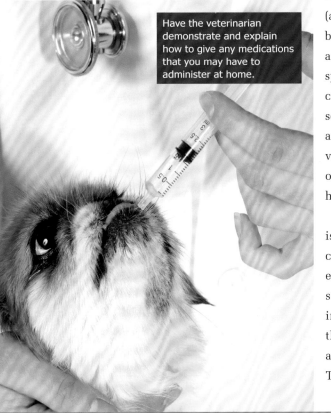

Have the veterinarian demonstrate and explain how to give any medications that you may have to administer at home.

keratoconjunctivitis sicca, or "dry eye" (a drying of the tissue around the eye), because of reduced efficiency at wetting and cleaning the cornea. The severity of symptoms varies from dog to dog. In mild cases, no treatment may be necessary. More severe cases can lead to chronic problems associated with eye irritation, and your veterinarian may choose to remove a wedge of tissue from the margin of the eyelid to help correct the issue.

The opposite of ectropion, entropion is the inward rolling of the eyelid, most commonly the lower lid. Resultantly, the eyelid hairs may rub against the smooth, sensitive cornea, ultimately causing visual impairment. The mode of inheritance is thought to be polygenic, with many breeds appearing to have a higher rate of incidence. Treatment may require surgical correction.

Homozygous Merle Eye Defect

The flashy blue merle coloring found in certain breeds and mixed breeds has a hidden agenda. Unfortunately, the same gene that is responsible for the desirable coat and eye appearance is often responsible for many developmental eye defects. Merle ocular dysgenesis is a group of eye defects found in homozygous merles—dogs that carry two merle genes as a result of breeding a male merle to a female merle.

Mathematically, the odds are that one out of every four puppies produced from a merle-to-merle breeding will have either an eye or a hearing problem. The eye defects occur in varying degrees and combinations and include: microphthalmia (abnormally small eyes), retinal dysplasia (abnormal development of the retina, resulting in its folding and detachment), abnormal shape and position of the pupils, irregularities of the iris, cataracts, incomplete development of the optic nerve and blood vessels supplying the eye, and lack of a tapetum (the part of the eye that helps dogs see at night or in dim lighting). These defects are often associated with or accompanied by excess white markings on the puppy's head, especially around the ears and eyes.

Iris Coloboma

Coloboma is a scientific word for a gap in part of the structure of the eye. An iris coloboma is a gap or missing part of the iris, which is the colored part of a dog's eye. The iris either dilates or constricts the pupil to regulate the amount of light entering the eye. In bright light, the pupil is small, but in dim light, the pupil is very large to let in as much light as possible.

The effect of an iris coloboma on a dog's vision is minimal. However, a large coloboma can cause your dog to squint in bright light because the iris does not contract enough to reduce the amount of light entering the eye. While some large colobomas may be visible to the naked eye, a canine ophthalmologist can make a definitive diagnosis.

Progressive Retinal Atrophy (PRA)

Progressive retinal atrophy is the name of several progressive, inherited diseases that lead to blindness. While many types of PRA are caused by different mutations, all of them have similar signs. Doubly frustrating for breeders and researchers is the mode of inheritance, which varies in affected breeds, with the genetic complexities remaining a mystery in other breeds.

A dog's retina contains photoreceptors called cones and rods. Rods help a dog see at night or in the darkness, and the cones allow a dog to see certain colors. Normally, the photoreceptors in the retina develop after birth until about eight weeks of age. The retinas of dogs with PRA either have arrested development (retinal dysplasia) or early degeneration of the photoreceptors. Vets say that dogs with the condition do not experience pain.

While the outward appearance of an affected eye is normal, PRA worsens over time, with affected dogs experiencing night blindness at first. Dogs may be reluctant to move from a lit environment to a dark one, such as going outside to potty in the evening. They may stumble on stairs, especially in unfamiliar environments. Eventually, the condition progresses with the degeneration of the cone cells, resulting in the inability to see bright lights and eventual failed daytime vision.

Gastric Dilatation-Volvulus

Gastric dilatation-volvulus (GDV), commonly called "bloat," is a potentially life-threatening condition and the mother lode of canine emergencies. While the disease has been studied for many years, the mechanics of the disease remain a mystery. When a dog's stomach distends, or bloats (usually from gas and air), and then rotates or twists, it's called torsion, or what is technically referred to as *volvulus* (imagine an inflated balloon that is twisted in the middle). Not all dogs that experience stomach bloating end up with volvulus. When bloating is accompanied by volvulus, the twisting pinches off the blood supply, causing immediate life-threatening problems. The passage of food is blocked, and the twisting interferes with the blood supply to the stomach and other digestive organs. It also impedes the return of blood to the heart, causing reduced cardiac output and decreased blood pressure.

In other words, in dilatation, the stomach swells; when accompanied by volvulus, the stomach, spleen, and other abdominal structures twist. GDV rapidly progresses and quickly becomes a veterinary emergency, thus requiring immediate veterinary attention.

Large, deep, narrow-chested breeds, including the German Shepherd Dog, Great Dane, Bloodhound, Boxer, Weimaraner, and Standard Poodle, among others, are considered at risk of developing GDV. Although the "why" remains a mystery, experts theorize that a deep, narrow chest allows the ligaments of the stomach to stretch farther when the stomach is weighted down with food. Over time, the stretched ligaments allow the stomach to move within the abdominal cavity, increasing the risk of twisting.

GDV has a 30-percent mortality rate and is considered the second leading cause of death, after cancer, among many large and giant breeds. Age and gender may also be factors. Symptoms often occur between eight and eleven years of age for dogs weighing from 50 to 99 pounds or 23 to 45 kg and between seven and nine years of age for dogs weighing more than 99 pounds or 45 kg. Males are believed to be twice as likely as females to suffer bloat. Again, the reasons remain elusive.

Recognizing the clinical signs and seeking immediate veterinary attention can mean the difference between life and death for your dog. The common signs that your dog may have GDV include a distended stomach, unsuccessful attempts to vomit, episodes of unproductive belching (attempts to expel air collected in the stomach), abdominal pain, heavy salivation, and general unease, demonstrated by behaviors such as pacing, whining, and unwillingness to lie down. Shallow, rapid breathing and pale gums are also symptoms. Rapid recognition of the clinical signs and immediate medical attention are necessary for the dog to survive. If in doubt, always seek medical attention right away. Left untreated, a dog will die. If caught early enough, survival rate runs about 90 percent.

Hypothyroidism

A very common condition in dogs, hypothyroidism (*hypo* = low) is the condition that occurs when not enough thyroid hormone is produced. The thyroid gland has a number of different and important functions, but it's best known for its role in regulating metabolism. A deficiency of the thyroid hormone affects the metabolic function of all organ systems. The cause can be either congenital or due to the progressive deficiency of the thyroid gland caused by the dog's own immune system killing the cells of the thyroid gland. Hypothyroidism in its noncongenital (primary) form is responsible for about 95 percent of canine cases. Hypothyroidism is most common in middle-aged dogs (between four and ten years of age) and usually affects medium- to large-sized breeds of dog. Some breeds appear predisposed to hypothyroidism. It can occur in both males and females, but spayed females appear to develop it most often.

Typical symptoms, which may be subtle in the beginning, include loss or thinning of fur, dull haircoat, excess shedding or scaling, weight gain, reduced activity, slow heart rate, and reduced ability to tolerate the cold. Ear infections, as well as itchy, red skin infections, resulting in sores on the body, may occur. Some dogs may have anemia and high blood cholesterol, too. These symptoms, combined with a blood test to check thyroid hormone levels, help confirm a diagnosis. Treatment for hypothyroidism is a synthetic thyroid medication that can do the thyroid's job and speed up the dog's sluggish metabolism. With daily medication, the prognosis for affected dogs is very good, and most return to normal condition and quality of life.

Multidrug Resistance Gene (MDR1)

Has your dog been tested for the MDR1 gene? If not, you may want to ask your veterinarian about it, especially if your dog is one of the commonly affected herding or hound breeds, as it can cause life-threatening complications. The name of the gene—multidrug resistance—is a bit of a misnomer because the dogs that test positive aren't really resistant to the drugs that cause them problems.

Here's how it works: in "normal" dogs—those who do not carry the mutation—the MDR1 gene encodes P-glycoprotein (P-gp), a large transmembrane protein that is an integral part of the blood-brain barrier. P-gp is responsible for pumping drugs and other toxins out of the brain and back into the bloodstream, where they can be safely metabolized. A mutation in MDR1, known as MDR1-1Δ, causes defects in the coding of P-gp; as a result, affected dogs do not produce the complete protein and therefore cannot pump out certain substances. Drugs accumulate inside cells, where they can reach toxic, life-threatening levels. Symptoms of neurotoxicity can include lack of muscle coordination, blindness, coma, depression, disorientation, excessive salivation, dilated pupils, respiratory distress, and vomiting.

In the grand scheme of things, the mutation would not be a problem at all except for the use of certain therapeutic drugs in veterinary practice. While these drugs are very beneficial for most dogs, they can be dangerous and even lethal to those with the MDR1 mutation.

A simple cheek-swab test available through the University of Washington School of Veterinary Medicine can identify dogs as negative or positive for the mutation. The test is a bit expensive but well worth the peace of mind it brings if your dog requires certain medications. Herding-breed dogs (and mixed breeds) should not receive some drugs until they are tested free of the mutation. The most common drugs to cause problems are loperamide, better known as the over-the-counter antidiarrheal agent Imodium, and ivermectin, the main ingredient in many heartworm preventives. Other important drugs are the chemotherapeutic agents vincristine and doxorubicin, acepromazine (a tranquilizer), and butorphanol (used for pain control).

The ivermectin dosage used in the commercial heartworm preparations is safe for dogs with the mutation, according to experts. Interestingly, though, affected dogs can experience toxicity if they eat the feces of animals that have been treated with larger doses of ivermectin. Those "road apples" consumed by dogs carrying the mutation can cause neurotoxicity.

Orthopedic Issues
Hip Dysplasia

One of the more frequently seen health problems in medium and large breeds, hip dysplasia (HD) is a defect in the conformation of the hip joint that can cause weakness and lameness to a dog's rear quarters, resulting in arthritis; severe, debilitating pain; and crippling. It is the result of a complex set of inherited traits, including failure of the head of the femur (thigh bone) to properly fit into the socket of the pelvis (hip bone). An imperfect fit can eventually lead to osteoarthritis.

HD is considered to be a polygenic inherited disorder, meaning that more than one gene influences the disease. Despite ongoing research, it is not clear which genes are responsible.

Environmental factors, nutrition, and exercise may also be contributing factors that influence the progression of hip dysplasia. The rate of progression of hip dysplasia is influenced by the growth rate of the individual dog.

The earliest of symptoms can appear between the ages of four to twelve months. However, symptoms vary from dog to dog and can range from practically nonexistent to crippling. Some dogs are very stoic and will keep plowing along, showing no signs of pain. As a result, many owners may not realize there is a problem.

Caloric intake, exercise, and weather can influence the appearance of symptoms, which may include a decrease in activity, walking or running with an altered gait, resisting movements that require full extension or flexion of the rear legs, stiffness and pain in the rear legs after exercise or first thing in the morning upon rising, difficulty rising from a lying or sitting position, and reluctance to climb stairs. Some dogs may have a swaying, unsteady gait or a bunny-hop gait in which they run with both hind legs moving together.

A preliminary diagnosis can be made through a physical examination by a veterinarian, which includes ruling out other issues, such as spine, knee, or elbow problems, or even Lyme disease. However, X-rays are the only means of reaching a definitive diagnosis of hip dysplasia.

The traditional method of X-ray evaluation is regulated by the Orthopedic Foundation for Animals (OFA). X-rays are sent to the OFA for evaluation and graded on a seven-point scale from Excellent to Severe (significant hip dysplasia). Dogs can receive a preliminary evaluation at one year of age but must be two years old to receive an accurate reading and OFA rating.

OFA certification was once the only method of grading a dog's hips. However, the University of Pennsylvania Hip Improvement Program (PennHIP) offers an alternative process using distraction/compression X-rays to obtain accurate and precise measurements of joint laxity, the primary cause of degenerative joint disease. The amount of joint looseness when the dog's hips are completely relaxed is assigned a distraction index (DI), which strongly correlates to future development of degenerative joint disease.

Crate rest is critical to an ailing dog's speedy recovery. Crate-trained dogs also find comfort and serenity in the familiar surroundings of their crate.

Treatment varies depending on the dog and the severity of the disease. Excessive activity like jumping and prolonged running should be avoided. Analgesic and anti-inflammatory drugs can help to relieve pain associated with bouts of lameness, but these medications do not halt or reverse the progression of HD. Depending on the dog's age and the severity of the condition, surgery to rearrange the bone of the pelvis or the femoral head to improve joint function may be recommended. Or, in some cases, a total hip replacement may be necessary.

Elbow Disease

Anatomically, a dog's elbow joint is similar to a human's elbow joint. A complicated yet efficient hinge-type joint, it is created by the junction of three different bones: the radius, the ulna, and the humerus. These bones fit and function together with little room for error, and all the parts must work harmoniously for maximum soundness and efficiency. Anything that alters the elbow configuration will affect a dog's ability to use his leg correctly. Elbow disease—frequently referred to as elbow dysplasia or elbow incongruity—is really a syndrome for different elbow abnormalities that include ununited anconeal process (UAP), fragmented coronoid process (FCP), and osteochondritis dissecans (OCD).

Symptoms of all three diseases are similar and can include a weight-bearing lameness in the front legs that persists for more than a few days, reduction in range of movement, and pain when a veterinarian manipulates the joint. Your veterinarian may recommend a set of X-rays and, in some cases, a computerized tomography (CT) scan or exploratory surgery in order to establish a definitive diagnosis.

Treatment varies, depending on the diagnosis. With FCP and OCD, many experts first recommend medical treatment, which includes a specifically designed exercise program; weight loss, if necessary; and the use of nutraceuticals, such as glucosamine, chondroitin, and methylsulfonylmethane (MSM), as well as nonsteroidal anti-inflammatory medications. In some instances of FCP and OCD, surgery may be necessary. UAP is generally treated with surgery.

Patellar Luxation

Patellar luxation is a medical term used to describe a slipped or dislocated kneecap: *patella*, meaning "kneecap," and *luxation*, referring to a joint that is abnormally out of place. Patellar luxation is a particular concern for breeders and owners of small and toy breeds.

There are three major components involved in luxating patellas: the femur (thigh bone), patella (kneecap), and tibia (lower thigh). The three components come together at the stifle, the anatomical equivalent of the human knee. A dog's kneecap, which is very similar to a human's kneecap, is the flat, movable bone at the front of the knee. Its job is to protect the large tendon of the quadriceps muscles, which are used to straighten the stifle.

In a normal knee, the femur and tibia are lined up so that the patella can slide up and down in a groove on the face of the lower end of the femur. The patellar ligament and the attached muscles hold the patella in place while the sliding motion allows the dog to bend or straighten his leg. All of the pieces fit together in a predefined way. If you place your hand on your kneecap while bending and straightening your knee, you will feel the normal movement of the knee as it glides up and down in the groove.

Dislocated kneecaps occur when the groove is shallow and not well developed and when the femur and tibia are not properly lined up so that the patella rests securely in the grove. Very little prevents the kneecap from shifting or slipping out of place and riding on the inner surface of the femur. If the patellar tendon lacks stability, it also can cause the kneecap to slip out of place. Either of these conditions, or a combination of the conditions, can result in a dislocated kneecap.

Patellar luxation is a congenital condition, meaning that the structural changes that lead to luxation are present at the time of birth. The actual dislocation may not be present, but the writing is on the wall, so to speak. In addition, luxated patellas are thought to be inherited, but the exact mode of inheritance is not yet known.

Diagnosis is relatively simple and can be done by a veterinarian who is familiar with orthopedics. In most cases, it entails a physical examination when the puppy is between four and six months of age that includes palpation of the joint and manual luxation of the kneecap.

Cranial Cruciate Ligament (CrCL) Ruptures

Your dog need not be a canine athlete to experience a torn knee ligament. The odds of a torn ligament may increase with active dogs. All dogs, however, are at risk because the primary cause of torn cranial cruciate ligaments is slow degeneration that takes place over time within the ligament rather than as the result of trauma. Torn knee ligaments are one of the more common orthopedic injuries in dogs and the major cause of arthritis of the knee joint.

The knee joint, unlike the hip and elbow joints, has no interlocking bones. Instead, it relies on an assortment of soft-tissue structures to hold everything in place while still allowing the knee to bend the way it should and prevent it from bending in ways it should not.

Two cruciate ligaments running in opposite directions crisscross inside the knee: the cranial cruciate (anterior cruciate) and the caudal cruciate (posterior cruciate). The function of each is to stabilize the knee and prevent excess movement in its respective direction. The cranial cruciate ligament tends to rupture most often, thereby allowing the tibia to move excessively in the forward direction. This causes joint instability as well as irritation and inflammation of the joint capsule and the soft tissues surrounding the joint.

To further complicate matters, a ruptured CrCL, the equivalent of a torn anterior cruciate ligament (ACL) in humans, predisposes a dog's knee to other painful injuries, including damaged cartilage—specifically, the medial meniscus that is sandwiched between the femur and tibia and reduces the pressure of bone against bone. Without proper treatment, the process of degeneration continues to snowball until the knee joint develops permanent osteoarthritis.

Although all breeds are at risk, some larger breeds appear to be predisposed to an inherent ligament degeneration—meaning that the ligaments surrounding the knee deteriorate and weaken over time, thereby making the joint vulnerable to injury under normal activity or minimal trauma. A dog's individual knee conformation may be a contributing factor. And there is direct trauma, with one of the more common causes occurring when the stifle turns while in full extension; for instance, when a dog is running at full speed and suddenly turns, skids on a slippery surface, or steps in a hole.

Symptoms of CrCL injury can occur suddenly or gradually, depending on the extent of the injury and the individual dog. The hallmark symptom is stiffness or limping in the dog's hind leg, particularly after exercise or prolonged periods of rest. Such limping may become progressively worse over time.

Diagnosis of a ruptured ligament involves a physical examination, observation of joint movement, and manipulation of the joint. Magnetic resonance imaging (MRI) is an option in making a diagnosis, but in many instances veterinarians rely on a thorough orthopedic examination. The primary diagnostic test is the anterior drawer motion test, which is a physical manipulation of the stifle joint to assess the tibia's forward movement in relation to the femur. Radiographs are frequently recommended to document the knee's condition.

Treatment options vary depending on the extent of the tear and can include conservative management and restricted activity for six to eight weeks. For a ruptured ligament, surgery to stabilize the joint is often the best option; without surgical intervention, large dogs will develop arthritis and become increasingly unstable.

Von Willebrand's Disease

When a dog bleeds, a cascade of more than twenty-five proteins and several types of cells and blood platelets go to work clotting the blood of the damaged blood vessels. These mechanisms are very complex, and all of the components must be present and working in a specific order for the process to work efficiently. Part of the complex mechanism of clotting requires that a production protein found in the blood, called von Willebrand's factor (vWF), be present to form a stable blood clot. When this large glycoprotein protein, which plays a key role in the blood-clotting process, is absent or deficient, abnormal (and sometimes fatal) bleeding occurs, hence the inherited bleeding disorder von Willebrand's disease (vWD).

Here are a few of the more popular veterinary specialties and the conditions they address:

- **Dentistry:** Diplomates are certified by the American Veterinary Dental College (AVDC) and treat conditions involving the teeth and mouth.
- **Dermatology:** Veterinarians are certified by the American College of Veterinary Dermatology (ACVD) and specialize in diagnosing and treating animals with benign and malignant disorders of the skin, hair, ears, and nails.
- **Internal Medicine:** Diplomates are certified by the American College of Veterinary Internal Medicine (ACVIM) in small- or large-animal internal medicine, cardiology, neurology, or oncology.
- **Nutrition:** Veterinary nutritionists are Diplomates of the American College of Veterinary Nutrition (ACVN). Veterinary nutritionists are specialists who are uniquely trained in the nutritional management of both healthy animals and those with one or more diseases
- **Ophthalmology:** Diplomates are certified by the American College of Veterinary Ophthalmologists (ACVO) and specialize in diagnosing and treating diseases and injuries to the eye, such as cataracts, ulcers, and glaucoma.

The AVMA has twenty-two recognized veterinary specialty organizations. Other areas of specialty include canine acupuncture, sports medicine and rehabilitation, pathology, pharmacology, and radiology, to name a few.

Affected dogs are deficient in vWF, but the deficiency varies depending on the severity of the disease. Similar to hemophilia in humans, vWD is classified into types 1, 2, and 3, with type 1 being the most common and type 3 being the most severe. In type 1, vWF functions properly but is seen in reduced concentrations. Type 2 is characterized by functionally abnormal vWF. In type 3, vWF is virtually absent in the plasma of affected dogs.

Decreased or absent vWF puts affected dogs at high risk for serious bleeding disorders should they undergo surgery or experience trauma. In dogs with type 3 vWD, minor bleeding episodes, such as nicking the nail's quick during grooming, can turn into a major bleeding incident.

The primary symptom is prolonged or excessive bleeding, such as during surgery, during an injury, when a female is in season, when a puppy is teething, and so forth. In some cases, spontaneous bleeding from the nose or gums may occur. Blood in the feces or urine may also be present. Diagnosis is based on tests that measure vWF in a dog's plasma.

No cure exists for vWD. If your dog is diagnosed with this condition, you will need to take special precautions to make sure he does not injure himself, as even a seemingly minor injury may need special attention. In some instances, you may be able to stop the bleeding by applying prolonged pressure. When in doubt, seek immediate veterinary attention. If your dog requires surgery, a veterinarian may recommend a transfusion preoperatively as a precaution.

CHAPTER 19

PUPPY FIRST AID

Chances are good that at some point in your dog's life, he may need first aid or emergency veterinary care. The most important step in first aid is preventing emergencies from happening. However, as you probably already know, puppies are ingenious and have the uncanny ability to get into any and all sorts of trouble.

Despite having puppy-proofed your home and yard, any number of situations exist in which injuries may occur, be it a bee sting, minor scrape or cut, torn toenail, or something more serious, such as choking, a broken bone or tooth, or poisoning. If your puppy is sick or injured, always err on the side of caution and seek immediate veterinary care, be it with your regular veterinarian or a twenty-four-hour emergency clinic.

Recognizing the difference between a minor situation and a life-threatening medical emergency will help you decide if the situation can be treated at home, coupled with a "wait and see" attitude, or if you need to seek immediate emergency medical attention.

The American Red Cross as well as several other organizations, such as Pet Responder and Wag'N Pet Emergency Management, offer pet first aid and CPR classes that teach you how to respond to emergencies and provide basic first aid. Knowing what to do in an emergency will help to keep you calm and focused. At the minimum, you should know how to perform the basic procedures, including:

- applying a muzzle
- sliding an injured dog onto a flat board or using a blanket as a makeshift gurney
- transporting an injured dog in a safe and stable manner for both dog and owner
- taking a rectal temperature
- checking a dog's heartbeat
- taking a dog's pulse (femoral artery)
- cleaning and dressing, if necessary, a minor wound

While first aid is not a substitute for veterinary care, a little advance preparation may be just enough to relieve your pet's suffering and possibly save his life until you can get to an emergency clinic.

Life-Threatening Symptoms

Most life-threatening situations involve deterioration of the cardiovascular, respiratory, or central nervous system. If your puppy exhibits any of the following symptoms, or if you suspect something is wrong, seek veterinary assistance right away:

- bleeding that is profuse and/or cannot be stopped
- difficult or labored breathing or no breathing at all
- collapse, coma, depression, extreme lethargy, or lack of consciousness
- uncontrolled or bloody diarrhea or black, tarry stools
- pale bluish or white gums
- pain
- seizures
- temperature above 105°F or 40.5°C (a dog's average temperature is 101°F to 102.5°F or 38.3°C to 39°C)
- broken, bleeding, or loose teeth
- vomiting blood or uncontrolled vomiting

Puppies that are exposed to trauma, poisoning, or gastrointestinal distress may need immediate emergency veterinary care. Situations that should cause you increased concern include:

- bite from a snake, poisonous spider, toad, or other animal, especially a cat or unvaccinated animal
- burns (hot liquids, fire, electrical blankets)
- electrocution (e.g., from chewing on an electrical cord)
- excessive heat or cold
- frostbite
- overdose of medications
- porcupine quills embedded in the skin
- puncture wounds
- trauma of any kind—hit by a car, kicked by a horse, fell from a deck, and the like
- smoke inhalation
- swallowing foreign objects (toy, marble, paper clip, thumb tack, sock

First Aid Kit for Dogs and Owners

As a dog owner, a well-stocked canine first aid kit is a must-have. If you travel frequently with your dog, you might consider one kit for your home and one for your vehicle. While many of the supplies in a human first aid kit can be used for pets, too, you may prefer to

Dog owners need to be prepared for anything!

have a separate one for your dog. Either way, appropriate first aid supplies will allow you to more readily deal with any canine medical issue that arises.

Whether you choose to purchase a colossal preassembled kit, a basic home kit, or customize your own, be sure to include:

- activated charcoal, available from pharmacists, or milk of magnesia (to bind or neutralize certain poisons)
- alcohol or alcohol prep pads for sterilizing scissors and tweezers; not for use on wounds
- eye wash for flushing out eye contaminants
- gauze rolls and gauze pads for wrapping wounds or muzzling an injured dog
- gloves (disposable latex) for protecting hands and preventing contamination of wounds
- hydrogen peroxide 3% USP or Ipecac to induce vomiting if necessary
- instant cold pack/instant heat wrap
- large eye dropper, bulb syringe, or large medical syringe without the needle for flushing wounds
- medications, including antidiarrheal medicine (e.g., Imodium, FortiFlora) and aspirin (not nonsteroidal anti-inflammatory drugs such as acetaminophen or ibuprofen)
- muzzle
- nonstick bandages, towels, or strips of clean cloth to control bleeding or protect wounds
- scissors and tweezers
- styptic pencil or cornstarch (an anticoagulant) to stop bleeding if a nail is broken, torn, or clipped too short
- thermometer designed specifically for dogs (the temperature of regular thermometers does not always go high enough for pets)
- triple-antibiotic ointment/spray to inhibit bacterial growth in cuts and abrasions

These are the basics of most canine first aid kids. You may also want to consider a few extras, including:

- antiseptic towelettes
- Benadryl 25 mg or Aller-tec (cetirizine hydrochloride tablets 10 mg) for temporary relief of itching and scratching due to allergies
- canned or dehydrated pumpkin (works as both an antidiarrheal agent and natural laxative); particularly recommended for any dog that carries the MDR-1 gene and may not be able to take certain drugs, including antidiarrheal medications
- EMT gel (applied to a wound to reduce bleeding, seal off nerve endings to reduce pain and itching, and form a protective barrier over the wound to reduce infection)
- Famotidine (available from a veterinarian or over the counter as Pepcid AC 10 mg) to remedy stomach upset/vomiting by reducing the amount of stomach acid being produced
- flexible cohesive wrap for securing wound wraps
- hydrocortisone cream
- list of emergency numbers for poison-control center, veterinarian, and twenty-four-hour emergency clinic
- rehydrating solution, such as Pedialyte, to replace lost electrolytes
- Rescue Remedy (Bach Original Flower Essences), a natural stress-reliever for calming dogs
- sterile saline wound flush
- wound-healing spray, such as tea tree oil, formulated for cuts, scrapes, abrasions, and hot spots

"An ounce of prevention…" goes the saying. While minor wounds can be treated at home, a canine first aid class will go a long way in preparing you for minor and serious emergencies. When in doubt, always seek veterinary care immediately. For more information about first aid kits or classes, contact your veterinarian or the American Red Cross.

There's an App for That

The American Red Cross has a pet first aid app that puts veterinary advice for everyday emergencies in the palm of your hand.

Common First Aid Emergencies

Unexpected emergencies can happen in an instant, whether due to health problems, accidents, or even everyday household items.

Antifreeze (Ethylene Glycol) Ingestion

Dogs are attracted to antifreeze, supposedly because of its appealing taste. All dog owners should be highly aware of its danger, as damage caused by very small amounts is irreversible and life-threatening. As little as a single tablespoon of antifreeze can result in acute kidney failure; about 5 tablespoons or 74 g can kill a medium-sized dog.

Nonexertion Heatstroke

Nonexertion heatstroke most commonly occurs when dogs are confined in an overheated enclosure, such as an automobile, or when they are confined outdoors during warm weather or high humidity and deprived of water or shade.

Symptoms can occur within thirty minutes to twelve hours and include, but are not limited to:

- uncoordinated movement, staggering, depression, seizures (usually within the first hours)
- nausea, vomiting
- excessive urination
- diarrhea
- panting
- rapid heartbeat
- weakness
- fainting
- coma

A dog may appear to feel better in a day or two, but more severe internal damage is still occurring. Recovery depends on how quickly your dog is treated by a veterinarian. Once your dog ingests antifreeze, a small window of time for treatment exists. The sooner your dog is treated, the better his chance of survival. Once kidney failure has set in, dogs can occasionally be saved with aggressive treatment.

Cardiac Arrest

If you realize your dog is not breathing, you should immediately get him to the closest veterinary or twenty-four-hour emergency clinic. Unfortunately, the outcome is usually not promising. According to the AVMA, less than 6 percent of dogs that experience cardiopulmonary arrest while in a veterinary clinic survive. If your dog stops breathing, cardiac arrest will soon follow. Only attempt cardiopulmonary resuscitation (CPR) in an extreme emergency, as this emergency procedure can cause fatal damage if not done correctly or if performed on a dog that is not in need of the procedure. Here is the basic CPR procedure:

- Lay the dog on his side on a flat, hard surface that will not bend when the chest is compressed.
- A dog's heart is located just behind his front legs (right around the point of the flexed elbow). Apply pressure with the flat part of your hand directly over the heart area with a force that is appropriate for the size of the dog at a rate of about 80 to 100 compressions per minute, again depending on the size of the dog.
- If you are the only person available, breathe into your dog's nose once for every five compressions that are done. If you have someone to help you with compressions, give artificial respiration after every two or three compressions.

- Continue with the CPR and artificial respiration until the dog begins breathing on his own and the pulse becomes steady.

No strict rules apply as to how long you should continue CPR. If the heart has not begun to beat within five to ten minutes, it may not be helpful to persist. It is worth noting that this is a basic CPR outline. A pet first aid class will give you firsthand experience at performing CPR, which will help you remain calm and be more effective.

Choking

Dogs can choke on any number of items from doll parts to safety pins to pieces of dog bones. Dogs that wolf down their food too quickly can choke, too. Any obstruction in your dog's airway is a life-threatening emergency and requires immediate medical attention to prevent brain damage or death.

Symptoms vary, but the most common signs include an acute onset of vigorous breathing efforts and may also include coughing, gagging, or a retching noise, and pawing at the side of the face. The coloring of the dog's gums and tongue will change rapidly (in as little as sixty to ninety seconds), and he may collapse. Seek immediate veterinary attention.

The dog's airway needs to be cleared immediately. Time is of the essence because once a dog goes unconscious, you may have less than one minute before his heart stops beating. You can attempt a modified Heimlich maneuver by following these steps: Position yourself behind the dog. Wrap your arms around his body, just behind his rib cage. Wrap one hand around the other to make a double fist, placing the double fist on his abdomen beneath or behind the rib cage, and apply a brisk compression. It may take several attempts to dislodge or expel the object.

If you are unsuccessful, and your dog is still not breathing, work on clearing the airway. Many veterinarians are adamantly opposed to sticking your fingers in the mouth of a choking dog. Instead, pull his lower jaw open and tilt his head upward. If an object is visible, try to remove it with your finger without pushing it deeper. Use extreme caution to avoid being bitten. Regardless of how friendly your dog might be, a panicked, choking dog is likely to bite as a reflex mechanism.

Brachycephalic breeds have more difficulty in hot weather. Provide your dog with shade, lots of cool water, and a place to take a dip.

Once you have cleared the dog's airway, have him examined by a veterinarian as soon as possible. As with most medical issues, a first aid class (or your veterinarian) can show you how to perform the maneuver well in advance of needing it.

Hot Cars

Did you know that a parked car acts like a greenhouse, trapping the sun's heat? That's why you should never leave your dog unattended in any vehicle. Despite a zillion public-service announcements, this point cannot be overemphasized because many people simply do not realize how quickly a car can overheat—yes, even with the windows cracked! Consider that on a sunny day, the internal temperature of a parked vehicle can quickly reach 134°F or 56°C, with the majority of the temperature rise occurring within the first fifteen to thirty minutes. Leaving the windows opened slightly does not appreciably slow down how fast the car heats up or even reduce the maximum temperature possible. A dog can suffer irreparable brain damage or death if his body temperature rises above 107°F or 41.7°C. In the amount of time it takes you to run into the grocery store, your dog could be exposed to life-threatening temperatures.

Heat-Related Issues

The average dog's temperature is 101.5°F or 38.6°C, with a normal range between 101°F and 102.5° F or 38.3°C and 39°C. These are core temperatures, based on rectal thermometer readings. While temperatures can vary throughout a dog's body, the core temperature is one of several constant (homeostatic) internal conditions, which also include blood pressure and blood chemistry.

Anytime a dog's body temperature goes above normal, it is a cause for concern. Heatstroke is associated with a marked elevation in a dog's body temperature. It is a serious, life-threatening emergency, yet it is almost always preventable. The most common causes include exposure to high temperatures, high humidity, or poor ventilation. While all dogs are susceptible, brachycephalic (short-nosed) breeds like the Pekingese, Bulldog, and Pug heat up faster than others.

Unlike people, dogs do not sweat. The only sweat glands they have are on the pads of their feet. Their primary cooling mechanisms are panting and conduction. When overheated dogs pant, they breathe in and out through their mouths. They inhale cool air and, as the air moves into their lungs, it absorbs heat and moisture. When they exhale, the hot air passes over their wet tongues and evaporation occurs, enhancing and maximizing heat loss and cooling their bodies.

Conduction, which is the second method of cooling, occurs when a dog lies down on a cool surface, such as a title floor, grass, or concrete. You may have seen your puppy do this, but you were not aware that the heat from his body was being transferred to the cool surface.

Of the four types of heat-induced illnesses (heat cramps, heat exhaustion, heat prostration, and heatstroke), you should be most concerned with heat prostration and heatstroke.

Heat prostration is considered a moderate case of heatstroke, with a dog's body temperature at 104°F to 106°F or 40°C to 41°C. Many experts do not differentiate between heat prostration and heatstroke, as both are serious medical issues. Symptoms include rapid panting, red or pale gums, weakness, vomiting, confusion, and dizziness. Seek immediate medical veterinary attention. Dogs with heat prostration can often recover without complicating health problems.

Heatstroke is the most severe form of heat-induced illnesses and occurs when a dog's body temperature is above 106°F or 41°C. Symptoms are often overlapping but are generally more severe than those of heat prostration and can include rapid panting, inability to stand up, collapsing, red or pale gums, thick and sticky saliva, weakness, vomiting (with or without blood), diarrhea, shock, fainting, or coma.

Cell damage begins to occur at body temperatures above 108°F or 42.2°C, resulting in multiple organ-system dysfunction, including the respiratory, cardiovascular, gastrointestinal, renal, and central nervous systems. Immediate veterinary attention is paramount.

Effective cooling of a dog can be accomplished by getting him to a cool environment immediately and lowering his temperature by submerging his body in cool (not cold or iced) water or applying cool water to his body with a shower or hose. When submerging a dog in cool water, always keep his head elevated above the water. If possible, use a fan to keep air moving over the body surface. Check his rectal temperature every five minutes. Once his body temperature reaches 103°F or 39.4°C, you can stop the cooling measures; even though he appears to be recovering, take him to your veterinarian or a twenty-four-hour emergency clinic to be checked.

The best prevention is to monitor your dog and his activities and never place him in a situation where he can become overheated. Limit exercise, such as playing, running, and games, to the cooler parts of the day.

When you invest the time, energy, and love into the proper care and training of your puppy, the rewards never end.

RESOURCES

Books

The AKC's World of the Pure-bred Dog. New York: Howell Book House, 1983.

The New Complete Dog Book (American Kennel Club). 21st edition. Irvine, CA: I-5 Press, 2014

Kaminski, Patricia and Richard Katz. *Flower Essence Repertory.* Nevada City, CA: The Flower Essence Society, Earth-Spirit, Inc., 1994.

McConnell, Patricia B. *For The Love of a Dog.* New York: Ballantine Books, 2007.

Mery, Fernand. *The Life History and Magic of the Dog.* New York: Grosset & Dunlap, 1968.

The National Geographic Book of Dogs. Washington, DC: National Geographic Society, 1958.

Scanlan, Nancy. *Complementary Medicine for Veterinary Technicians and Nurses.* Ames, Iowa; Blackwell Publishing, Ltd., 2011.

Scott, John Paul and John L. Fuller. *Genetics and the Social Behavior of Dogs.* Chicago: The University of Chicago Press, 1963.

Scientific Journals/Papers

Boudrieau, Randy DVM. "Managing Cruciate Disease: Where Are We Now?" Paper presented at the World Veterinary Organization Conference, Bologna, Italy, 2010.

The Center for Food Security and Public Health. "Canine Influenza." Paper presented at Iowa State University, 2007.

Crawford, C., et al. "Influenza Virus Infection in Racing Greyhounds." Paper presented at the North American Veterinary Conference, 2006.

Demers, Joseph DVM, CVA, CVH, HMC. "An Introduction to Homeopathy." International Veterinary Information Service, 2007.

Lauten, Susan, PhD. "Nutritional Risks to Large-Breed Dogs: From Weaning to the Geriatric Years." *Veterinary Clinics Small Animal Practice* (2006): 1345–1359.

Mueller, Ralf. "Sarcoptes, Demodex, and Otodectes: Treatment Options." Paper presented at the North American Veterinary Council, 2007.

——. "Update on the Diagnosis and Treatment of Fleas and Mites." Paper presented at the World Small Animal Veterinary Association, Sydney, Australia, 2007.

Nash, Holly, BVSc. "Acupuncture in Small Animal Practice." (2011): 26, 204–206.

Ness, R.D. "Integrative Therapies." *Clinical Avian Medicine.* International Veterinary Information Service, 2007.

Schwartz, S. "Use of Herbal Remedies to Control Pet Behavior." International Veterinary Information Service, 2000.

Websites

American Heartworm Society: www.heartwormsociety.org/veterinary-resources

Baker Institute for Animal Health, Cornell University College of Veterinary Medicine: www.bakerinstitute.vet.cornell.edu

Companion Animal Parasite Control: www.capcvet.org

Centers for Disease Control, Canine Flu: www.cdc.gov/flu/canine

Hemopet Canine Blood Bank: www.hemopet.org

The Merck Veterinary Manual: www.merckmanuals.com/vet

Pranic Healing: www.pranichealing.com

The Reiki Center: www.reiki.org

Washington State University College of Veterinary Medicine: www.vetmed.wsu.edu

INDEX

ear mites, 205
ectropion, 212
elbow disease, 218
epilepsy, 209–210
entropion, 212
external parasites, 180–183
flea-allergy dermatitis, 91,
    199–200
gastric dilatation-volvulus,
    214–215
growth-plate injuries, 114, 187
heat prostration, 228
heatstroke, 118, 226, 228–229
hemangiosarcoma, 207
hip dysplasia, 216–218
homozygous merle eye defect,
    213
hot spots, 201–202
hypothyroidism, 215
illness, signs of, 167–173
internal parasites, 183–186
iris coloboma, 213
lethargy, 170
limping, 170–171
loss of balance, 170
lymphoma, 207–208
motion sickness, 150–151
multidrug resistance gene,
    215–216
nuclear sclerosis, 211
obesity, 188–189
patellar luxation, 218–219
pawing at the mouth, 171
progressive retinal atrophy,
    213–214
rabies, 176–177
scratching or itching, 171
shaking or trembling, 172
stiffness, 170–171
swelling, muzzle area, 172
temperature, above normal, 172,
    228
urination changes, 169
vaccinations, 51, 173–180
vomiting, 172–173

von Willebrand's disease,
    220–221
water consumption changes,
    168–169
wellness, signs of, 16, 166–167
. See also natural dog care
healthy puppies, signs of, 16,
    166–167
heartworms, 183–184
heat prostration, 228
heatstroke, 118, 226, 228–229
Heimlich maneuver, 169, 227
hemangiosarcoma (HSA), 207
hepatitis, 176
herbal remedies, 194, 195
herding, 162
hiking, 115–117
hip dysplasia, 216–218
holistic medicine and
    practitioners, 105, 191
homecoming, 18–29
  bonding, 29
  boundaries, 18–19
  children and puppies, 26–27
  first day, 25–26
  first night, 28
  household rules, 29
  other household pets, 27–28
  puppy-proofing, 18–19
  supplies, 18–20
homemade diets, 97–98
homeopathic care, 191–192
homozygous merle eye defect,
    213
hookworms, 184
hot spots, 201–202
household rules, 29
house-training, 36–41
  accidents, 41
  breed size, 38
  crate vs. paper, 36–37
  length of time for, 40–41
  plan for, 38–40
  schedule for, 37–38
  submissive urination, 149

urine marking, 146
verbal cues, 40
when to begin, 31–32
humane societies and shelters, 17
hypothyroidism, 215

I
identification information, 23–24
ignoring Come command,
    147–148
infections, protozoal intestinal,
    110–111
in-store adoptions, 17
integrative medicine, 105
interactive play, 32–33
internal medicine, 221
internal parasites, 183–186
International Association of
    Reiki Professionals (IARP), 197
International Disc Dog Handlers
    Association (IDDHA), 160
International Weight Pulling
    Association (IWPA), 161
iris coloboma, 213

J
jogging, 116–118
Journal of the American Animal
    Hospital Association (JAAHA),
    51
jumping up, 143

K
Kennel Club (England), 15
kennel cough, 177–178
kennels, boarding facilities,
    154–155
kibble, 95

L
learning theory, 54–57
leashes, 22–23
leash-training, 42–44, 129
leptospirosis, 178
lifestyle considerations, 8–9
Lin, Sophia, 134

Photo Credits

Tracy Libby

Tracy Libby is an award-winning writer and photographer whose work has won multiple awards from the Dog Writers Association of America (DWAA) and the Alliance of Purebred Dog Writers (APDW). She holds a Bachelor of Science degree in Journalism from the University of Oregon and has been writing about pet care for over two decades. Her articles have appeared in most mainstream magazines including *Dog Fancy*, *Modern Dog*, *Dog World*, *Puppies USA*, *Dogs USA*, and the *AKC Gazette*, as well as online for Embrace Pet Insurance.

She lives in Oregon with her husband, five cats, and five Australian Shepherds. She has been involved in the sport of dogs for nearly three decades, exhibiting her Aussies in agility, conformation, and obedience.